SOMEWHERE IN TIME
(A Mid-Life Memoir)

By Michael W. Hall

Copyright 2016 Michael W. Hall All rights reversed.

This is a work of fiction. The characters and events described herein are imaginary and are not intended to refer to specific places, things or persons alive or dead, existing or not. All rights are reserved. No part of this book may be reproduced or utilized in any form or by any means; electronic, mechanical or otherwise, including photocopying, recording or by any informational storage and retrieval system, without permission in writing from the publisher and author.

ISBN

978-1535387415 (13 digit)
1535387416 (10 digit)

First Edition

Printed in the United States of America

Dedication

This book is dedicated to my parents, Wayne and Laura Hall, without whom none of these mid-life ramblings would have been possible. Additionally, I wish acknowledge my eternal gratitude to the many other cosmic wanderers I have had the privilege to share precious time with, be they casual acquaintances, family members, lovers or friends. Remember, we are all reoccurring players in this ongoing cosmic-drama, and none of us gets out of here until the last holds hands with the first.

SOMEWHERE IN TIME
(A MID-LIFE MEMOIR)

By Michael W. Hall

Chapter 1

HALF-TIME PAUSE

It's not so much a mid-life crisis, as a desperately needed half-time pause, to gather myself. Like when the veteran football coach is accosted by the female reporter after a tough first-half and brashly asked over the crowd noise, "Coach...! What are you going to tell the team in the locker room?" Glancing at the camera with a feigned look of seriousness, trying not to blurt out what's really on the tip of his tongue (*How the Hell do I know),* the aging icon keeps walking, leans toward the foam-tipped microphone bobbing in front of his face, and hoarsely delivers the obligatory sound-bite: "We're going to keep on doing what we've been doing... and try to do it better in the second half."

That's just about what I've been feeling these past few months, or even years, of this middle-aged existence of mine. Going through the motions of being a fifty-something husband, dad, slash, small-town-lawyer (and vicarious fly-fisher), with a lovely wife and four rambunctious children, all in various stages of development. And like the wily old coach, I know what I need to do. I just hope I can figure out how to do it better in the second-half of life.

Actually, 'the second-half' may be a bit too optimistic in my particular case, given the dismal track-record of my not so distant paternal family history. My grandfather, Charles Lindley Hall, the husky, three-hundred-pound Washington State Patrolman, died in his sleep from a heart-attack at age 73. And my own father, Charles Wayne Hall, the Columbia University educated PhD, died from his second myocardial infarction at the tender age of 49. I don't know very much about my great-grandfather, the legendary Charles Wesley Hall, who, rumor has it, played football for West Point during the beginning of the 20th Century. Nor do I know much about the rest of the "Hall" branch of my family tree.

Needless to say, my own swiftly approaching mortality is becoming more self-evident every time I bend over to pick something up and find the floor a little farther away. As a consequence, I try not to drop things, and when I do, I find plenty of reasons why whatever I just fumbled, should *'damn-well' lay there a while*.

In my case, the situation may be more like a seventh-inning stretch than anything else; when everyone stands up to work out the kinks, sing an old song, and glance around to find there are more than a few other poor slobs in the same precarious position. So, reluctantly, you vow to stay until the end, no matter how it turns out, because there's always hope. And who knows, perhaps God will grant a miracle in the bottom of the ninth. Besides, you've got too damn much invested in those season tickets to throw it all away at this stage in the game.

Many unsettled feelings this past summer, when the weather was good, and the warm breezes blew in off Puget Sound. Lingering memories of younger days, rattling around in my aging, baby-boomer brain. Sweet thoughts of college days back on campus and the ivy-covered walls of the old frat-house. Those care-free post-graduate years living large in L.A., rooming with my younger brother, trying hard to get 'discovered,' as an actor/singer/writer/whatever, while Greggy attended the "Fashion Institute of Design and Merchandising," hoping against hope to become a famous Hollywood costume designer.

Those were the days. My first post-graduate corporate position as "Shaker the Country Bear" at Disneyland. Roaming the park in a steaming, hot polyester-and-artificial-fur costume, trying to stay "in-character," while twisted, little, brats poked and prodded my private-parts with their newly purchased Davy Crockett long rifles. Then my graduation to the "Main Street Electrical Parade," trading off playing a different Disney character each night, earning minimum-wage and proud of it, just killing time until that 'big break' came along.

Snapping back to my current middle-age reality, I resume the mind-numbing routine of shaving that same old face in front of the downstairs bathroom mirror. Hiding out as it were, grabbing some early-morning 'alone-time,' while my wife and kids jostle for position upstairs: brushing, spraying, washing their faces and trying on different 'Sunday-best' outfits, one after another. The whole scene builds to a predictable frenetic storm, as we make our way, collectively, to the trusty family-wagon for another of our more than weekly pilgrimages to church. My wife and I are committed to the adult choir, which practices on Thursday nights. The kids have youth choir and various programs, with their attendant meetings, rehearsals and special events. We all arrive for Sunday pre-service choir rehearsal by 7:30am and usually don't drag ourselves to a late, post-second-service, brunch until well after the Free-Methodists have grazed through the choicest fare at the local Family Buffet. Then, there's Tuesday night prayer meeting, and the miscellaneous marriage and parenting classes my wife and I periodically attend, but aren't currently, thank God. After a while, if you're not vigilant, you find yourself way too busy to hear that 'still small voice' the Good Lord typically employs when trying to get your attention over the din of your overly-committed, maxed-out, church, home and work life.

It was during one of those rare slices of solitude, when I was fighting to be elsewhere in my mind, that I actually noticed it for the first time. It was subtle, but unmistakable. I was standing before the mirror shaving, staring at nothing in particular, when a slight glitch in the reverie had me perceive, for a split-second, that I was shaving with an old-fashioned, straight-edged razor, like the one my Grandfather used to use, before he surprised everyone and switched to one of those fancy 'safety-razors.'

What a rush!, I thought to myself, as the subliminal shock jolted me back to reality with a heart-thumping shot of adrenaline. I vowed to myself, *"I've got to lay off those "Hemi-Sync"© relaxation tapes."*

I had, indeed, become a bit of a night-owl lately, listening to late-night talk-radio and soaking up the latest juicy tid-bits on UFO's, Bigfoot, and the most recent J.F.K. assassination theories. I embraced my self-imposed, sleep-deprived lifestyle like an old friend, utilizing its tantalizing distractions to buffer the stark realities of my current, soul-sucking, mid-life situation. So, as I mentally scolded myself in front of the steamy, bathroom mirror, I convinced myself I was only paying the price for my late-night indulgences with the likes of Art Bell, George Noory, and those millions of other sleep-deprived "Coming Global Super Storm"/"Workers in the Light."

At any rate, that's when I first consciously remembered musing myself completely out of time and space and evidently into 'somewhere else!' But, in the back of my mind, I wondered whether something more mysterious and meaningful was responsible for the sudden onset of such seemingly unrelated mid-life incongruities.

I had purchased a few Hemi-Sync™ audio CD's at one of those health-fairs downtown Seattle. The ones created by the Monroe Institute and sold by Dr. Nick Begich, the Ph.D. mind-control expert, who teaches people how to maximize their cognitive powers by syncing both hemispheres of their brain.

Now, I consider myself a God-fearing man. Indeed, I'm proud to have served as Vice President and adjunct professor at "Puget Sound Christian College;" a small, non-denominational institution of higher learning over-looking the blue waters of Puget Sound. But, ever since I was diagnosed with sleep apnea in my thirties and had a full-blown, clinical, sleep-study, with those 'Frankensteinian' electrodes pasted to my head, I've come to appreciate the fact that our brains are capable of much more than we can even imagine. And being left-handed as well, and intuitively working from my emotional right-brain, I figured, since I've reached the official 'pre-Alzheimer's' age-bracket, I should explore all my baby-boomer options, before I fill every nook and cranny of my house with lost sets of car keys.

Besides, I have a hard time believing that God is such an inept time-space manager as to create the vastness of the universe and only populate one inconspicuous speck of it with inefficient hominids whose separate sides of their brains can't effectively communicate with each other. *And what that has to do with anything is anyone's guess.* But then, that's exactly what I'm talking about. The brain does some mysterious things, if you let it.

Strange synchronicities started happening more and more often, and more unpredictably, when I transferred the Hemi-Sync® recordings to my little iPod and began using their soothing white-noise sound-tracks to mask the industrial-strength roar of my bedside CPAP 'snore-machine.' (CPAP stands for: "Continuous Positive Air Pressure," as my fellow 'sleep-apneacs' will tell you). Periodic flashbacks seemed to come from some long-ago scene, complete with all the accoutrements appropriate to their historical era. Somewhere around the turn of the century (that's the turn of the 'Twentieth' century for those 'Gen-Xers' and their progeny who may be forced to read this dusty tome, as some macabre form of post-modern punishment). Fortunately, I usually was able to wrap these somnambulistic time-travels around my favorite daydreams of fly-fishing on the old Payette, or being on safari in some exotic locale; somewhere 'Hemingway-esque,' like the "Big Two-Hearted River" or "The Snows of Kilimanjaro."

Eventually, as a kind of cerebral defense mechanism, I mentally retrofitted my bathroom hideaway into a middle-aged man-cave, fantasy façade; a real 'sportsman's sanctuary,' reminiscent of our families' rustic, summer cabin on Cascade Lake, high in the western wilds of central Idaho. Periodically, and with no effort at all, I am there in a heartbeat, living the outdoor-life, contemplating the many things a man must do, as 'the sun also arises' over the lake, on the mystical cove the kids have dubbed "Belly-Button Bay."

There's the sawing and splitting of firewood. Stacking and stoking the old wood-stove. The cleaning of old duck decoys and oiling steel-blue gun barrels. Endless meditations at the fly-tying bench, and the mending of cherished fishing poles. The primal smell of woodfire. The welcoming aroma of coffee, bacon and eggs sizzling on the griddle. The ambient scent of rough, cedar walls, mixed with old-leather and mothballs.

A wafting, summer breeze blows in through the tattered screen-door. The well-worn "Daisy" lever-action, 200-shot, BB repeater proudly hangs over the cabin door, ever-ready with the famed "Red Ryder" logo carved into its wood-grain stock.

    The cozy cabin interior is decorated, hodge-podge, with ancient outdoor-gear, hovering somewhere between 'antique' and 'plain old junk.' Here and there, faded photographs frame the walls with generations of classic fishing and hunting scenes from seasons gone by, printed on paper, but etched in the soul.

    The coming of twilight brings a cool stillness. The autumn sun pours its golden hue on the dappled lake. Far away loons giggle, signaling the end of another lazy day. The crackling pop of the campfire. Marshmallows roasting, golden-brown, on hickory-sticks Grandpa cut long ago. Bats flit to and fro out of sight, like tiny angels slipping through time. The sweet night-song of birds settling in their nests.

    Then evening falls and the stars twinkle to life, whispering from heaven, close enough to the touch. The glorious night-bloom of the Milky Way spreading from horizon to horizon. The soothing sound of an old owl hoo-hooting outside the cabin window. Gossamer curtains floating ghostlike on the evening breeze. Laying still and content in the cabin loft, on crisp cabin-sheets, beneath the heavy, patch-work quilt that travels, nightly, through time, bringing back memories of familiar dreams and easy, younger days.

    And so it was, with these warm feelings and impressions still fresh in my mind, that I enthusiastically jumped at the unexpected invitation from my Hollywood-costumer brother to attend the annual reunion of a film we both worked on, back in the summer of 1979. The movie, which has become a classic, worthy of inclusion with other all-time-great, romantic pictures like 'Casablanca' or 'Gone With the Wind,' is called, "Somewhere in Time," starring Christopher Reeve, Jane Seymour and Christopher Plummer. It's the endearing love-story of a handsome, young playwright (Richard Collier), played so well by Chris Reeve, who falls in love with a beautiful, turn-of-the-century actress (Elise McKenna), played by the incomparable Jane Seymour, after seeing an old photograph of her at the gorgeous 'Grand Hotel' on sun-swept Mackinac Island, in Lake Huron, on Michigan's Upper Peninsula. The romantic adventure is all about love and loss and triumph, as Richard travels back in time to find Elise. And despite the jealous machinations of her ever-controlling stage-manager (William Fawcett Robinson), impeccably portrayed by Christopher Plummer, they fall in love and share a lifetime together in the short span of a few days.

Neither Greggy nor I had been back to Mackinac Island in over twenty-five years. He called me from L.A. to inform me that one of our mutual friends, Jan Flannery, a beautiful, young actress who was an 'extra' in the film, had told him about the annual event, which is held on Mackinac Island at the Grand Hotel in October each year.

I remember Jan Flannery as a vivacious good-looker with personality galore, who my brother introduced me to when I was also working as an extra on the film. Even then, you could tell Jan would succeed in whatever she put her mind to. I remember having a major crush on her at the time; being single and rebounding from my long-distance relationship with a beautiful southern belle. But, my purely platonic crush on Jan Flannery was shared with every other guy on the island, including as I recall, Christopher Reeve, who at the time was the most eligible bachelor in Hollywood. Jan, however, being a happily married woman, conducted herself with the utmost dignity and grace, spending a lot of time with Chris and Jane Seymour during the summer's filming.

I eagerly jumped at the opportunity to be my brother's 'date' for the 'S.I.T.' weekend on Mackinac Island. Greggy was recently divorced and as wild and crazy as ever, something I always admired in him. He already paid for the hotel room, which we would share, along with the registration fees. And since I hadn't taken much of a vacation last summer, or the summer before that, I posited I was long overdue. Besides, as I explained to my wife, with as much feigned confidence I could muster, it would be good for Greggy and I to do some sibling bonding again, after all these years. "Him being so far away in Hollywood and all... and approaching his mid-fifties... like me."

As it turned out, I didn't have to do much marital-negotiation at all, an unanticipated bonus that perplexed me at the time. But what the hell, a good mid-life crisis can do that to people. Perhaps my lovely wife was experiencing her own pre-menopausal condition that affects the female gender at roughly the same time their husbands get the overwhelming urge to take off cross-country on a Harley. Whatever the reason, I wasn't going to second guess providence, and immediately made plans to clear ten days from my calendar; figuring three motorcycle travel days each way from Seattle, plus the three-day reunion weekend and an extra day thrown in as a cushion.

Everything was going along fine, as I prepared for the trip and doted appropriately on each family member, as pre-penitence for the wild and crazy times Greggy and I would undoubtedly attempt, but never actually consummate, during the much anticipated Somewhere In Time reunion weekend.

Then, as one can imagine, I was devastated when my brother called a few days before I was to leave on my cross-country road-trip, with some bad news. Something had come up with his boss, Arnold Schwarzenegger. Greg had been Arnold's 'personal costumer' for over 20 years, through the good times and the bad. And Arnold had proven himself a loyal friend to my brother, as well as the other close-knit filmdom-buddies who have worked with him over the years. Nicknamed "Team A.S," Arnold's loyal rat-pack consists of those special people who take care of his hair, makeup, transportation and stunts, along with my brother the costumer, and a few others. As always, Greggy dropped whatever needed to be dropped, to attend to his boss's current needs, whatever they were and wherever they occurred.

I resigned myself to calling off the whole glorious 'road-trip-thing' when Greggy unselfishly declared, "What the hell... you should go anyway! Use the pre-paid reservation and eat double for me." He didn't have to prod me much to accept his generous offer. The only problem was, finding the right moment and appropriate phase of the moon, to inform my dear wife of the slight change in plans. So far, everything thing was working out to be the perfect 'mid-life-crisis-road-trip' of a lifetime. I guess I just didn't want to spoil the beauty of it all.

Chapter 2

MID-LIFE CRISIS HERE I COME
or
(Zen and the Art of Motorcycle Flatulence)

Anticipating my early Monday morning alarm, I bound out of bed with a purpose I have not felt in a long while. I spent most of the weekend packing and polishing my middle-age pride and joy; the one luxury item I somehow was able to convince my wife, "would be a great investment... a Harley-Davidson "Heritage Softail Classic," fully loaded and leaning sturdily in the driveway, gleaming cherry-red, in the autumn sunrise. I usually keep the beautiful beast in the garage to protect her from the elements. But, last night I thought, *What the hell, I should let her 'season' overnight...* just as she'll be doing on my much-anticipated road-trip odyssey to mid-life 'Neverland.'

There's no real reason I have to leave this early in the morning; well before my wife and kids get up for work and school. But, I hurriedly pull on my traveling clothes and donned the smooth, black-leather chaps. The ones with the butt cut out for maximum riding comfort. Before leaving, I check on the kids, vicariously soaking in the peace on their slumbering faces. I won't see them for almost two weeks, as I make my first, and most likely last, middle-aged pilgrimage to Mackinaw Island... *searching for something... a feeling... that I can't put into words.*

I said my formal goodbyes last night, because, as I noted, "I want to beat the morning commuter traffic." *My kids truly are my hope and joy; the reason I want to live a long life, to watch them grow and soar.* But, even if I don't live to be a ripe old age, I'm excited for their future and the opportunities and challenges each of them will face. *I think we raised them well.* I ask God to *bless them while I'm gone... and keep them safe.*

Tip-toeing down the hallway in my biker boots, I peer into my wife's room and watch her sound asleep... dreaming of something sweet I hope... peaceful and resting. She deserves the rest. We both do at this stage in the game. Hers may come in her dreams. But, I have chosen a more restless respite, searching for something, heading "East of Eden" on a Harley, like Steinbeck searched for himself and his country. I grab my stuff-sack, with my peanut-butter and jelly lunch, from the fridge and step into the crisp, morning air and my new adventure.

Wiping the dew from the bike's leather seat, I methodically fold the rag and stow it in the leather side-bag. I step back a moment to admire the lady-hog's classic design. Then, donning my brain-bucket and sunglasses, I throw a cautious leg across her wide girth and feel her substantial weight beneath me. I strike the starter, unleashing her pent-up power, then quickly throttle down, remembering my slumbering family and neighbors, as the lubricated cylinder's flop between my legs. Pulling her upright, I stow the kickstand, adjust the mirrors for a long-distance-gaze, far and away behind me for the long eastward run. A couple of finely-tuned twists of the throttle, one last look to survey the familiar, and I'm off... *to whatever lays ahead.*

Sliding through my neighborhood, it feels like Saturday instead of early Monday morning. Normally, I'd just be starting my morning routine, as my sleepy neighbors are now starting theirs. "Sam," the old contractor, who owns the neighborhood, 'alarm-clock' rooster, is probably wondering, *"What the hell is he doing up this early on a Monday morning? On his motorcycle yet?"* I hear the old cock crowing in his backyard, *the rooster, not Sam,* dopplering away as I rumble past. The minimal hilarity of my early morning 'joke-to-myself' brings a care-free smile to my face, exponentially larger than it has the right to be. I soak in the feel-good-feeling of freedom as it slowly fills my bones, flapping past familiar abodes filled with familiar, foreboding people, as if I have found the lost elixir of life, exempting me from the mind-numbing grind of humanity; that life-sucking routine you don't even realize you're in, until for some reason or another, you find yourself looking at it from the outside, at what used to be you.

Stopping briefly at the intersection of my street and Main, I make a right turn and blast through downtown, unleashing my churning emotions with the bike's full, unbridled compression, heading to the freeway and into the rising sun.

Man, forget about trying to beat the commuter traffic! These poor bastards must get up at five a.m. to be on the road this early. At least I can fly down the transit lane without much delay. The I-5 merge at Northgate Mall is pensive as usual. Then, the normal slowing at the 'U District' exits and the Ship Canal Bridge. Rising over the crest of the bridge-span to the breath-taking view of Lake Union and downtown Seattle, with its landmark Space Needle looming in the distance, I quickly glance to the left and catch the morning sun rising over Husky Stadium and the 'U-Dub' campus.

Flying down the fast-lane with the cool wind in my ears, I think of my eldest daughter, my grown-up baby-girl, as she most assuredly slumbers in her over-priced, upscale Seattle apartment. No-doubt, catching up on the beauty-sleep she so eagerly deprives herself of each weekend. *Like father, like daughter.* I reminisce about her recent college days; the football games in Husky Stadium, the wild sorority functions, and crunching through the autumn leaves on Greek Row. I liberally applied whatever fatherly advice I could muster, as she made her way through the mandatory minefields of youthful growing pains and minor tribulations. She graduated with a B.S. in something I didn't even know existed; something to do with maps and computers and 'demographics.' She's all grown up now. A beautiful, young woman, living on her own, working for one of those surviving 'dotcoms,' and frantically looking (a bit too hard I think) for 'The Guy;' that one special, forever relationship that will fix everything for her. *God bless him, whoever he is. And Lord... give him patience.*

Passing the downtown high-rises, already bustling with Monday morning 'drones,' clutching their hot, sleeve-covered, coffee cups filled with "Starbucks," "Tully's" and "Seattle's Best" brews. Myself, I prefer the local mini-brands, like "Mukilteo Coffee Roasters" or "Emerald Hills Coffee," only because I grew up in their namesake communities and enjoy the local persona. I tap into the passing thoughts of the zombied 'employees' trudging to their work stations, making someone else a lot of money. But, who am I to think such pompous thoughts; an old, general-practice small-town-lawyer, living from client to client, retainer to retainer, eking-out a semi-respectable feast-or-famine existence. At least I haven't succumbed to the trap my father fell into; highly-educated, highly-stressed and dead the year before he was to retire. I really love that guy. He never complained. And he seemed to have the perspective of God, or at least the patience of Job. He's probably the reason I have a hard time taking things too seriously. I suppose that's not a bad legacy to leave a son... really.

Leaning through the wide eastbound turn onto I-90, I relish the traveling music flowing from my "iPod" ear buds. My current 'road-group-of-choice' is "The Lost Vaurnets;" one of our local, Rockin'/Blues 'MBA-biker-bands,' made up of middle-aged, white-collar, working stiffs like myself. Highly educated business owners; most with advanced business degrees, who jam together on a not-so-regular basis, downtown Brackett's-Landing, at Engel's Pub. Talk about carving out a handsome existence. Playing "Jerry Garcia," coaching your kid's soccer team, and operating your own small business. Man, that's the ticket. The ultimate, hybrid-lifestyle! I can see their wives now; all rabid, 'Dead-Head-Soccer-Moms.'

The freeway stretches out as far east as I can see. And I'm already there in my mind, beyond the horizon, catching bugs in my teeth.

Chapter 3

MID-LIFE RELATIONSHIP-REVIEW

It came to me in a flash, through the fog of my random morning reverie.... W*hat would my life be like, if for some inexplicable reason, I had not married my lovely wife?* And I don't mean, what if we just decided to 'live together.' Rather, what if I had made an earlier 'commitment,' and settled down with one of the other serious girlfriends I had put so much time and energy into in my youth? *What a tantalizing rumination.... Now, that's a day-dream worthy of some serious windshield time.*

Let's see, there was Sheila, my long-time, high-school sweetheart. Wow! What would life have been like with her? What a beauty! Long wavy, auburn hair that caressed her slim, broad, shoulders. Her lovely face, so full of wisdom, even at the tender age of 19. Her long, tanned legs. Sheila looked fantastic in a bikini... back when the word "bikini" really meant something. Not like today, where it can describe anything from an X-rated 'thong,' to a modest two-piece number. I remember marveling at how fortunate I was, to be born at the right time in history, to witness such a remarkable thing as a 'bikini,' especially Sheila's bikini!

There were dream-like summers at her family's summer-cabin on the leeward south-end of Whidbey Island, just a short, twenty-minute run, north, in my beat-up, sixteen-foot outboard. I'd leave our little waterfront harbor (where Sheila's Dad, the Port Commissioner, got me my first job at our public boat-launch) and scurry across 'the pond' to spend the weekend with Sheila, her mom and dad, and two older brothers. We'd boil up a bucket of freshly dug butter-clams over a driftwood fire on the beach. I can still feel the contentment, sitting on a drift-wood log next to Sheila, forking the clams from their steaming shells, dipping them into melted butter and washing them down with sloppy chunks of garlic-bread on a cool Summer's eve.

Those were the days. Summers in the sand, the smell of cocoa-butter on the salty sea air, Sheila's luscious body glistening, golden-brown, in the hot, summer sun. It was our own tropical paradise, where 'island time' moved slow and sweet like molasses. The rhythmic waves set a slow cadence for the day, melding with the thrum of bumble-bees tip-toeing on sweet-clover. The soft sea-breeze would periodically interrupt the bake of the mid-day sun, as lazy aromas from a nearby meadow carried the hint of wildflowers and sage.

Our respective families took it for granted that Sheila and I would marry someday, settle down and raise our kids close to home, to be spoiled by everyone in town. But, something happened during our college years that stretched our fates too thin, sending us spinning into our own separate space and time. I remember being devastated at the time. Looking back, I should have seen it coming, and probably did subconsciously, but didn't want to acknowledge it. I see it now as one of those inevitable realities; one of those "best things that ever happened to me" events you never would have contemplated at the time. Like that fork in the road you never saw coming. I would have preferred to stay quietly in the slow-lane, on the main drag, rather than veering off wildly at the next exit to nowhere… or so I thought.

But then, had I not been so damned depressed over my break up with Sheila, I probably would never have made that impulsive trip from Pullman to the University of Idaho to attend that 'Up With People' concert one fateful spring-evening in 1974. I noticed the brightly colored posters advertising the international performing troupe that were plastered around campus. I was a junior at Washington State University, living at Alpha Tau Omega fraternity, licking my wounds from my recent long-term relationship, when for some reason I still can't explain, I attended the Up With People show, by myself, on a Friday night, passing up a much-anticipated fraternity function, featuring the highly-touted-and-more-than-willing (Kappa Alpha) "Theta" sorority babes. *Go figure….*

Anyway, after a great show put on by over one-hundred young people from around the world, I was prompted to interview for an opportunity to travel with the group. To my utter surprise, I was accepted as a cast member, somehow raised the necessary tuition and found myself in Tucson, Arizona that July, learning to sing and dance with an entire cast of unique characters from around the globe, each of whom, over the next year of world-wide travel and performances, I would learn to love as one big, happy family.

I'll admit, I eagerly developed a consoling relationship or two with a few of my fellow, female cast-members and at least one special host-family daughter. But generally, I just enjoyed the travel and the life-changing experiences; touring North, Central and South America, and staying in such exotic and far away locales as San Juan, Puerto Rico, Mexico City, Caracas, Venezuela and Snake Navel, Idaho.

Our multi-lingual troupe stayed in host families' homes wherever we traveled; two or three "Uppies" to a local family. You really get 'the feel' of a place when you stay with the people who live and work where you perform. I had the opportunity to live with folks from every socio-economic strata you can think of. Usually, we experienced decent and sometimes deluxe accommodations, and were treated royally by our excited hosts, who eagerly rolled out the red-carpet to impress us.

I especially remember one precious host-family in a small village, deep in Southern Mexico, where I and a buddy of mine (Mitch, our cast drummer) were allocated with a very poor family. They had nine children of their own, and extended family-members, living in a small, three-room shack on the outskirts of town; across the railroad tracks… literally. Being reminded of Up With People's informal motto, "Be Flexible," neither Mitch nor I complained, as we stoically waved to our fellow, wide-eyed, cast-members from the back of our host-father's early model (and I mean way-early model), dented and primered pick-up truck, pulling away with four of our newly acquired host-brothers and sisters, and their dog, jumping excitedly around us. I remember thinking to myself; *Thank God it would only be for a short two-night stay.*

Mitch and I were indeed a little self-conscious at the prospect of further burdening our host-family's obviously limited resources with two more, rather large, American mouths to feed. And, if the truth be known (being young and very single males), we (or at least I) had selfishly held out hope for an adventurous romance or two in this little south-of-the-border town. Thoughts of Marty Robbins' classic, Tex-Mex ballad, "El Paso," plied my imagination during our "Grapes of Wrath-like" ride through the dusty wilderness. Visions of the nightlife at 'Rosa's Cantina' stirred the primal recesses of my brain, dimly lit by naked, forty-watt lightbulbs suspended in the smoke of some small, out-of-the-way saloon, with dirty, brass foot-rails and the full-figured Felina pressing her way through sweaty bodies to introduce herself to the dashing, young 'Americanos.'

But, our hopes for 'gonzo-good-times-in-Guadalajara' seemed to sieve through our fingers like parched, desert sand, as we jerked to a dusty stop in an innocuous, run-down neighborhood that, if it weren't for the cheery locals waiting there to greet us, I would swear looked like one of those stark "Christian Children's Fund" television commercials. Fortunately, our trepidations were quickly abated with our first taste of real "Mexican hospitality."

Our short, rosy-cheeked host-mother, who I never saw without her apron on, was constantly cooking and creating delicious, aromatic concoctions in her small, but efficient, kitchen in the corner of their bare living room. Our wiry host-father was constantly shuttling in neighbors and relatives for formal introductions, and to partake in generous portions of fresh, home-made, Mexican food that Momma Gutierrez continually supplied to the large, family-style table, which was generously packed with food and drink and eager bodies, thigh to thigh.

For a large family on a limited income, our hosts displayed amazing resources and a huge spirit of giving. Each evening, after Papa G. had proudly driven us and his entire family to and from the show in his ragged work-truck (requiring multiple round trips), the real celebration began back home. A late evening breeze filled with the rich aromas of home-made tortillas, black-beans and rice, fried eggs (from their free-range chickens) and home-made salsa, smothered with pan-fried chilies, onions, garnished with sweet orange-wedges, and deep-fried churros dusted with sugar and cinnamon for desert.

One night a relative or neighbor, and mostly probably both, brought over a freshly deceased fowl of some kind, with the sparse pin-tail feathers still clinging to its limp carcass. It was cheerfully accepted, quickly cleaned and added to the ever-boiling pot that Momma G. constantly attended to, while simultaneously cooking, baking, frying and stirring her next creative concoction. There was always more than enough wonderful food to go around, even for those who came late after walking from the show-arena because they had no vehicle. Momma and Papa Gutierrez made everyone feel at home, sharing all they had, while making sure their honored guests, the American gringos, could not eat another bite.

Each night when our stomachs were full, Poppa would bring out his battered, gut-string guitar and play, flamingo-style, old folk-songs and Mexican ballads, just like I imagined it to be at Rosa's Cantina. At some point during the festivities, a single bottle of 'especial' tequila was ceremoniously produced and the successive toasting of shot-glasses began. The young ones sparingly partook with their thimble-sized cups of diluted wine and tap water. Soon, the music and the glow of the drink in the low, hazy light, brought me back in that West Texas town of El Paso, and Rosa's cantina, listening to the music, watching Felina, the beautiful Mexican maiden, dancing and whirling in my head.

The richness of life flowed effortlessly from our host-families' simple abode, long into the night. Eventually, as the celebration slowly wound down, the children were lovingly laid to bed in the next room, on thin, thread-bare blankets on the floor with clean, cotton sheets for covers and well-worn chair-cushions for pillows. The whole scene could easily have been misunderstood as pitiful to a casual observer. But, we caught a deeper meaning… a lasting impression of love and caring, as each child was doted on and tucked-in by both parents, as if in a canopied, four-poster bed.

That first night, Mitch and I were embarrassed and quite reticent to discover we were to sleep in the one and only bed in the entire house, which was being given up for us by our humble host-parents. We tried to insist on sleeping on the floor, like everyone else, including

Grandma Gutierrez, but soon found ourselves approaching a cultural ingratitude if we did not accept their gracious offer.

So, there we were, two young gringos, sleeping in an old-fashion hospital bed, minimalistic and white-metal framed, on a thin but comfortable mattress, snoring away, while the entire Gutierrez clan slept contentedly around us on the cleanly-swept wooden floor. I remember drifting to sleep on those warm, Mexican nights with my soul full and content, feeling thoroughly loved by those gracious and caring people; a beautiful, humble family I realized I would most-likely never meet again in this lifetime. *God bless the Gutierrez family... and all those millions of other generous host-families who have lovingly cared for Up With People cast-members around the world.*

It was in this glamorous setting of world-travel to exotic places that I fell in love again with a beautiful, gentle soul named Claudia. She was from Folsom, California and had the patience and insight of a saint... a really good-looking saint. She had a beautiful smile, and her voice had the best qualities of Joan Baez and Bonnie Raitt. As one of our Cast's featured performers, Claudia kept her dark-blonde hair short and straight, curving in at the base of her angelic face. To gaze into her eyes, with no one else around, was a joy I'll always remember. Despite the pressures of performing nightly; her as one of the featured performers and I as the Master of Ceremonies, we quickly became special, forever friends. On late-night bus trips, or in those long, hurry-up-and-wait lines, or during dance warm-ups before the show, she'd always lend a supportive ear. And I would give her a sympathetic, encouraging glance whenever I could.

It was a relationship that grew slowly over time, with a hug here, a hand-held there or a quick goodnight kiss. We built a life of mutual love and respect despite the unpredictable, short periods of time we had to spend together, traveling from that 'somewhere' we had hurriedly just left to the next 'somewhere' we were always heading to. Like rolling through midnight on a Greyhound bus out of Barstow, California, with her angelic face sleeping softly on my shoulder. I watch with sleepy eyes the staccatoed centerline of the highway flowing out beyond the bus headlights. Feeling the soothing balm of simply 'being together.' Drifting in and out of dreamland with the rhythm of the road. I always thought if we had a normal courtship, without the accompanying frenetics of road-life, we would have either swiftly married or become too close as friends to want to complicate things with a permanent relationship. As it turned out, we (mutually, I think) chose the latter scenario, as our fast-paced tour droned on into reality. I remember wondering whether I had done something wrong or whether, perhaps, we had found something just too right.

Damn! I'm not accustomed to having such long, uninterrupted conversations with myself. I pop out of a brief highway hypnosis to find myself blasting eastward into the fall colors of eastern Washington, relishing the idea of ruminating on my impromptu 'relationship-review.' Suddenly, I realize there is no one to tell me what to do, or when to do it! I think I could get used to this.

I settle into the good vibrations of my bike beneath me, the road framing a dream-like boundary at both shoulders, inviting me into the endless possibilities that lay ahead. There must be something out here for me to discover... to experience... or perhaps just to remember.

But, my most haunting relationship memories come back to me in lapping waves on a sun-drenched beach, with the lazy smell of lilacs in the air, one magical summer in 1979. I had decided to spend the summer of my twenty-sixth year far away from my then prestigious position as a Universal Studios Tour-Guide, visiting my brother, as he worked 'on location' on a small Universal Studios production on Michigan's Mackinaw Island. The movie was called "Somewhere in Time." The cast and crew were filming at the gorgeous turn-of-the-century "Grand Hotel," which was then, and still is, the epitome of everything romantic and suave. I had opted not to bum around the country with my back-pack and guitar that summer, or climb Mount Rainier, or attempt any number of things I had vowed to accomplish before it was too late, and instead, I decided instead to hang out with my younger brother (*we are only eleven and a half months apart and raised like twins*), to earn some cash as an "extra" on the film.

Greggy had been on the Island about a week when he called me during a break in the filming. He described the magical scene to me, including the old-fashioned setting on a small, secluded island, where no cars are allowed. All transportation is restricted to horse-drawn buggies and fat-tire bicycles. He said the Producers were desperate for "background actors" for the film. It seems the studio had allocated a modest production budget for the picture. And they had not been able to do much advanced publicity to attract enough 'locals' to compliment the film's casting needs. Additionally, the picture was being shot on an isolated island in Michigan, with no easy access except by ferry boat. Consequently, the pool of local actors was somewhat limited. I'd been taking acting classes ever since Greg and I arrived in L.A. three years ago and had already been in a few films. But, at the time, I was trying to wean myself from being type-cast as a 'bottom-of-the-rung-actor,' and was concentrating on my singing career at the local open-mike cabarets around the San Fernando Valley.

But Greggy, sounding a bit lonely for his 'old bro' (and trying to hide it), sweetened the deal by mentioning, "They're paying a hundred bucks a week, plus room and board. Oh, and there are some luscious Babes you might want to meet! If you know what I mean."

Suddenly, I found myself re-evaluating my summer itinerary. *Damn, the choices a single guy has to make.* "I'll be there on the next stand-by out of Burbank," I told him. What the heck! It doesn't take long for a single guy to pack.

Stepping off the quaint ferry onto Mackinac Island for the first time, just a few, short 'L.A. hours' after my brother's initial telephone call, was like stepping back in time. My first impression was one of total 'peace and quiet.' Coming from the hustle and bustle of Los Angeles, to the clean, laid-back atmosphere of this little Victorian hamlet was a pleasant culture shock. I remember being amazed at perceiving each individual sound as it occurred around me, instead of the constant, jumbled, cacophony of the big city. Greggy took a break from his costuming duties to meet me at the ferry-dock and got situated in his room at the Grand Hotel. He then took me on my initial round of introductions at the costume trailer, then the make-up and hair department, where without warning, I was transformed into a short-haired, turn-of-the-century dandy, in a snazzy cream-colored, three-piece suit, high-top brown boots and, for effect, a white, Panama-style hat.

There weren't as many people milling around the set as I was used to. And Greg wasn't kidding when he said "Somewhere in Time" was not your typical big-budget movie. Even the hotel employees (most of whom were already appropriately dressed in Victorian-style work-clothes) were utilized as background actors, while they went about their daily routines. Being the 'new face' in a small crowd, I took a bit of good-natured ribbing from Greggy's colleagues on the crew, who joked that Greg was going to fly in his mother next, and his cousins from Walla Walla, to work on the film. I already knew many of Greg's 'studio-lifer' buddies from other pictures he had worked on. It was good to see them again and catch up on their current life-news. Show-business is, indeed, a small family when it comes right down to it. And sometimes, it's the only family they really have.

I met Jan Flannery for the very first time that day in 1979, with the afternoon sun highlighting her golden tresses. Her strikingly-blue eyes sparkled as my brother introduced me to her. She shook my hand and immediately, I was enamored by her timeless beauty. Handsomely dressed in a form-fitting costume, fit for a leading role in the film, initially, I thought s*he was Jane Seymour's 'stand-in,' or perhaps, had a featured role in the film.* I remember contemplating to myself, *'What is such a delicate soul doing with the rest of her life?'* My brother eventually nudged me back to reality with a well-placed elbow, as I realized my mouth had been hanging open way too long without a response to her introductory remark.

"Yes hello!" I responded, to whatever she said while I was wallowing in my stupor of admiration. Her radiant beauty affected everyone in a similar manner. I was especially dumbstruck at the unique 'something' she possessed that seemed to exude from her very essence. *Was I the only one who sensed this powerful attraction?* Her evident charms could hardly be resisted by the most blasé member of the human race, at least that portion of the population who eats, breaths and appreciates beauty when they see it. I soon found out that Jan was married. But, strangely, my fascination for her did not diminish. It was a unique, larger than life feeling, which I found peculiar at first. There was definitely a "something else," over-arching our current, individual circumstances. Something meaningful had descended upon my heart; deeper and more mysterious than a mere passing crush.

Undeniably, over the intervening years, Jan has become my perfect, unreachable star; the prized pearl of some great quest I had always contemplated, but never had time, or perhaps the fortitude, to embark upon. And now in my graying, middle years, the memory of that summer so long ago, that dreamy, sun-swept island and Jan's timeless beauty, still haunts my heart. I will always remember the innocent foreverness of it all.

Chapter 4

CAMP COFFEE WITH ROXANNE

    I wake stiffly and slowly before fully realizing where I am, clutching my goose-down sleeping bag tightly to my head. Lying on the ground, under a make-shift awning I rigged up last night, I lift one eyelid and survey the morning reality of what, around the flickering campfire last night, looked much more ominous and surreal. *Good morning,* I think to myself, fumbling for my glasses to bring the new day into focus. I stretch and my iPod ear buds fall from my ears. The cold air invades my warm cocoon. I have officially survived my second night on the road and my first 'camp-out' experience, since I left the family cabin the night before.

    It was strange to have the cabin to myself, in peace and quiet, seeing the silent mementos of our families' countless summer vacations displayed on the knotty-pine walls. The faded family photos, preserving the past in innocent snapshots, just as we lived them, so unawares.

    It wasn't the same without the old lodge jam-packed from kitchen to loft with all our stressed-out, excited, sunburned-selves (plus a few of the kid's tag-along friends), everyone competing for hot-water and air-time on another traditional 'Hall family vacation,' or as I call it, our annual interlude into "The Twilight Zone." I would love to have stayed another day, to hike the familiar trails and visit Belly-Button Bay, where we'd take the kids fishing. Or relax in the secluded hot-springs where my wife and I would sneak off to by ourselves. Then there's the 'zip-line-from-hell,' skimming over the croaking frogs at "Hubba-Bubba Pond." And the late-night campfires, telling real-life ghost-stories. Playing charades around the wood-stove. Four generations of extended-family bouncing on the edge of their seats, fully engaged. And those legendary family stories, handed down over the years, told and retold, until they approached biblical proportions. Like the annual recitation of "Boomer the family dog, versus the Cabin

Skunk." A classic, semi-authentic yarn of high-mountain adventure and heroics, including an under-the-cabin rescue (of both dog and dad) from the clutches of the biggest, baddest, stinkiest, skunk this side of Boise. And the resulting, repeated, tomato-juice baths (of dad and dog) in the tool shed. Then, the quarantining of both of them in the backyard tent for the rest of the vacation. Like all our other "Tales from the Crypt," everyone would take turns adding their own hilarious recollections to each fabled story. Then, those soft, summer nights with nothing much to do. Grandma playing cards with a couple of her many grandsons. Parents and kids alike, reading, knitting and nodding by the fire. All on a late-summers-eve at the cabin on the lake. A million miles away from reality, but lovingly catalogued only an instant away in my mind.

    I wake again on the hard ground, the morning smell of fall in the air. I wiggle from my sleeping bag and stand awkwardly, emerging like a hulking moth to the late-autumn sun. *Man am I hungry!* My metabolism must have kicked into overdrive to keep my core from dipping into hypothermia. I slept fully-dressed in my jeans and flannel shirt. But, the thin morning-air cuts to the bone. I unfold my leather jacket, which I used for a pillow, and slip it on and zip the collar to my chin. I walk stiff-legged, downhill to a towering pine tree to relieve myself, blinking with blurry eyes through the dense morning mist clinging to the nearby meadow. Thanks to my aging prostate, I get a long look at the new day as it slowly presents itself.

    Standing there waiting, a peculiar thought forms in my head. *What if trees absorb everything from their surrounding environment and assimilate it into their DNA, or whatever molecular building-blocks trees have?* Would that mean a small part of me will be forever melded with this growing monolith, along with every other passing deer, bear or middle-aged hominid that pauses to relieve itself and contemplate its awesome majesty? *Man, I've got to stop this sappy, grandiose, thinking so early in the morning. I'm supposed to be on vacation, not trying to posit some new 'trans-genetic theory of flora and fauna!'* Besides, people with more impressive abbreviations *behind their names are, no doubt, on top of such things.* It's probably my hemi-sync, white-noise tapes again.

Climbing back up the hill, I slap my arms briskly around my chest to beat the chill from my jacket. Standing there, cocked on one leg like John Wayne, my thumb in my front pocket, surveying my 'fortress of solitude,' it suddenly dawns on me. *What a perfect morning for "Camp-Coffee!"*

Back home, my fishing-buddy, John ("Doc") Dearborne, and I, treasure the "Camp Coffee" chapter in one of John Gierach's rustic, outdoor-life, fly-fishing books. Gierach's well-crafted tomes are like vicarious field-trips for us middle-aged working-stiffs, (or "Sports," as Gierach affectionately calls them); those who hold down 'normal jobs,' but keep their vehicles crammed with 'camo' and 'bug-out-gear' for the next, 'always-swiftly-approaching,' safari into the wilderness. Gierach's classic, roman a' clef novels like, "Trout Bum" and "Another Lousy Day in Paradise," or "Standing in a River Waving a Stick," are just a few timeless examples of the free-flowing prose that has allowed Gierach to transform a simple, unassuming past-time like fly-fishing into a quasi-respectable living. I can't exactly remember which of his books has the "Camp Coffee" story, but they are all gems, and well worth every precious moment one can fritter away reading them. My friend, "Doc," (he's really an Emergency Medical Technician) typically buys one of Gierach's volumes each month or so, and we trade off reading and sharing various chapters; rehashing their sporting details and angling hilarity, over our own cup of 'church coffee,' between services during our duties in the tenor section of the local church choir. *"Church-coffee!" Now, there's a chapter begging to be written.* Gierach's wise and humorous 'books of the angle,' mixed with Doc's and my ongoing commentary on everything 'outdoors,' provides a much-needed distraction, as we struggle to maintain a precarious grip on sanity, during those long, pre-holiday choir rehearsals. My humble attempt at "Camp Coffee" won't be as tasty as Mr. Gierach's, or his crusty companion (and legendary 'tier-of-flies'), "A.K. Best." But, it sure sounds good on this cold October morning, somewhere next to that thin, blue line, on the map in eastern Montana.

The foundation for genuine trout-bum 'camp-coffee' is a strategically built 'stick fire,' designed to burn hot and fast, with just enough fuel to bring local lake or stream water to a rolling boil in a beat-up, and preferably only partially-glazed, metal coffee pot, minus the inside guts (for the true purest), which Gierach says, "just get in the way." Then, either John or A.K. would unceremoniously throw in a couple palm-fulls of good, American coffee (with no mention of the washing one's hands, *of course*), letting the aromatic brew free-flow, deep in the bowels of the smoke-smudged cauldron, which may or may not have been washed out, but never actually cleaned. The pot itself typically dangles precariously over the flames on what barely passes for a wire handle hooked over the fork of a tree branch that has been shoved at an angle into the soil and propped over a rock, next to the crackling fire. Taking in the full-bodied aroma of real 'camp-coffee,' as it hangs in the morning air, mingled with wood-fire smoke, is an exquisite experience not easily forgotten, especially in such rustic locales as this, with no alarm clock or any real schedule to adhere to. It's like living vicariously in the corner of a Terry Redlin outdoor painting.

    I gingerly lift the lid of my boiling coffee pot, splash in some cold water to settle the grounds and let the pot steep at the edge of the coals, as per the 'Gierach-Best' recipe (or is it Best-Gierach?). The only thing missing is the optional egg shells from the morning's 'camp-breakfast,' which I haven't made yet. *Maybe I'll throw them in later, when I sizzle-up the thick-sliced bacon in the soft-sided cooler in my saddlebag.* For now, I'm perfectly content leaning against my lady hog, slurping from my red-speckled tin-cup, brimming with strong, hot "camp-coffee," staring into the fire, thinking about... nothing.

    Gazing into the flames, the vestiges of a tantalizing dream back-drafts into my consciousness for further potential scrutiny. There was this particular buxom babe I passed on the highway yesterday. I was cruising along with the warm, afternoon sun at my back, alternating road-tunes and hemi-sync white-noise in my ears, on a deserted two-lane road that was laid out to infinity between my legs. Suddenly, almost surreally, something caught my eye in the distance off to the left, swiftly approaching my peripheral awareness, materializing like a wavy mirage. By the time I was upon her goddess-like vision, my sideways-glance was fleeting at best. But, quite memorable to say the least... even outrageous!

  The full-figured waif was obviously plying her wares, looking for a ride. I, being a good boy, God-fearing and church-going, never even throttled down. Then, in a flash she was gone, like some ghostly apparition. *I mentally kicked myself the rest of the day for such outdated, Puritan thinking.* And now, through the morning brain-haze, with my 'camp-coffee' in hand, I remind myself, *Hey! Whose mid-life crisis is this anyway?* After a thorough mind's-eye review of her sumptuous body, I resolve not to let a similar opportunity pass by so quickly without at least mulling over the reasonable, if not completely moral, options. At least before the opportunity to 'mull' becomes a moot point.

  Standing there, mesmerized by the fire, I continue to nibble at the celebrated image I've so fastidiously reconstructed of her in my middle-aged brain. Unabashedly, she presented enticingly short cut-off jeans, frayed or unfrayed I cannot say, perched precariously atop long, well-defined, tanned legs. Each limb glistened, as if freshly shaved and moisturized. If she was wearing anything at all beneath her fetching ensemble, I imagine it to be lacy and thong-like, unmentionable actually, mercifully providing a stunning view of her firm gluteus-maximi beneath. Her ample chest was a bona fide architectural wonder, and the first road-side attraction I found worthy of closer inspection. Her torso was firmly wrapped in a bright, yellow tube-top, bodaciously stretched over her thick breasts, miraculously, without minimizing their admirable lift and girth. I could not verify this at the speed I was traveling, but, upon pure speculation after-the-fact, I posit the evident pounds-per-square-inch stress placed on the tube-top's enviable fabric must have made it slightly transparent, if fortuitously gazed upon in close proximity. *I shall call her Roxanne.*

  Staring into my coffee cup like a tenacious suitor, straining to recall the manic minutia of my lucid, even lurid, dream, it all seems so real. I can almost feel Roxanne straddling my bike, clinging firmly to me from behind, her bare legs splayed generously to accommodate my broad, middle-age rump, eagerly grasping my belt with her slim, 'au naturale,' fingers, her unbridled breasts pressed firmly into my back. The hot wind blowing through my graying sideburns into her young, blonde hair. *Oh man, I must have been crazy!*

It was only a dream. But, a damn-good dream, *or was it...?* I pour myself another steaming cup of camp-coffee and hunker down, attempting to interpret the meaning of this startling vision. Eventually... slowly... I begin to focus on the day, and the quest ahead. *Who knows what the new day will bring?*

Chapter 5

FRAT BOY AND THE BABES

Rumbling down the highway with the road beneath my heels, I smile to the mellow sounds of "Chicago" filling my ears and the warm sun rising ahead. From here to the horizon, I don't see a care in the world. Taking a deep, easy breath, I admire the picture-perfect postcard I find myself in. Chicago's classic horn section belts out the dramatic chorus of that classic tune I've long since forgotten the name of, but, which is forever imprinted on my soul, along with so many sweet memories of younger days.... *"Bah... bah, bah, bah, bah... Bum, bum, bum...."*

The early morning smells of Minnesota beckon me onward. *Man, I am in hog-heaven!* I should have done this years ago. I think I'll plan a dose of mid-life-crisis every summer. *This is the most time I've had to myself since... since....*

My mind flows backward, as the road provides the foundation for further daytime reveries; back to another life, when I was much younger, just getting my toes wet in adulthood, seemingly at the top of my game... invincible.

June, 1976.... I'm lying in the Eastern Washington, sun on the front-lawn of Alpha Tau Omega fraternity, back at ole' "Wazzu." I just finished the final, brain-busting, exam of my collegiate career. Confidently assuming I 'b.s.ed' sufficiently to graduate, I now sport the coveted B.A. in journalism from W.S.U's "Edward R. Murrow College of Communication," having successfully crammed four long years into five. The same memorable 'Chicago' tune (I remember it now, appropriately titled "I've Been Searching So Long") is blasting from 'Birdman's' third-deck sanctuary on the top floor of the frat-house, the bulky speakers of his high-fidelity stereo propped precariously out the corner window. The sun is shining hot, as it does this time of year in the farm-field heat of south-eastern Washington; Pullman to be exact, where green ivy clings to the bricks of the ole' 'Tau-lodge,' as it has for generations of 'ATO Brothers' before me. Real men who made the grade, who stuck it out to garner the rewards of the good life. Sequestered, pruned and protected, here in the hallowed bowels of Greek Row, the center of my known universe.

Life is good indeed. The keg on the front porch is fresh and icy-cold, pumped and primed to minimize the froth. School is officially out for the summer. And in my case... forever! For the past eighteen-plus years (nineteen, if you count my doing kindergarten over), I've been doing what everyone has been telling me to do; studying, homework, utilizing sports as a distraction, swimming, baseball, football, wrestling, toeing the line on a road I had little or no input in choosing. But now, the dusty, dog-eared, book of my life has turned a new page. From here on, there are nothing but blank pages that only I can write.

The mid-day sun glistens from the baby-oil on my flat abs and modestly buff pecs. My mirrored sunglasses glint in the wavering heat. I stretch lazily on a beat-up lounge-chair, tanning everything not strategically covered by my tastefully-short and purposely frayed cut-off jeans. Yes, from my point of view, it would seem the skies the limit! It's balls-to-the-wall and tits-up from here, as far as my blazing intellect and unquenchable enthusiasm will take me. Slurping the foam off another plastic cup of cold "Coors Light," I nonchalantly contemplate my impending, illustrious future.

Currently, I'm staring down my last full-week of down-time here on campus, with nothing to do until my annual summer-job starts; life-guarding at the lake back home, if you call that a job. Mostly, it's doing exactly what I'm doing right now, minus the beer; tanning myself and watching the babes in the sun. All I really have to do today, and more impressively, for the rest of the week, is lie here next to this 'never-ending-keg' and scrutinize the scantily-clad sorority babes, as they frolic to-and-fro with their newly acquired tan lines and freshly painted toes. Yes, life is good, and I have complete confidence that it's going to get nothing but better from this point on.

In the Fall, I'm moving to L.A. with my younger brother, to work on becoming famous like all those other star-struck, 1970's overachievers, who, en-mass, are currently preparing to leave their respective non-descript home-towns for the glories of "Hollywood!" My brother is already there attending summer-school at the "Fashion Institute of Design and Merchandising." The little punk actually beat me to graduate-school, and interestingly, I don't feel the slightest twinge of jealousy. "Greggy" finally found something he actually enjoys, and indeed, excels at; designing clothes of all things! *Go figure. Hard to believe, coming from one of the 'wrestling Hall brothers.'*

    We were both 'jocks' growing up; football, wrestling, baseball, especially wrestling, where at 165 lbs. and 175 lbs. respectively, he and I stood next to each other in Coach Hess' legendary "Fighting Tigers" line-up at Edmonds High School. Some of our old records still stand, rusting away on the brass plates of old hard-wood trophies, gathering the dust in some long-forgotten glass case. A stunning testament to something that, at the time, seemed really important. We both placed at 'State.' Then I, being a year older, blazed the trail to Washington State University, lettering in wrestling and swimming, and of course, girls... or 'Babes,' as I affectionately called them (no sexist overtones intended). Probably, because my Dad called my mom 'Babe.' That, or her childhood nickname, "Tootsie." Either one, when yelled in public by your Dad, searching for your Mother in the local grocery store (when you're thirteen), was quite embarrassing. But, that was my Dad. It took a whole lot to embarrass him. And at the time, very little to embarrass me.

    Greg was the only male that year to graduate from the Home Economics College at WSU (with an emphasis on fashion design). At Commencement, he humorously stood out like a sore thumb, dressed in the only blue gown in a sea of red-gowned co-eds. We had always talked about going to Hollywood; he and I, and making it big in showbiz. So, this was our chance. Dad got in touch with one of his former fifth-grade students who was now an L.A. cop. He and his gracious wife helped us get settled in a small oasis of an apartment in the once neo-hipster, bohemian neighborhood of Eagle Rock, near South Pasadena. Greg began his studies in clothing-design and I worked at odd jobs, sang in local clubs, and began writing movie and television scripts. What a life! Such anticipation. Such confidence....

Back on the road again, retuning to my many-moons-from-then, middle-aged self, somewhere on the eastern edge of Minnesota, astride my broad-framed 'Sophie' (thus, I have affectionately named my bike, for no apparent reason), I can't believe all that has happened in the short lifetime I've lived between college and now. Marriage, kids, career... stress and depression... a few fleeting victories, and larger, lingering challenges. Then, it hits me. Oh my God! I've become my father! And he didn't last long; checking out at forty-nine after his second heart-attack. I sure love that guy, and his quiet, lead-by-example, guidance and work ethic, his sense of humor, and the way he could tell stories. I only hope I can be half-as-good being me, as he was being him.

Chapter 6

'PAPA' AND 'BAD BOY'

I roll up to the toll booth to purchase my ticket for the Mackinac Island ferry with a twinge of anticipation welling in my gut, remembering the last time I was here over 25 years ago. A whole generation and then some has passed since then. For me, it seems that multiple lifetimes have gone by in a flash. Revisiting any fond memory is a treat; a classic human experience to be relished and never rushed. Like discovering my childhood playground again as a college student, back home on a visit. I stood there watching the kids playing where we once played, playing the same games we used to play; reminiscing about those long-ago heroes of the tarmac, each of them still haunting the recesses of my cerebellum. This whole mid-life trip is hauntingly similar in some ways, like some inevitable odyssey. As if, knowingly or unknowingly, I've stumbled onto my own secrete memoir, which is only partially written; an old story, chocked-full of metaphors and bold plot-lines, just waiting to be acted out. I don't know why, but I'm enjoying every moment of this uncertain quest of mine, anticipating each new moment that finds its way into my unfolding story.

I extend a crisp twenty-dollar bill to the pretty toll-booth attendant and greet her with, "One ticket please, passenger only." Her bubbly continence changes, slightly.

"Aren't you taking your bike to the classic car show?"

I give her a surprised look and glance around to notice quite a few old-fashioned vehicles parked in the holding lanes, along with a vintage-blue "Indian" motorcycle, with a boxy side-car, carrying a hip-looking couple about my age also waiting for the ferry.

"The ferry has limited space for vehicles, but your bike could make the next one no problem, the attendant says with a smile.

As she holds my bill in abeyance, I say, "Sure! What's going on? I thought they didn't allow vehicles on the island?"

"Normally, they don't. But this is the annual "Somewhere in Time" weekend, and they've added a classic vehicle show to the festivities. Motorcycles are welcome, especially nice ones like yours."

Accepting my change from her slim, 'French-nailed' hand, I thank her and roll into the holding lanes, sliding next to the Indian motorcycle. Methodically, I attend to my dismount routine; rocking the old-girl onto her kick stand, pulling each finger of my leather gloves and flopping them into my helmet, which I then hang on the handle bar. Then there's the stiff-legged, 'duffer' dismount, waiting momentarily for my land-legs to kick in. Whoever said "The legs are the first to go," had it about right, unless you count my now bi-focaled eyesight. Stretching the kinks out, I lose, then quickly regain, my balance. That's another trippy thing to deal with as one ages; transitory vertigo. It feels good to stand again, breathing in the rich smells of Lake Huron and Michigan's crisp upper-peninsula. I can't believe I actually made it.

The couple with the blue Indian easily mount a friendly conversation, initially focusing on our mutual admiration for each other's rides. Come to find out, they are also from Washington State, Whidbey Island no less, just north of my hometown! Both Ph.D. psychologists; Doctors David and Amanda Johns have driven their 1952 Indian Chief and sidecar all the way to Mackinaw Island for what has become an annual romantic get-away to the Somewhere in Time weekend. What a coincidence to come this far and meet two fellow-Washingtonians in the Mackinac Island ferry line.

Like most 'Somewhere in Timers,' they have a fascination with time-travel and author Richard Matheson's classic novel, "Bid Time Return," which is the book the movie "Somewhere in Time" is based on. Dr. David is tall, thin and pensive, exuding intelligence and an inquisitive mind under his balding pate. His "partner," Amanda, is curvy, petit and outgoing, with classic features and penetrating eyes that are difficult to hide from. But, given her free and open personality, her close scrutiny eventually becomes quite pleasurable. At first glance, they seem an unlikely couple. But, their "life-partnership" becomes self-evident as you get to know them, despite their intriguing incongruities. We pledge to spend some relaxation-time together at some point during the weekend's festivities.

It is nice to find someone else to relate to during this unique experience of mine. Now that I'm actually here, the butterflies begin to flutter in my gut, as I contemplate the question, *What I've gotten myself into?* As the two doctors wander off in search of a morning latte, David casually responds to my, "See you later," with a curious remark that is almost lost in the wind.

"As time allows...."

What an interesting couple... I'll look forward to getting to know them better on the Island.

Arriving on Mackinac Island again is a full-blown nostalgia-trip for me, rolling up to the Grand Hotel on my fully-loaded Harley, fishing gear and all. I vowed to bring only what I needed for the trip, as some sort of green, minimalistic statement. My sleeping bag and ground-cover are rolled tightly behind my seat. The bulging side-bags are strategically packed with nominal changes of clothing and food. My travel CPAP-machine, and whatever fishing gear I could stow, are tucked in here and there. Grandpa Ned's 9 foot, 6.4 weight, graphite, 'Loomis,' fly-rod, with its large-arbor 'Orvis' reel, and my spare split-cane 'special,' are creatively lashed in a leather case to Sophie's side. Just like the cowboys used to do; scabbarding their Winchesters to their horse's flanks.

I consider myself fortunate to have inherited some vintage fishing and hunting gear from my wife's grandfather. If only, perhaps, by default. And I've prided myself in caring for his stake of quality outdoor gear, vicariously enjoying his legendary field-and-stream life-style through the classic fly-rods and antique shotguns he used and loved so much.

Edgar ("Ned") Rodiger is an interesting icon from my wife's side of the family. Ninety-eight years young when he finally cashed in his chips with a peaceful whisper. Despite his life-long lean frame and cool-eyed persona, Ned ate like a horse all the way to the end. His still thick shock of hair went pure white in his later years. And despite the many colorful exploits he would tell and retell around the family fireplace, it's been independently established that he made a decent living in the nineteen-thirties, forties and fifties as a frontier nightclub owner and a hunting/fishing guide based out of Ketchum, Idaho. He owned and operated the popular, rustic, night-spot called "The Ranch House" and piloted his high-rolling 'sports' in and out of the backcountry camps in his own, single-engine, Piper Cub. 'The Ranch House' is still in operation today, in the same location, pumping out good times and memorable night-life under a new name.

Legend has it, whenever Ernest Hemingway was in Ketchum, he wouldn't plan a hunting or a fishing expedition without consulting his old friend, "Bad-Boy" Ned. "Bad Boy" was the moniker Ned picked up during his professional gambling days. No one really knows who tagged him with the ominous nickname and he never adequately explained the details himself. Suffice it to say, the title must have been appropriate, as it still evokes whispers of clandestine respect from certain old-timers in-the-know.

They say you could find "Papa" Hemingway holding court at end of the Ranch House's well-worn and crowded pinewood bar or playing checkers and smoking fat Havana's at the pot-belly stove, blending in seamlessly with the locals. Periodically, you'd find him urgently pontificating a point of pressing social significance with the other Hollywood regulars, like Gary Cooper, Ingrid Bergman and Howard Hawks. It was at the Ranch House where the giants of the day could be themselves and re-load their souls, without the usual trappings of fame and notoriety to hinder their recuperation. Yes, it was said, "The Ranch House was quite a place."

I often wonder which of Ned's vintage gear might have actually felt the expert fieldsman ship of Hemingway's hands. And I fantasize about the many unpenned short-stories 'Papa' might have written, based on the escapades of 'Bad-Boy Ned' as the 'grace under pressure' sidekick to his legendary protagonist, "Nick Adams," if only he had lived as long as Ned did. I've read many of those unwritten tomes in my mind's eye. All of them crafty best-sellers, reissued in numerous celebrated printings, now dog-eared and lovingly sequestered in countless, sacred bookcases, next to roaring hearths in fishing-cabins and hunting-lodges anywhere a quixotic explorer can be found, restless and reminiscing, planning the next great adventure. Perhaps one day, someone will carry on the tradition of such great sporting legends as "Papa and Bad-boy," for all our vicarious reading pleasures. As for me… I have a memoir to write.

Chapter 7

WELCOME TO THE GRAND HOTEL

I spy Jan Flannery for the first time in over twenty-five years at the busy registration desk, welcoming the Somewhere in Time guests and looking even more gorgeous than I remembered. She's elegantly dressed in a white antique gown and matching Victorian hat. I purposely register with another volunteer at the opposite end of the table, not wanting to reintroduce myself to her just yet... wondering whether she will recognize me after all these years. I hurry through the crowded lobby with my clothes and toiletries and my CPAP, stowed in my compact "Filson" 'Pullman,' cotton-twill suitcase. ("Might as well have the best!")

Sidling up to the hotel's ornate registration desk, which is arranged with turn-of-the-century accoutrements, the thought occurs to me to ask the gentleman behind the desk, "Would room 420 be available...?"

I was astonished I even remembered the old room Greggy and I stayed in during that dream-like summer of 1979, so many years ago. *It couldn't hurt to ask...* I think to myself.

The dapper and efficient clerk checks his computer, "Yes, it's available. However, most of the "Somewhere in Time" guests are staying in the lower level rooms, and the..."

I interrupt before he finishes his explanation, "Actually... it's kind of a sentimental thing." I say, rather mysteriously, leaning in and laying on the thespian charm, which has laid dormant inside me all these years. With a sideways wink, I add, "If you know what I mean."

My little charade seems to perk up the staid employee, as he welcomes the dash of intrigue I unexpectedly inserted into his most-likely predictable day.

"Oh, of course, of course. Not a problem Sir," he whispers under his breath, his beady-eyes darting side-to-side with a certain panache that he, no doubtedly, has been longing to utilize. He spins on his heel and reaches surreptitiously into one of the old-fashion, hardwood, cubby-holes at the back wall and grabs a heavy, gold-plated key with the number "420" inscribed on its ornamental tag. The clerk then ceremoniously rotates the large guest register and presents me an antique pen, after courteously dipping it into the cut-glass ink-well. Not being accustomed to such enthusiastic service, but enjoying our continued clandestine role-play, I scratch my name onto the parchment register, just as the good doctors, David and Amanda, stroll up next to me.

"Hello stranger!" Amanda says, her off-handed salutation unknowingly complimenting my veiled mystique in the eyes of the fastidious registration clerk, whom I have informally deputized as a comrade-in-arms.

"Doctor… Doctor…" I acknowledge them with a stealthy wink and a secretive nod to the clerk. Then, as if to shield our conversation from close public scrutiny, I add in a guarded tone, "He'll take care of you. He's one of us." With that, the clerk almost bursts with glee, assuming he has been secretly initiated into some covert, "James Bond" operation.

Just then, a young, college-age bell-boy dutifully presents himself at the registration desk, having no doubt been summoned by the clerk. David and Amanda intuitively confirm they are onto my charade with a wink, playing along for fun. David steps in closer, leaning sideways toward me and the clerk.

"Mr. uh… Four-twenty?" David asks, under his breath, glancing at my room key in the hand of the desk clerk.

"Why yes, uh? Mr…?" David and I instinctively synchronize a slow head-turning gaze to the desk clerk, as if to cue his next strategic move. The fastidious clerk snaps-to like an anxious "Mr. Whipple" just caught squeezing the "Charmin." He quickly dashes to the cubbies and retrieves another gold-plated key and holds it next to mine, allowing our conversation to continue….

"Ah yes… Mr. and Mrs. Ninety-Nine." I say, consummating our new code-name introductions. I barely get the fortuitous phrase 'Ninety-Nine' out of my mouth without breaking character, thinking I sound like Don Adams playing the comedic television spy, Maxwell Smart, addressing his leggy side-kick, "Agent 99." I struggle to continue without laughing.

"Shall we rendezvous in the Cupola Bar at the appointed hour?" I suggest to my mysterious compatriots.

"Indeed..." Amanda intones, like the exotic 'James Bond babe she could truly pass for, while David adds in parting, just to mess with the clerk's obviously fragile psyche, "As time allows, Mr. Four-twenty... as time allows."

Damn, they're good actors, despite being shrinks. Either that or some basic thespian training was standard during their doctoral training.

The bellboy, who is dressed in a turn-of-the-century bell-hop outfit, complete with a red, pill-box hat incongruously perched atop his modern-day haircut, cautiously takes my room key from the registration clerk, not knowing what to think of the mysterious scene he has just come upon. The clerk cautiously brings the bell-boy into our covert operation.

"Mr. Hall, I mean, 'Mr. Four-twenty,' will be staying in room... uh, four-twenty." Then, with a surprising 'Dr. Strangelove' flair, the clerk adds with a smile, "Enjoy your stay with us, Sir. Arthur here will show you to your room. And please, don't hesitate to let me know if I can do..." (pausing for dramatic effect, now fully engaged in our secret plan, he adds) "anything at all." The clerk seals his perceived allegiance with an exaggerated wink, as John and Amanda give a last clandestine nod before turning to finish their own registration process. The bell boy grabs my Filson bag and leads me in the direction of the lobby elevator.

Man, that was fun! I wouldn't have had the nerve to do that back home. There's something about being anonymous in a foreign land that brings out one's carefree spirit. Too bad my brother isn't here for some of these random acts of hilarity. Of course, I can't hold a candle to Greggy's unpredictable antics. He's naturally off-the-wall 24/7. He would have probably secured complimentary room-service and a free massage by now. I'll just have to make the best of things without him and see where it takes me.

Waiting for the elevator, I glance into the adjacent dining room, beautifully spacious and bustling with a crowd of mid-morning breakfast guests. My senses awaken to the aroma of thick-sliced bacon, hotcakes, stacked and brimming with real butter and dark maple syrup, eggs over-easy or 'Benedict,' and fresh, percolating coffee. All that from one long whiff. I'm instantly torn between coming back down to the breakfast-buffet or following my original plan to seek the solitude of the first fishing hole I can find.

The elevator opens and interrupts my momentary reverie. I follow the bell-boy inside.

"Floor please?" the festooned elevator operator intones.

My young porter flashes the older gentleman my room key and replies, "Four-twenty, George. For uh, 'Mr. Four-Twenty.'" the bell boy adds with emphasis, continuing my mysterious charade without explanation to the elevator operator. He smiles, as if he could care less. I manage a belated, "Thank you," and automatically stare at the antique floor numbers above the elevator door.

Since it's just the three of us, myself being the unknown entity, the bell-boy takes the opportunity to engage in some small-talk with the elevator attendant.

"How's that energetic wife of yours George? The young man asks, with a mischievous smile. "Still leading the charge for preserving those sub-Saharan tree frogs?" The attendant nods a disgruntled affirmation without glancing our way.

"You know my wife Art; as busy as a body can be. Bless her little, green soul." Then he adds sarcastically, "If I could only get her to pay half as much attention to me!"

I smile to myself, enjoying their workplace repartee. The gentleman slides the elevator open at the fourth floor without leaving his stool and touches the brim of his hat. "Have a wonderful stay here at the Grand Hotel, 'Mr. Four-Twenty.'"

"Thank you," I say, following the bell-boy down the richly carpeted hallway. Belatedly, I wonder if I should have tipped the elevator operator for his services. Being too late on the uptake, I dutifully follow the bell-boy down the plush corridor, taking in the pastoral scenes arranged in elegant frames down the hallway and the plants and antique furnishings appropriately spaced along the tastefully papered walls.

I can't help but notice the competent stride of the young lad before me, even with the full weight of my luggage in his hands. For a moment, my own indestructible youth flashes before me. I could run all day and do as many push-ups as I wanted, until I was bored, and have plenty of energy left over to 'party-hardy' at the slightest provocation. If only we seasoned veterans could pass our hard-earned knowledge to the younger generations. And, if only the young bucks would heed our advice and take advantage of its power and perspective, I doubt there would be as many wars, divorces, or messed up kids as there are now. Then, again, if I'd followed the sage advice of my own father's accumulated life-experience, I probably wouldn't even be here now, thinking these wispy, hypothetical thoughts. Or, perhaps I would. Obviously, I am.

We reach room 420 and the young man turns the gold key in the tumbler, flipping the deadbolt, and pushing the brass door-plate open before him. I follow into the room as an exhilarating wave of *déja'vu* washes over me. It's been twenty-six years since I was in this very room. The furnishings have changed a bit, but not much. The space seems so familiar and intriguing. Two Queen-sized beds still parallel each other to my left, with a fashionable nightstand and lamp between them. It all beckons me, like a long-standing invitation, as it did then so many years ago, when Greggy and I bunked together during the filming of Somewhere in Time. I bounce my shoulder-bag onto the closest bed and breathe in the subtle scent of fresh linens and polished mahogany. In reality, this was my brother's room. Greggy and the rest of the crew had their own rooms during that summer in 1979. This is the room he called me from on that fateful day, knowing I'd be sweltering in our little flat back in L.A., slugging it out on 'the hill' at Universal Studios. He accurately described the room as spacious, bright and clean, with breath-taking views of the lake and the old saltbox lighthouse, and the cool breeze blowing in off the water. Of course, I didn't need much convincing to leave the smog and the heat, and our lonely apartment. And since I hadn't yet squandered my summer vacation, I quickly found myself on Mackinac Island.

Yes, Greggy and I shared this very room; young and naïve and so full of hope. Actually, we only used this luxurious place when our heads finally hit the pillow in the early hours of the morning. Then, the cruel wake-up call would startle us awake in what seemed like a matter of minutes. Since Somewhere In Time was shot on a modest budget, the cast and crew were under enormous pressure, working long hours at a frenetic pace, to get as much raw footage 'in-the-can' as possible during the tight shooting schedule. Watching my brother and his colleagues working so hard, I remember thinking: *being a lowly tour-guide isn't so bad after all.*

While the bell-boy goes through his room-readying routine, I gaze more closely around. On my right next to the bathroom door is an antique cherry-wood bureau with a large beveled-glass mirror. To my delight, I notice a small, well equipped, writing table strategically placed next to one of two, large 'lake-view' windows over-looking the fall-colors of the hardwoods and yellow birches below. Farther out, the Grand Hotel's spacious lawns slope graciously toward the blue waters of Lake Huron. The cathartic beauty of the scene seems too good to be true for this weary, middle-aged traveler, who could really use some 'alone-time.' Luckily, with the off-season swiftly approaching, and the hotel about to close for the winter, there are typically more rooms available than guests this time of year. I consider myself blessed to have finagled this quiet and spacious room, so full of memories, yet far enough away from the madding crowd.

The bell boy finishes stowing my gear, then expertly dashes open the lace curtains with the flare of a Victorian actor. He then launches into his canned introductory narrative, pointing out the room's amenities and the local points of interest within view of the spacious windows.

"Off to the left in the distance, is the famous 'Round Island Lighthouse' featured in the movie Somewhere in Time. It was built in

1895 and restored again in 1978 for the filming. Christopher Reeve rowed Jane Seymour out to the secluded island during one of the famous romantic scenes. All the lights, cameras, equipment and crew had to be transported by boat."

Listening with one ear, I surreptitiously reach into my pocket and thumb through my current life-savings for an appropriate gratuity. Perusing my measly wad of cash, I find it ironic that one of the selling points to my wife; to be able to make this trip in the first place, was I that had recently made a whimsical search on the internet and found some of my forgotten and unclaimed MCA/Universal stock investments, which had been steadily earning interest all these years! It took a lot of patience and mounds of paperwork, but I eventually recovered the funds from a successor, 'Take-over Company' I didn't even recognize. And here it is; the remains of my entire stock portfolio from all those years in L.A., $783.34. Thus, I was able to convince my wife that the unexpected windfall was additional confirmation "I should take this old 'tour-guide money' and attend the annual reunion of that classic film my brother and I had worked on together, so long ago." Looking back, I believe my humble performance was worthy of an "Oscar," or at least a "Golden Globe." Indeed, it was one of those rare moments in one's married life when, even with all the cards stacked against you, and with the many innumerable reasons why 'it just won't happen' staring you in the face, somehow, God winks in your direction and the miraculous happens. In my case, my wife inexplicably agreed I should take the whole week off work, ride 'our' new motorcycle half-way across the country to the annual Somewhere In Time weekend, and stay with my crazy brother at the luxurious Grand Hotel. *"Yes, Virginia... there is a Santa Claus!"*

Before leaving, I gave my frazzled wife an appreciative hug and a kiss, and with the guilt nudging at my conscience, I seriously thought about not going. While I'd be gone, she'd be doing everything herself; getting the three younger kids up and ready for school, making the lunches, being the 'soccer-mom' for their respective after-school practices, music concerts and church activities, as well as being the 'on-call counselor' for our fledgling, just-out-of-the-house, elder daughter with her current 'crisis-of-the-moment.' Then, there's the grocery shopping, making sure everyone does their homework before it's time to 'brush, flush and P-Js,' just so she can do it all over again the next day. Fortunately, my twinge of marital compassion was fleeting. And by the end of our hug, mentally, I was already on the road with the wind dancing through my sideburns.

In all fairness, as the initial euphoria cleared in a later, reflective moment, it occurred to me that my wife does all those things anyway, even when I'm at home. I went to bed that night feeling a bit conflicted and much more appreciative of my spouse and how much she does. Thinking deeply of how I fit into it all, I finally dropped off to sleep, and dreamed about one of my old girlfriends… again.

Attempting to make up for my earlier potential faux pas with the elevator operator, I hand the bell boy a generous tip as he turns to leave. In a glance, I see he is pleasantly surprised at its denomination. I remember being in his position as a young man; not feeling appreciated by those I was serving; busting my butt, attending to those who had plenty of monetary resources, but were unreasonably hesitant to spread it around. I rationalize that since I'll only be on this wonderful island for the weekend, and I brought more than I plan to spend, and also, in honor of my generous brother who already paid for my room and board, I should tip well in celebration of my current good fortune. Come to think of it, with this small gesture of unsolicited gratitude, I'm feeling a little richer already.

As the young man turns to leave, I remember to request some local information.

"Say, ah, what's your name?"

"Art, Sir… uh, Mr. Four-twenty? At your service."

"You can call me Michael. 'Sir' sounds too much like my grandfather. And 'Mr. Four-twenty' was just a little inside joke. I'm afraid my friends and I were having a bit of fun at the expense of your front desk clerk."

"Well, you couldn't have picked on a more willing victim," the young man retorts, with noted sarcasm.

"Well, Art, you wouldn't happen to know of any good fly-fishing spots around the island would you?" I ask. With that, the young man perks up, as if I hit upon a favorite topic of discussion.

"Sure do." he says with a grin. "And speaking of grandfathers, mine used to take me fishing right down in front of the hotel," he says, gesturing out the window. "There's a nice cove, just across the road at the end of the lawn. I've fished every inch of this island and that's about as good as they come." I move to the window for clarification.

"You mean right across the road?"

"Yep, the walleye and white bass circle the island picking off the bait fish as they ball-up in the coves and rock points. You won't find any better place to catch a mess of bluegills 'this side of the Mississippi,' as my grandfather used to say. Did you bring any woolly-buggers or flashy buck-tail streamers?"

"Of course." I reply, thrilled that I seemed to have asked the right question to the right person.

"I'd try anything that simulates a smelt or lake herring," the young man continues, "either early morning or evening, between twilight and dusk. Anyway, that's how we used to do it. Those were some good times...."

Chapter 8

THE RULE AGAINST PERPETUITIES

Suppressing a middle-age urge to use my time efficiently, I find myself just standing there with the bell boy staring at the lake.

"Your grandfather sounds like quite a fellow," I say, gazing reflectively toward the blue water. For a time no reply is necessary, as we stand with hands in our pockets, enjoying our respective by-gone imagery.

"Yeah, he was," the young man finally admits. "He's the one the "Arthur" character is based on, in the movie Somewhere in Time?"

"Really?" I say, genuinely surprised.

"Yeah. That was his name too… "Arthur," just like me." The young man then relates a few personal stories from his family's history, which has no doubt been passed down through the generations. He too, seems to be somewhere else in his mind.

"My great-grandfather, Arthur's father, came to the Grand Hotel in 1910. He was sent here to keep an eye on things by his father, Obadiah Biehl, who was the Founding Trustee of the Public Benefit Trust that was set up by the railroad to build and manage the Grand Hotel, before the turn of the century… you know, the Twentieth Century."

I attribute his unnecessary clarification to his youthful perspective. Either that or an unconscious comment on my graying sideburns.

"My grandfather, "Arthur," was only ten years old when he came to the island. He used to catch hell for terrorizing the guests, bouncing his big, red ball around the lobby."

As the young man shares his family history, the past and present begin to meld together as certain scenes from Somewhere In Time flash before me: The young Arthur sitting patiently in the hotel lobby waiting for someone to play ball with him; the elderly Arthur dutifully going about his business as a cheerful bell boy and one-man

Chamber of Commerce, gracefully sailing into his golden years, helping out any way he can. I then envision both "Arthurs," grandfather and grandson, in old waders and fishing-vests and cane-poles, fly-fishing in the cove in front of the hotel. 'The old man and the boy,' sharing the passing of time.

My awareness shifts back to the bell boy, still eulogizing the memory of those cherished days. "We'd fish, and he'd tell me about the hotel, the people he met, the memorable ones; like Jimmie Durante and Esther Williams when they made a movie here on the island back in the forties. It was called "This Time for Keeps." They used the Hotel as a backdrop just like Somewhere in Time did. They built the big outdoor swimming pool down by the lake for the picture; for Ester Williams' swimming scenes. Grandfather said the hotel was never the same after Obadiah's death. As the original hotel trustee, his grandfather took pride in treating everyone like family, guests and employees alike. He was involved in their lives. That's why Arthur's father was sent here to be the hotel manager; to keep an eye on things for the family. 'The personal touch' they used to call it."

"There was a clause in the original Public Benefit Trust that allowed the Board of Directors to take control of the Hotel after Obadiah's death. They voted in their own trustee and cut my family out of any say in how the hotel was to be run. The Board hired some fancy Philadelphia lawyer who cited some obscure legal theory, something about 'a perpetual rule,' that prevented Obadiah's son, Arthur's father, from succeeding as trustee. Some say it was because he started showing signs of minor memory lapses, which the Board used as grounds to disqualify him from being trustee."

"But through it all, they never let their disappointment interfere with their duties as life-long hotel employees, especially Arthur. Even as a lowly bell boy, Arthur carried on the original intent of the Public Benefit Trust, which was to provide a haven of rest and relaxation for all those who came to the island, along with that personal family touch. Arthur was voted 'employee-of-the-year' so many times they finally just gave him the plaque to keep. He hung it in his little bungalow down in front of the hotel. I often wondered why they let him live there so long, with all the political wrangling's about the property's "highest and best use." But you know, Arthur enjoyed every minute of his life right up until the day he died. Toward the end he checked himself into the hotel as a guest. He died right here in the hotel he loved so much, in room 313; the same room Richard Collier died in in the movie."

Drinking in the bell boy's touching soliloquy, I find myself overwhelmed by how awestruck one can become with the simple meanings of life... even in small moments like this.

"I'm only working here to pay off my student loans, and to kill time before deciding what to do with my life. I really can't see myself staying on the island forever... like Arthur did."

Mentally reposed at the young man's feet, relishing his reminisces about his grandfather; it's as if time has stopped in honor of the moment. Still looking at the lake, I let his sage-words settle in the intimate atmosphere around us, contemplating their deeper meaning. My thoughts then drift back to my first year of law school and its frenetic paper-chase for the meaning of such oblique legal concepts as "the Rule Against Perpetuities," "In Rem Jurisdiction," and the seemingly simple, but highly complex issue of "Standing." Back then, we would read a hundred and fifty pages a night, try to digest the accompanying case-law, and stand terrified before our crusty Constitutional Law professor, sleep-deprived, fighting periodic panic-attacks, attempting to recite the appropriate rule of law that so obviously presented itself in the seminal case of <u>Brown v. Board of Education</u>... *"Mister Hall...!!!"* The reoccurring dream still haunts me.

I begin to contemplate the legal issues presented by the bell boy's unique case concerning his great-grandfather's Public Benefit Trust. On a whim I ask him, "What kind of document was used to appoint your great-grandfather as the original trustee? Do any copies still exist?"

"It was my great-great-grandfather Obadiah. You can read the cover-page of the founding document in the display-case downstairs in the "Hall of Records," along with the other hotel memorabilia.

Obadiah Biehl is listed as the original trustor and trustee on the first page. But, it's hard to understand the rest of the old fashioned legal-jargon."

Interesting... I muse to myself, continuing our vigil at the window. "I'd love to look at it sometime." I confirm to Art. "Antique legal documents are a kind of hobby of mine. If nothing else, I enjoy trying to decipher their meaning. Besides, the Rule Against Perpetuities is a rather complicated legal doctrine. It can be confusing for even a seasoned lawyer." Then, and for no particular reason, I begin an informal lecture on old, English common law.

"The Rule Against Perpetuities" was created by the English courts in response to certain controversies concerning estates of the landed-gentry. Basically, it limits how long one can pass real property, in trust, from generation to generation, after death. The courts ruled that you could only pass an interest in real estate down to a limited number of generations. And potentially, in your family's case, that could have been a relative who was already living within twenty-one years of the original trustor's death. Theoretically, that would have been twenty-one years after your great-grandfather died. Assuming the Board of Directors had adequate cause to disqualify your great-grandfather, Arthur's father, as trustee because of his periodic memory lapses, the question is, whether your grandfather, Arthur, was born within 21 years of Obadiah's death? If he was, and if what you've told me is true about the intended succession of your families' authority to manage the hotel, it may be that Arthur should have taken over as the hotel's trustee as per the terms provided for in the trust document." With that, the young man's gaze diverts from the lake to me, as he attempts to digest what he's just heard. "You mean Arthur should have been in charge of the hotel all those years?"

"Well, the first step is to find out when your great-great-grandfather died. And here's where it gets down to splitting hairs, and potentially how the Board of Director's claimed control over the trust. The traditional Rule Against Perpetuities has a little-known provision that allows for the normal nine-month gestation period in defining a human life, in addition to the twenty-one years, to cover the contingency that a trust beneficiary may be conceived, but not actually born, at the time of the trustor's death." I turn to the bell boy, "You said Arthur came to the island in 1910, when he was five years old? That would mean he was born sometime in 1905 or 1904. If you back that up by nine months... and if that date is within twenty-one years of Obadiah's death... you may have quite a case. Unless, of course, the whole thing's barred by some applicable statute of limitations. The bottom line is, you and your family may still have a claim!"

Art looks at me with his mind whirling and says, "Whoa...."

"When did Arthur pass away?" I ask, continuing to track my admittedly thin line of legal reasoning.

"Oh... uh, about four or five years ago. I was in college at Millfield at the time.

"And your own father...?"

"No one knows.... He took off shortly after I was born."

"Well, it sounds like you've got some legal research to do." I say, sounding strangely like my old 'con-law' professor. My rambling legal analysis seems to have flowed from somewhere else. I have no idea whether Art picked up on any of the details or not. He then turns to leave with a quizzical look on his face, blinking himself back to reality.

"Well, thanks Mr., uh, sorry... Michael. I'll see you around." he says, as he heads toward the door. Then stopping short with his hand on the door-handle he adds, "Oh, and don't forget, right down in the cove at the front of the hotel... the best fishing on the island. You can't miss." The young man leaves in a rush, as if he suddenly remembered something. "And thanks for the legal advice!" he says over his shoulder, as he disappears into the hallway at a determined pace.

A beautiful silence returns to the room, as I sit on the bed taking in the pleasant memories; thinking of the myriad of emotions that must have expressed themselves to these textured walls over the many years. I wonder... why am I here? What has compelled me at this time in my life, with all the other things I should be doing; things that still need to be done, to journey to this place, again. I feel a profound anticipation, as if something important is about to happen... something I am destined to be a part of, for some unknown, or perhaps deeply known, reason. *What have I done with my life?* Perhaps, that's what I'm here to find out.

After unpacking and methodically dressing for my first impromptu fishing expedition, I glance into the bureau mirror and catch the sobering view of a hefty, middle-aged man, dressed in a plaid shirt, fly-fishing vest and baggy chest-waders... hiding under an old fur-felt fedora. I smile at the comical image staring at me and flick the brim of my hat. "Might as well have the best!" I say, to no one in particular, the "Filson" Out-Fitters 'motto' popping incongruously into my head. At least my choice of quality gear shows a little class: "Filson," "L.L. Bean," "Cabela's" and "REI." As my Dad always said, "You get what you pay for." Or was it Granddad? I pause another moment, sizing up my 'ready-for-fishing' self... looking like a paunchy version of "Papa" Hemingway himself... without the beard of course. Maybe I should grow one.... Of course, it's hard to look dashing in chest-waders and a fully-packed fishing vest. Even if I were fifty pounds lighter and twenty years younger, I doubt many romance-oriented women would vote me onto their 'fantasy calendar' any time soon. So, this is what I've become; baggy waders, floppy hat and all the rest. Even after all these years, it takes a little getting used to; adjusting to my aging image in the mirror. It's as if the reflection comes from another dimension; a more sobering place that lacks the subjective, self-flattering impressions one tends to liberally apply to oneself, as a futile defense to reality. For a brief moment, I see a more sterile, and most probably, more honest self-image, without the frosting and filters I have lavishly layered on over the years. Then, without the distracting 'rush of time' that generally keeps me from looking too closely, I catch a glimpse of the 'real me' hiding there in plain sight, through the wrinkles and the extra pounds, beyond the temporary triumphs and disappointments, all of which only amount to a hill of beans. It's interesting to glimpse yourself as you truly are, looking back in real time; timid, but accepting, confident and humbled at the same time. That's who's staring back at me now.... His wise, aging eyes meet mine. A slight grin. I smile in a mystic moment of recognition, confirming that we see each other for who we really are. I hope he sticks around for a while this time. We should get to know each other better.

"Ahhh, Mr. Four-Twenty, have a secret rendezvous with a brook trout?" says George, the elevator operator.

"If I'm lucky," I respond, smiling, and stepping from the hallway into George's office.

"Rumor has it, you're either government black-ops or a little off-center, or both," he says, closing the elevator door for the short trip down to the lobby.

"Well, off the record, I can only confirm that I'm not black ops. But then, with all the covert mind-control stuff going on, you never can tell."

"Sounds a bit 'Art Bell-ish,'" adds George, with a twinge of intrigue.

"Oh yeah..." I eagerly respond. "Sleep apnea and late-night talk-radio, the perfect recipe for your basic altered-state lifestyle."

"Amen brother. You're talking to a fellow CPAP 'Ethernaut.'" George smiles knowingly, as if he has determined I must be O.K.

"I'm afraid my friends and I had a little too much fun at the expense of your front-desk clerk. I hope we didn't freak him out too much." I say apologetically.

"Well, we could use a little excitement and intrigue around here, as you probably can tell. They don't let us out much, if you know what I mean."

As the elevator door slides shut, the entire pantheon of potential local fisheries swirls in my head. In addition to the easily accessible cove in front of the hotel, the other possibilities beckon to my instincts. I studied a few of the Island's websites before I left and one of them showed a beautiful, rustic scene and noted, "[t]he Hemlock-White Pine hardwood forest has a rich undergrowth of birch, elm and maple..." on a landscape comprising of, "... fields, meadows, marshes, swamps, bogs, coastline, boreal forest, limestone formations and caves." Another local fishing spot showed a thumbnail photo with the romantic title, "Tahquamenon Falls." It was a picturesque scene with a placid free-flowing creek cascading over a stately 'falls' into the perfect fly-casting splash-pool, surrounded by flaring autumn colors of red, yellow and pumpkin orange. A great photograph worth more than a thousand words, especially for a part-time 'Sport' like me.

As we begin our descent, I decide to inquire of George....

"Say, do you know anything about Tahquamenon Falls?"

"Indeed, I do." my fellow middle-ager calmly intones. "It's like fishing in the middle of a postcard. When I want to be alone and think... I go to Tahquamenon Falls."

"Any fish there?" I ask.

"Not many. You'd probably catch closer to your limit in the cove in the front of the hotel. But, deep down in those slow-moving pools, they're monsters. Big browns.... If you've got the patience, and the right match for the hatch, they'll show you a good time."

With eyes that reflect his own eager enthusiasm, I lap up George's flowery word-picture like sweet molasses. Then comes his caveat.

"But, you can't get there from here. It's on the mainland... farther up north. Well worth the drive though, if nothing else for the 'colors' this time of year."

I could tell, from George's far away gaze, that something primal was smoldering inside him. Something wonderful and longed for; like breaded, pan-fried trout, sizzling in butter and onions over a secluded camp-fire. In an instant, I tap into his reverent moment. I've known a few such precious spots. But, not as many as I'd like to admit. Those special places in the universe where the noble 'wasting-of-time' takes place on a semi-irregular basis. Where those few consecrated moments of pure bliss exist. When everything is still and clear and meaningful. Like standing crotch-deep in a cool, clear-running 'stream of paradise,' fly-fishing some small corner of heaven, soaking it all in. Waiting for whatever it is we all wait for. Suddenly, I am somewhere else, on another sacred day....

Running through Valley County, just out of McCall, Idaho, the winding north-fork of the Payette River is like heaven on earth to me. Late summer hatches of mayflies scurry over crystal-clear rocky runs, making for a fly-fisher's dream, and for me, a veritable spiritual paradise. Of course, no one expects to see a "Gone Fishing" sign hanging on your regular spot in the church pew on Sunday morning. But, every once in a while, I've been known to commune with "The Great Fisher of Men," rod and reel in hand, even on the Lord's Day.

For me, fly fishing is more than an excuse not to shave on the weekends. For me, it's pure unadulterated worship. "Fishing" itself is of course totally biblical. But, there is something sacred, even holy perhaps, about immersing oneself in a cool mountain stream, casting to a slow-moving, deep-blue pool, feeling the presence of creation all around without a steeple in sight.

I'm quite certain that if God fishes in His leisure time, He has a beautiful, secluded spot just like mine in some rugged, remote corner of heaven. I imagine the great "I AM" to be a strict 'catch-and-releaser,' sharing His angling secrets with just a few private 'confidantes,' like Michael and Gabriel, both of whom I presume to be dry-fly fishers. With the patience of Job and the Kingly wisdom He imparted to Solomon, the Lord is obviously the ultimate angler. In my day-dreams, I visualize the long, looping arcs of the Lord's fly-line, and the rhythmic casts of His glistening fly rod, whipping to and fro in the rising mist of an early morning sun. I also assume, with some confidence, that "The Ancient of Days" prefers natural, cane poles over even the best synthetic-polymers. Then again, like most other 'not-so-important things in life,' there are pros and cons to both schools of thought.

Falling in slow-motion, like the down of thistle, the good Lord's elegant pattern settles ever so lightly onto the deep-blue pool, dancing as if on the surface of a mirror. Then, with a 'slap!,' a big speckled-brown trout smacks the surface and dives deep, making a bold downstream run against the Lord's bending rod and screaming reel. The wily, old Trout is hooked and he doesn't like it. It's a familiar fight, one that happens again and again on any given day; the sudden tension between free-will and divine providence. *"He's a Big One!"* the Lord says, smiling proudly, letting the fish take his initial, unencumbered run with nothing but the weight of the line. Indeed, the

Trout is a big one; one of the biggest and smarter than most. He's speckled-brown, broad and sleek, with powerful lines... magnificent from nostrils to tail.

From the fish's perspective, he's 'earned' everything by his cunning and wit. He should have known better than to fall for the unconventional, the unknown, a fact that makes his current predicament all the more perplexing. How could this happen to him? Perhaps, it was the unique presentation, the subtle approach, that caught his inquisitive eye. Or perhaps, it was the simple message? Whatever the attraction, it triggered a deep primal response that rose quickly within him without warning.

Now that he's hooked, all he can do is what he knows best; fight for his life, and everything he knows to be dear and familiar! So, he struggles on with all his might against 'The Lord of the River,' and His subtle 'Holy Spirit,' that has caught him so unawares. Frantically, he thinks about his life and how good it has been. Yes, even the bad times. He must not give in to the very thing that could end all he knows to be 'himself.' He <u>must</u> escape or he will surely die; die to everything that is his.

Not even his friends can help him now. He, alone, has taken the bait, and the battle is on for his very soul. How foolish he feels, fighting alone in the deep, writhing in his own whirling pool of blue. Of course, most of his kind have had their own brush with this same Noble Angler. Yet, most, in this bend-of-the-river, have escaped the 'Heavenly Hounding' through their own frenetic squirmings and machinations (even unto death's door), only to live on in fear, endangered, longing for something more.

In his youth, he had contemplated the seductive dangers of those forbidden thoughts; the nefarious nibbling at which he knew he shouldn't. Yes, he had eyed with envy those crafty imitations: the wet-flies, the streamers, those dancing dry ones. Boldly, he even brushed a "Pale Morning Dun," and gazed longingly at the "Blue-Winged Olive." He once nudged a delightful "Nymph" and toyed with a sassy "Bucktail Streamer." He was briefly hooked on one occasion. Yes, long ago, as a young fry, but large for his age. At the time, he had resigned himself that *the end had come*; like so many other foolish fingerlings that had strayed away from the familiar and the wise. But, by some strange twist of fate, and nothing clever he could claim as his own, he found his time had not yet come. Instead, it seemed, he was predestined to grow bigger and stronger and become better at doing what big speckled brown's do, day in and day out, living in the main-stream, basking in the shallows, eating and living and creating others like himself... down in the smooth-moving, deep-blue pool, on the old Payette.

Yes, the old Trout should have known better. His great pale belly, displaying its glorious girth, testifies to his many years at the top and to his legendary cunning. His sterling reputation has spread far up and down the winding river; the 'Great Speckled-Brown from the deep-blue pool, down by the bridge'... a real force to be reckoned with by all who venture through his part of the old Payette.

Even now, as he struggles, the rumors fly like the frenzy of a full-on hatch at feeding time. *The 'Big Speckled Brown' has taken the bait!* In solemn tones they say, *But, don't count him out yet. He'll fight the good fight, as he always has. He'll not back down nor give up, not in a great fight such as this.* But eventually, most of the inhabitants of the old Payette just don't care enough to intervene. To be sure, *what could they do?* Indeed, they've each got their own challenges to deal with; coping with the unpredictable river and the good and bad things it brings their way. They tell themselves they will wait, *to see how it comes out... whenever it's over, one way or another.*

And so, as the legend goes, after a long and valiant fight well-fought, using everything he has in his well-worn bag of tricks, the majestic old-Brown, with the honor of Jacob having just wrestled with the Angel of the Lord, finally rolls over with a great convulsive gasp and gazes ominously into the face of his Maker.

Then, unexpectedly, something remarkable happens. Something so awesome they still talk about it on warm summer-nights under the fullness of the moon. The 'Old Man of the River' gathered the exhausted fish into His caring hands, gently removed the Heavenly fly from his gaping mouth, and blessed the trout with a puff of His own life-giving breath... sweet and strong and everlasting. And with a knowing smile, He placed the old fish back into the fresh, free-flowing stream and let him go.

Thus, the "Old Speckled Brown" was caught and released, for good, by the "Ultimate Angler" of all. And yes, just as they say, miracles do happen... even in such unlikely places as the slow-moving, deep-blue pool, down by the bridge on the old Payette.

Wow! There I go again... drifting off to God knows where? I wrote that so long ago. I have got to focus. Or perhaps, I should do just the opposite. I am here to relax....

"Thanks George," I say, stepping from the elevator into the hotel lobby.

"Wet one for me brother," he says.

"You got it." I pledge.

I flash back a 'Peace' sign and throw him an archaic 'Art Bell-ism,' as a parting gesture of middle-age solidarity... "East of the Rockies."

Chapter 9

BEHOLD A PALE GODDESS

What a glorious autumn afternoon! And what a classic place to be. Alone with a fly-rod, standing in the clear, shallow cove across the road from the Grand Hotel, breathing in the crisp fall-colors of Mackinac Island, taking advantage of a lull in the Somewhere in Time festivities, before tonight's kick-off dinner and dance.

It was strange to see Jan Flannery again after all these years... still bright and gracious and even more beautiful than I remembered, with the enticing maturity that middle-age womanhood brings. I purposely signed in at the opposite end of the long registration table; hiding in the crowd. I didn't have the courage to re-introduce myself to her just yet. I wonder if she'll remember me after all these years? Well, I'm sure she'll remember me, but not the same way I remember her.

She really is quite beautiful. Such a classic face. And those striking blue eyes. She has more beauty and grace than most women half her age. The passing of time has only served to polish the sparkle of her extraordinary continence. I guess I wasn't ready to burst the carefully crafted fantasy-bubble I had so meticulously fashioned around her these past twenty-five years. Not that I have any right to so cavalierly tamper with our long-ago friendship. In fact, at some appropriate time, I must apologize to Jan for commandeering her goddess-like image for my own middle-aged fantasy. But, there are times in one's life when escaping to a better place or a long ago, wished-upon, memory can prove helpful in getting over 'the hard times.' Indeed, the periodic musings of my summer-time crush on Jan, has served as a mental safety-net on more than a few occasions, during those fleeting and frenetic years since that fairy-tale summer of 1979.

Reveling in my current rustic surroundings, I drink in the feel-good-feeling of my well-worn, but functional, fishing gear. My Filson wool-jacket, designed for the Klondike Gold Rush 'Stampeders' in

1914. It seems fitting somehow, that I'd be wearing a "Mackinaw Cruiser" here on Mackinac Island. Just, another of life's little synchronicities that have always intrigued me.

It's soulfully satisfying to watch my familiar gear effortlessly do what it's supposed to; waiving my "Ray Gould" 'Double Parabolic,' eight-foot, six-weight, split-cane fly-rod, rhythmically back and forth in the blue Michigan sky, shooting its florescent-green, sink-tip line through the crisp, fall air in a loose unloading curl, landing fly-first on the surface of lake. A quick strike instinctively sends me lurching backward, as the rod instantly bends, jerking and bobbing before me. The sweet rush of adrenaline pumps through my veins, as I play a rather substantial fish at the end of the line; or rather, the fish seems to be playing me. I take another step to recover my balance, and, uh… it's *gone!* As fast as it hit, he or she, is gone. I caught a glimpse of its ghost-like body as it momentarily flashed below the surface. Then it plunged into the deep. A check of my line confirms that the fly is broken off. I smile and sigh and enjoy the familiar feeling of my heart racing in my chest. Catching my breath, I draw in a healthy dose of earthy air and pause… and thank God for the moment. Then, I fumble for a heavier tippet and something similar to the pattern I just lost to the jaws of that 'she-monster,' and wonder and worry… about nothing at all… for the first time in a long while.

I hereby proclaim this to be my new 'favorite-spot!' Particularly, at this glorious time of year, with the fall earth-tones in full-blaze and the warm, autumn sun slanting its golden hue. The hardwood forests with their ancient, aromatic smells, so sweet and pungent, like 'apples and cinnamon' wafting from a warm, winter stove.

Blinking from my diffused gaze at the surface of the lake, I am drawn to another good-size fish gliding along the bottom of the sandy cove. Having lost track of how long I've been so dreamingly engaged, again, for the first time, I realize, I don't even care....

Lifting my eyes from the wavering depths, my peripheral vision catches a soft, gossamer reflection undulating on the surface of the lake, extending in my direction from the shore. The impression of a

Greek goddess materializes before me, in the wind-wept figure of Jan Flannery, majestic and glowing, on a bluff in the late afternoon sun! I startle us both with my surprised recognition, and my aborted back-cast falls embarrassingly around me like a wet noodle. Jan's beautiful figure is draped in cream-colored lace. I'm in baggy hunter-green. She benevolently returns my sheepish grin and says, barely audible over the breaking waves, "Is it really you?"

I turn awkwardly and waddle toward the shore, happy to hear her voice again. I clear my throat and reply, "Yes, it's me. Or rather, the 'twenty-five-years-older' version of me." I try not to slip on the rocks in my clumsy boots, walking as suavely as one can in chest-waders and a bulky fishing-vest, resigned to the fact I've totally blown my chance to make a classy, "John Wayne" entrance.

"I was worried you might not recognize me," I say, admiring how well she fills her vintage-dress; straight out of 'Somewhere in Time'… all beads and lace, with a small parasol and dainty, high-top boots, as if she were suspended in time. Tottering towards her, a powerful déj`avu moment hits me. It was here on this very beach that Jan and I first walked together as movie extras, both in period costumes, laughing and sharing our lives and dreams, during that summer so long ago? It was also here in the small grove of trees that Richard and Elise's forever-relationship began. Yes, it was this same secluded shore that Jan Flannery's endearing qualities first stirred my youthful soul.

I slosh to shore with an intended bravado that is instantly neutralized by Jan's close proximity and her timeless charms, which linger so gracefully after all these years. Her glowing complexion is still fresh and wise and full of vitality. Standing before her with whatever awkward panache I can muster, in hip-waders and floppy hat, holding in as much middle-age girth as the laws of physics will allow, I extend my fingerless wool-glove toward hers, which are elegantly covered in lace. I bow for a classic movie-style kiss of her hand just as a large wave crashes at our feet, sending Jan leaping sideways to avoid soaking her boots. In her haste, she pulls me with surprising strength, causing me to lose my balance. In an instant, we are sprawling toward higher ground... rod, reel, parasol and all... me thudding backward in the sand and Jan falling intimately onto my chest. For the longest moment, I feel her heartbeat pounding with mine, staring wide-eyed into her crystal blue eyes, linked by some strange sweet memory, with the blush of eternity flashing between us.

Jan eventually blinks us back to reality, wriggles embarrassingly off my chest, and begins brushing the fine, white sand from her elegant dress. I stand as quickly as a middle-aged man can, clad in bulky fishing gear, and extend my hand to help her up. Jan instinctively shifts to her best Elise McKenna persona, nods gracefully, takes my hand and elegantly rises up. I take the opportunity to kiss her gloved hand, then stand speechless, beholding her and marveling at this moment that has finally come. Here we are, together again, in one of the most romantic settings on earth, with nothing to say. We finally break out laughing and hug each other like old friends.

"You haven't changed a bit," I say with all sincerity. "Still as beautiful as ever!"

"Neither have you," Jan returns, blushing at my compliment.

"Well, your compliment is more generous than mine," I say, patting my stomach through the unflattering layers of fishing gear.

"The only thing I see, is the 'you' I'll never forget," she says, as if in a dream, with a smile that causes my heart to 'thunk' in my chest. I struggle to compose myself, feeling as if I've finally returned from some long journey, from a place and time long ago that seems like... yesterday.

With our comical reunion now complete, we assume the oddly comfortable roll of life-long friends again, strolling the beach, arm in arm.

"How have you been?" Jan asks, taking the conversational lead. "And what have you been doing with your life?"

"I'm fine, I guess, for a middle-aged, small-town lawyer, with a wife, four kids, and an insatiable mortgage that insists on being fed every month." Jan laughs at my sarcasm and continues to probe.

"What brings you back to Mackinac Island after all these years? I haven't seen you since we worked on the movie together... back in..."

"The summer of 1979," I chime in with her, admitting how ancient we are.

"Don't remind me," she says. "I don't feel that old."

"Neither do I," I say, trying to sound convincing. "Except when I get out of bed in the morning... and after lunch, when I fall asleep at the Rotary meeting... or on the couch after the seven o'clock news."

"You..." Jan affectionately punches my shoulder with her dainty fist, like she used to do so many years ago.

"No, really, if I had an internet profile, which I don't thank God, it would read something like a "Far Side" cartoon. "Michael Hall, age fifty-three, bifocals, arthritic knee from high-school football, morbidly obese, or so say those damn weight-charts, carpel tunnel in the left wrist, and forgets where he puts his car-keys half the time." Jan giggles delightfully at my sorry self-appraisal, encouraging me all the more.

"I've got these ugly 'skin-tags' popping out all over my body, like sprouting eyes of an old potato. One of which looks oddly familiar, like some long-lost twin absorbed in the womb."

Jan, punches me again, laughing hysterically. I continue my comedic routine, now definitely on a roll.

"Major complaints? It's getting harder to put my socks on in the morning, or take them off at night for that matter. And every trip to the bathroom is becoming a major expedition thanks to my ever-enlarging prostate! My sleep-apnea has relegated me to sleeping in the guest bedroom. I'm pre-diabetic, on blood-pressure medication, and I take baby-aspirin to stave off my family history of heart attacks, stroke and cancer. The only food-groups I'm supposed to eat are limited to various shades of green."

Jan is now struggling to catch her breath, and totally relating to everything I'm saying, encouraging my further editorial comment.

"Significant stress factors? Let's see. I've got three more kids to put through college, with no visible means of doing so. I'm still paying my own student loan, which is so old it was originally issued in confederate notes. I've worked my ass off for almost thirty years now, well, not literally as you can see, and have no retirement or savings to speak of. My calculated Social Security benefit won't even cover the medications I'll need by the time I am able to draw on it. And that's assuming the 'Generation X-ers' behind us aging 'Baby Boomers' all have ten kids who hold down good-paying jobs for the next thirty years to support us. I can't afford medical insurance. The kids need dental work. And I'd love to get one of those gastronomic 'lap-bands,' so I can go from being 'morbidly obese' to just 'normally obese!'"

"My only hope in the short term is that one, big personal-injury case I've been working on for the last five years. If I can only convince the damn insurance company to mediate a decent settlement, I might be able to pay off our back-taxes and set something aside for my funeral… if I live that long! We've refinanced our house so many times, it's like we're renting it from the bank. And with the economy the way it is, we're spending our kid's inheritance like water. Speaking of water, along with global-warming and the next approaching ice-age, I hear they're predicting another drought next summer, despite the record flooding and snow their calling for this winter. Other than that, and assuming an asteroid doesn't hit the earth tomorrow, life couldn't be better!"

After laughing through most of my off-the-cuff soliloquy, and commiserating with me point by point, Jan wipes the tears from her cheeks and says, "Unfortunately, most of us baby-boomers can relate to everything you've just said. But, I've never heard it put so succinctly before." We both enjoy the levity of the moment, taking pleasure in each other's company.

"Actually," I continue, trying to be a little serious. "It's not all that bad. I just had no idea I would ever live this long. All my youthful hero's died a long time ago; Jimmy Hendricks, John Belushi… Lawrence Welk." Jan laughs again as I continue, "And I totally blew my window of opportunity to go out in a youthful, "James Dean-ish" blaze of glory."

"James who?" Jan says, feigning the ignorance of a much younger woman. "Just kidding," she says, admitting her membership in the bygone generation of "Giant," "Gone with the Wind," and "Key Largo," or at least their late-night re-broadcasts on cable. Catching her breath again, and regaining a bit of composure, she adds, "But, why did you come to the Island now, after all these years?"

"Now, that is the 'sixty-four thousand dollar question,'" I say, almost seriously. "No, strike that, Dr. Joyce Brothers and nineteen-fifties television? Now I'm really dating myself."

"Wait a minute, you're not that much older than I am," Jan says, with another poke to my fortunately padded shoulder.

Her kind caveat is encouraging and confirms that she still feels younger than her years. Just as do I in many ways. Walking together and talking again, brings back soothing, reflective thoughts, matching the mood of the falling leaves fluttering around us. Uncharacteristically, I feel I can share my closest thoughts with Jan as we walk, thoughtfully and purposely, she, holding onto my arm.

"This Island seems to have a strange, reoccurring significance for me," I say, thinking out loud as we move along the shore-path. "It has been winding itself through my life, literally and figuratively, for a long time, maybe longer than I realize. From my youthful 'Up With People' days, to 'Somewhere In Time,' and you. And now, back again." Jan graciously allows me to unburden my rambling emotions, smiling with tender acceptance of their apparent significance to me.

"I've always had a lingering feeling about this place; something beautiful and mysterious at the same time. Somehow, I am drawn to the romance of it all, for no apparent reason."

"I know what you mean," Jan says, basking in her own reflections. "I've obviously found it difficult to stay away myself, both emotionally and physically. Something keeps drawing me back to this island, year after year. I've been coming to the Somewhere In Time weekend for so long now, it's as if I've become part of the story, connected to something that keeps returning to me, again and again."

"You'll always be a special part of my Somewhere In Time memory," I say, never tiring to see her blush. Then, without thinking, I add, "It seems, I know you by heart." My words sound as if they are spoken from another time, pulling us somewhere else; someplace soothing and familiar, expressing a long-held 'knowing.' If we weren't both married, and so thoroughly propagandized with middle-aged morals, things could swiftly get out of hand. Fortunately, Jan gracefully clears her throat and changes the subject.

"Do you remember our big movie scene together; the gorgeous outdoor breakfast scene?"

"Of course! How could I forget?" I say, following her lead and remembering another fond memory. "You, strolling regally on the front lawn in your Victorian, equestrian outfit, riding crop and top hat, while Christopher Plummer and Chris Reeve square off in a clash of strong personalities?"

Jan laughs at my characterization of her small, but memorable, role in one of Somewhere In Time's classic scenes.

She adds, "As I recall, you had the good fortune of sitting all day, in the shade, partaking in the exquisite cuisine that the Grand Hotel generously supplied for the scene… crepes, fresh-fruit and crab-benedict!"

"Yeah, well, as you can see," I retort, holding my gut. "I'm paying for my youthful indiscretions." Jan laughs again while we walk. "But hey," I add, "we both made the final cut! And sometimes, that's about all you can ask for."

A few meaningful heartbeats pass between us, as Jan's manner subtly changes, to match the statement I just made.

"Your charm and countenance have not diminished." she says. Her flattery floats like a whisper on the leaves swirling at our feet. The next few moments flow in meaningful contemplation, as we match each other's stride, with only our footsteps marking the time.

Jan asks, "You didn't bring your wife… your family?"

"No, it was a spur of the moment thing. Greg surprised me with the tickets. He booked the room. But, at the last minute, he couldn't make it. Something about his boss, Arnold Schwarzenegger, needing him for a costume gig in Japan. We were going to make it a crazy, mid-life-brother-bonding-sort-of-thing. You know, ala 'Thelma and Louise?'"

"I see. The notorious "Hall Brothers!"

"You got it. The convertible Thunderbird over the cliff. The whole bit! Greggy probably saved us from something regrettable by backing out."

Suddenly, and somewhat inconveniently, I realize something about myself, perhaps for the first time. I am pretty good for the first few minutes of any serious, personal conversation. Then, I typically find the need to poke fun at myself, or someone else, as some kind of defense-mechanism. I quickly file this annoying thought in my aging memory-banks and vow to work on it, at some other, more opportune, moment.

"How is your brother? Jan enthusiastically asks. "We had some wonderful times together during the filming, sneaking off with Chris in his private plane; Greg, me and Jane Seymour, bowling and eating pizza until the wee hours of the morning. Now <u>those</u> were some crazy times!"

"He's doing fine... once we finally figured out he's bi-polar. Then came the challenge of convincing <u>him</u> he was bi-polar, and not just crazy. Eventually, he realized, if he stays on his meds, he doesn't have to be the first Marine on the beach every day."

Jan's genuine concern and empathy for my hyper, younger brother is truly touching. She and Greggy were, indeed, great friends during those long-ago, simpler times.

"I am so sorry, I didn't know...."

"No really, he's doing quite well; married for a short time, no kids. A Hollywood costumer's life is hard on relationships. Always on location somewhere, racking up those travel per-diems. He lives in the Hollywood Hills now, in a wedge-shaped duplex he calls 'The Hotel Cheese.' Don't ask me why. Probably, because it looks like a huge wedge of cheese. He lives in one side and rents out the other. Greggy worked for Arnold for fifteen years, before he became 'Governator.' Then, he finally got a 'nine-to-five' job at "Western Costume," supplying the major studios with movie clothing. He's got weekends off for the first time in his life! I think he's finally catching up on all those years he missed, working so hard. He says his goal is to retire one day, then keep on working for the rest of his life.... Typical 'Greggy-kind-of-thinking.'"

Suddenly, embarrassed, I realize I've been monopolizing our entire conversation; talking about me and my brother, and neglecting the one person I've always wanted to know more about! In her typical, polite manner, Jan has been content to let me ramble on with my disjointed thoughts.

"But hey, look at me carrying on!" I say. "What about you? What about your life? Let's talk about Jan Flannery!" Taken aback, Jan gathers herself, and contemplates where to begin.

"Well, I've filled my life with lots of 'things,' like everyone else," she says, placing quotations around the word "things," with her lace-gloved fingers. "I was in radio before Somewhere in Time. Then, our movie experience totally changed my life. With encouragement from the cast and crew, including Chris himself, I became a commercial actress, specializing in corporate training-films, mostly on the east coast. Then, after years of collecting antiques, I became a dealer myself of vintage ladies' accoutrements' from the Somewhere in Time era. I still act, and produce a few infomercials. But, mostly my life is focused on my family, and my activities as the official product licensee for Somewhere in Time, and the SIT website."

"Our world-wide fan club is called "INSITE;" the "International Network of Somewhere in Time Enthusiasts." It was founded in 1990 by Bill Shepard from Glendora, California. We publish an elegant quarterly journal on all aspects of the film. You should check out our on-line store! We have lots of wonderful "Somewhere In Time" memorabilia, including a gorgeous antique pocket-watch commemorating the movie, with Richard and Elise's photo inside." Jan produces a stunning gold watch from her antique purse, complete with a chain and fob. She opens it to reveal the romantic image of Christopher Reeve and Jane Seymour, as Richard and Elise, in a romantic scene from the picture.

Then, as if catching herself in the midst of a tabloid interview, she pauses apologetically.

"Oh my, look at me. See how I get, when I talk about Somewhere in Time? Before that magical summer, my life was the epitome of normal. And I wasn't very happy about it either. Then, I took a chance and grabbed a fleeting opportunity that changed my life. Do you know what I mean?"

"Yes, I do" I say, reflecting on her words and comparing them to my own admittedly lackluster life, and my propensity not to grab such fleeting opportunities.

"Well.... We will have to catch up more, later." Jan says, with a wistful sigh. "I have to work on tonight's Welcoming Ball. Can I count on seeing you there?"

"Of course my dear," I intone, in my best Richard Collier imitation. "And may I request you save a dance for me?"

"Of course, you'll be at the top and the bottom of my dance card, so it won't matter if you're early or late."

"I'll be there with bells on!" I say, humorously jingling the clunky 'bear-bell' attached to my fishing vest. Jan laughs at my lame attempt at 'outdoor humor.'

We say our temporary goodbyes and I take a long, lingering moment to enjoy Jan's provocative figure disappearing up the path toward the hotel. Then, for another long while I stand alone, watching the lake, slipping between now and then, and that long ago summer, thinking, with a smile on my face.

Chapter 10

THE 'WELCOME BACK' BALL

Wow! What a re-introduction! It suddenly occurs to me that this time, as we walked together, Jan and I delighted in talking about the past. In 1979, on this vary spot; we talked about the future, wondering what our lives would be like when our magical movie-making experience was over. Jan went back home and attempted to explain her life-changing experience to her husband, with words that could never do justice to the wondrous feelings and emotions of actually being there. Eventually, I moved on as well, allowing the sweet memories of that wind-swept summer and the allure of beautiful Jan Flannery to fade to a more distant, but 'forever,' part of me.

At one point, I woke up to find myself married, with a family, then law school and a busy career as a small-town lawyer. It's funny, how Brackett's Landing is so similar to Mackinac Island; with our own quaint ferry-dock at the foot of Main Street, the rustic board-walks and fishing pier, the waterfront shops and restaurants, just like on the Island. We even have our version of Mackinac Island's 'fudgie' tourists, who frequent the outdoor markets and cobble-stone crosswalks, buying sweet-treats, artwork and antiques.

I fondly remember working at the boat launch of our little marina during high school, spending those golden summers launching boats and sailing my thirty-six foot, woody, "Sea Bird Yawl" around the misty islands of Puget Sound. My parents were pillars of the community. And after Dad died, Mom became the town's beloved Mayor for many years. Now retired and loving it, she still holds court at the local bakery on Saturday mornings, solving the world's problems with her cronies. Her name is engraved on a bronze plaque at City Hall; a small testament to a life well-lived.

I've always been proud of our little water-front community, even before it was named the 'Friendliest Town' in the State. It was a good place to grow-up and a great place to settle-down. Waiting and dreaming in 'Mayberry R.F.D' or as Greggy calls it, "Opieville," just biding my time, longing for something else.

Being on Mackinac Island with Jan again, has brought a flood of latent feelings about my life and the path it has taken, and where it seems to be heading. I remember my youthful musings of being a Nobel Laureate, for inventing something earth-changing, like 'squeezable ketchup' or the 'binky-leash.' Then, of course, some other genius beat me to it... again. *There I go, with the inevitable comic interlude.*

But, have I made the right choices? Do any of us really know if we've made the right choices? Those all-important, life-changing, decisions seem to come at us willy-nilly, approaching at warp-speed, from the haze of our unrehearsed future. There seems never enough time to debrief or digest, before another of life's conundrums is thrust upon us; like Lucille Ball struggling to keep up with the assembly line from hell. And once those 'teachable moments' pass by, they're gone forever, quickly accumulating into what we've so uncontrollably become.

So, what is it about the past that keeps bubbling over into my current reality? Is it the normal function of my stage in life; a mid-life review of the stark reality of what I have become? So many strange and intriguing questions are occurring to me that I've never contemplated before; thoughts too deep for my middle-aged brain to adequately respond to, until now; now that I've finally taken the time to slow down and think. *Can we truly live in the present without understanding how the past affects our current existence? How do we know if we've lived a good life, or what a good life actually looks like?* Perhaps the answers to these questions are what I've been quixotically searching for all these years, tentatively approaching mid-life, still naïve and unawares. Then again, perhaps that's what a good mid-life-crisis does for one; provide motivation to pause and reflect at the exact point in time you assume it's too late to do anything about it.

So, with a lifetime of perspective alternatively enveloping me like a warm blanket and a wet towel, I wonder what I might have become had I taken one of those other paths less-traveled. I wrestle with these and other random thoughts while I leisurely shave and shower in my hotel room. I've always enjoyed the time-honored ritual of my personal grooming routine; a detailed process handed down to me through generations of 'Hall family' fathers and sons. *Now, that I think about it, I just assume my great-grandfather shaved his cheeks first, then his sideburns, then his chin and neck, as his son would have done, and as my father did before me."* I smile in the mirror, amused at my contemplating such trivial thoughts. Then again, our daily routines are an integral part of who we are, though I don't consciously recall thinking this hard about my shaving habits before. I seem to be doing a lot of deep thinking on this unconventional odyssey of mine. Perhaps, it's because I've had scant opportunity to spend much reflective time alone. So far, I'm enjoying this lack of structure that has become my middle-aged quest for... who-knows-what?

It's been a long while since I've enjoyed the sweet fruits of a good, narcissistic indulgence. Perhaps a brief refresher-course would do me good. As I ready myself for this evening's formal event, I wonder what other latent mysteries lay buried in my subconscious, now that my lumbering psyche has begun to stir from its dormant, middle-age hibernation... *an intriguing thought at this time in my life.*

"The Welcome Back Ball" is the first big 'schwa ray' of the Somewhere in Time reunion festivities. The formal dinner-dance brings everyone together; the guests, staff and volunteers, for the first time since arriving on the island. Fortunately, the local tux shop had a 'big and tall' section stocked with old rentals that could respectably pass for turn-of-the-century-finery. The last person to don the masterpiece I'm wearing must have been William H. Taft himself (that hefty, twenty-seventh President of the United States from 1909 to 1913). At least there's plenty of room, a commodity I have found increasingly harder to find these days. The elastic cummerbund sets off a formal presentation that could almost be considered debonair, if I do say so myself. Fortunately, the style of men's evening wear hasn't changed much in the past century or so. A generous splash of 'Old Spice' to my rosy cheeks, a dab behind the ears and 'bingo!' I've reached the apex of whatever my current circumstances will allow.

"What the Hell," I think to myself, looking squarely at my tuxedoed image in the bureau mirror. *"Time to throw caution to the wind, and see what the evening brings!"*

I feel like a peacock, as I step into the hotel hallway. But, also, I feel about as good as I've felt in a long while. I reach to deposit my room key into my right vest pocket and am reminded that it's already occupied by my great-grandfather's pocket-watch. I place the key in my other vest pocket and ceremoniously bring out C.W.'s gold timepiece to check the hour. I'm glad I thought to bring the old family heirloom. The watch is the last vestige of the Hall family tree still in my possession; having been handed down from father to son, to son, to me through the years. Adding to its sentimentality, I also used it as a part of my costume during the filming of Somewhere in Time. It added further authenticity to the handsome 1912-era outfit my brother had so carefully picked out for me. I remember Greggy letting me know, in no uncertain terms, that he held back one the best outfits for me to wear (other than Chris Reeve's custom-made costume, which was designed by Jean-Pierre Dorléac). "And you damn-well better appreciate it," I can still hear him saying. I do remember being impressed with my natty, cream-colored suit, its light-beige vest and high-collared, pleated shirt and string bow-tie. The ensemble even included a dashing Panama hat I could wear or carry conspicuously for effect. My great-grandfather's pocket watch, with its heavy fob and gold chain, provided the crowning touch to my movie-making attire.

Stepping into the crowded elevator, I instantly fall into character with the other assembled Somewhere in Time guests, all similarly garbed in their turn-of-the-century evening-wear. Comically, I see George, the affable elevator operator, pinned to the wall by the close proximity of an ample pair of costumed breasts, attached to a large woman in little red shoes and a small hat that seems sorely understated given her overall visual effect. I flash George a commiserating look as a shift in the crowd sends the twin behemoths intimidatingly close to George's face, tipping his hat off-kilter. I chuckle and quickly mask a barely audible laugh with a strategically-timed cough. George takes it all in stride; just another hazard of the profession.

I fix my eyes on the ornate floor numbers above the elevator door, trying to ignore the fact I've apparently under-estimated the square footage needed to comfortably mingle my girth with that of the elevator's current occupants. Mentally making myself as thin as possible (a daunting task worthy of "The Amazing Kreskin"), I worry I might inadvertently set off the elevator's weight-limit alarm. Miraculously, the door slides shut; just missing my vest buttons, as George expertly guides us on our appointed journey.

As we glide downward, a lighthearted frivolity breaks out amongst the costumed guests behind me, centering on the much anticipated events of the evening.

"Oh, Rollo, I do hope they hand out dance cards again this year," an excited woman exclaims from somewhere amongst the crowd, presumably to her husband. "It's such a wonderful ice-breaker," she continues. "Don't you think; to get to know everyone better? Don't you agree dear?" Her escort fails an immediate reply, as we lend a collective ear, anticipating his dutiful response.

"Yes dear," he intones, as if expected to do so. Then, sarcastically he adds, just loud enough for general consumption, "However, I wouldn't worry about breaking the ice my dear. That outfit of yours will surely melt the frigidity of any 'victim,' I mean 'partner,' on your list." A muffled burst of laughter erupts from the close-knit group, providing a jump-start to our festive mood.

"Oh, Rollo," she says, with a rap of what sounds like a loosely folded Victorian fan to his shoulder.

"Oh, Maude," he drolls dryly, in quiet acquiescence.

Suddenly, it dawns on the group that the affable couple has just role-played an ad-libbed routine, loosely based on the film's beloved supporting-couple "Rollo and Maude!" Led by someone's astute, "Bravo!" everyone joins in a round of slightly hamstrung applause at the professional actor's impromptu performance for our benefit.

Thank God I'm the first one off the elevator as it bounces to a halt at the lobby. I couldn't have held my stomach in much longer.

Disembarking, we must have looked like stylish penguins popping from a sardine can. Poor George. Had we not quickly disembarked, he may have needed mouth-to-mouth resuscitation. I rearrange my jacket and straighten my bow-tie, paused to take in the majesty around me. The Hotel lobby is exquisitely appointed in dark hardwoods and beautiful Victorian accents. The pleasing ambiance suggests that one is, indeed, back in 1912. Jan and her hard-working volunteers have strategically placed Somewhere in Time mementos throughout the hotel, to provide a touch of realism and romance to the evening. Directional placards written in old-fashioned, marquis-style, script, lend an authentic feel to our journey back in time. It's hard to tell which details were added for effect and what is the normal fare of the hotel. As I take it all in, the juxtaposition of fantasy and reality begin to blur with each passing moment. I believe I would have enjoyed this time in history; the pomp and circumstance, the formalities. Though, I have nothing to base this notion upon. These and other vague feelings of familiarity are coming with unpredictable regularity on this interesting adventure of mine; this vacation or retreat… this 'whatever-it-is' I am doing.

Chapter 11

QUEEN OF THE BALL

I briefly pause for a final self-appraisal in the lobby mirror and attempt to tame the leading-edge of the male-pattern bald spot at the top of my head. A quick side-view, to scrutinize the tuxedoed character that currently passes for me these days. Then suddenly, a synchronistic remembrance wells up within me, and my thoughts flash to another time and place, where I was similarly coiffed and costumed and filled with anticipation.

It was prior to my movie experience here on Mackinac Island... the winter of 1977, or '78? I had unexpectedly been invited to New Orleans to renew the acquaintance of a young 'Southern Belle' I had become acquainted with while traveling in "Up With People." Back in 1974, I had taken time off from college; having auditioned for and been selected as the master of ceremonies for the international singing and dancing troupe. Affectionately referred to as "Uppies," our rambunctious cast of 130 students from literally around the world traveled the globe spreading an upbeat, musical message of good-will and tolerant understanding. At the same time, we partnered with local non-profit organizations and community groups to facilitate volunteer projects in the communities that hosted us.

Standing in the lobby of the Grand Hotel, unexpectedly recalling this fond 'blast from the past,' a strange synchronicity hits me! Up With People got its start here on Mackinac Island in the 1960's. At the time, the group was described as a bold, new experiment, providing the youth of the world with a positive outlet for self-expression during those turbulent, anti-establishment times. What a coincidence, that decades later I would find myself back on Mackinac Island playing out another unique life-experience, or mid-life-crisis, depending how you look at it, during my own turbulent, anti-establishment time. It's as if I have some mysterious connection to this enchanted place, that inexplicably persists through time.

Suddenly, I feel compelled to explore these synchronistic threads of my life, as if something important and meaningful depends on it. Slowly, I am enveloped in a pleasant fugue-like state, as the regal trappings of the Grand Hotel fade and swirl around me. Willingly, longingly, I drift to another place, and special time; a separate reality indelibly etched in the heart of my past, present and most likely, future self. Soon, I find myself before the flickering flames of the hotel fireplace, sinking into a plush wing-back chair, with the present anticipation and excitement shifting to a savory muse of treasured memories... as they come... from wherever they come.

Ashley, or "Sissy," as they call her in "New Orleans," is a real 'Southern belle,' in the truly wholesome, traditional sense of the word. Her blue-blood family heritage runs deep in the time-honored traditions of the 'South,' since well before anyone kept track of 'slow-time' in "The Big Easy." "Southern Belle," is a perfect description for the curvaceous, raven-haired beauty I was so infatuated with as a young, traveling troubadour. Despite being surrounded by some of the most fascinating and attractive women in the world in my fellow Up With People cast-mates, even then, I recognized Sissy to be one of those rare jewels a young man meets, perhaps, only once in a lifetime. And then, only if that lifetime is truly blessed.

I was winding down from one of the most rewarding experiences of my life; one that included world-wide travel, educational opportunities galore, and hundreds of live performances, including the 'Super Bowl' half-time! Wherever Up With People traveled, we stayed in host-family homes, from all economic and social backgrounds and every station in life. I remember my time on the road as some of the most rewarding and challenging of my life.

I opened the classy, personally-addressed envelope, sitting alone in the tiny, $168-dollar-a-month, bachelor apartment that I shared with my "Fashion-Institute-of-Design-and-Merchandising" younger brother, both of us (like everyone else) trying to make it in 'show business,' living off "Top Raman" and whatever fast-food we could afford. My curiosity was definitely stirred by the vaguely familiar scent of perfume, which accompanied the surprising words so graciously scripted on its parchment stationary.

Sissy, a particularly memorable 'host-daughter' of one of our Up With People host-families, was inviting me to be her "escort" for a prestigious New Orleans 'Mardi Gras' event called, "The Olympus Ball!" She (being a young and privileged debutante) had been selected as "Queen of the Ball!" Reading further, she explained that the "Olympus Krew" is one of the largest and most prestigious of the time-honored Mardi Gras organizations, and that my presence is being requested for the entire week of festive celebrations, including both weekends, before and after, all expenses paid. *Holy ----!*

My head was spinning, as I thought to myself, *"What an interesting time in my life to receive such an intriguing invitation."* Of course, my current corporate position as "Shaker-the-Country-Bear" at Disneyland would be tough to give up for ten days, with all those understudies waiting in the wings to bump me off my pedestal. But hey, as Sissy proudly points out, her father (a well-to-do southern architect), is generously springing for the cost of my flight, tuxedo-rental, food, lodging; the whole shebang! So, the decision was; the highlife in New Orleans, renewing my acquaintance with a beautiful young babe, or Top Ramen and ketchup with my brother here in Eagle Rock. *Damn, what a decision…!*

No sooner than you can say, 'Newahlins,' I found myself stepping off the plane in 'Fat City,' naively staring at one of those once-in-a-life-time 'forks-in-the-road,' with only the briefest glimpse at the road sign that was poorly posted.

Looking around the terminal for the gorgeous Sissy, I instead, am surprised to see a very large, very black-skinned, man, nattily-attired in a chauffeur's cap and uniform, discretely holding a sign with the professionally scripted notation, "Master Hall." I pause and look around for someone with celebrity status who may have arrived on the same flight. Not recognizing Anthony Michael Hall or Monte Hall, or someone else who might fit the bill, I sheepishly approach the towering gentleman.

"Excuse me... Sir? My name is Michael..." Before I can finish my stammering statement, the big man's countenance beams with a bright, welcoming glow.

"Wull, Masta Michael, it's a plesha ta meet ya'll," he drawls as slow as road tar on a hot day. "Miz Sissy is so excit'd ta see yuh agin," he continues, taking my bag from my hand. Immediately, I'm thinking one of Sissy's three mischievous brothers, or two younger sisters, must have hired this guy to play a good, old 'southern-style' joke on me. He's probably an out of work actor like me, messing with my head, so they can have their 'yuks' at my expense. *What the heck*, I think to myself. Despite the fact this guy looks like a "New Orleans Saints" defensive-lineman, and probably could crush me with one hand behind his back, he appears harmless enough. And having not yet lost my youthful delusion of invincibility, I figure, if worse comes to worse, I can probably out-run the old duffer, if given half a chance.

Arriving shortly thereafter at Sissy's families' real-life sugar-cane plantation, and surviving my formal reintroduction to her and her impressive parents (both of whom look like they popped out of 'Harper's Bazaar' magazine), I'm feeling a bit uneasy and definitely under-dressed. My best outfit, which I am currently wearing, consists of a forest-green, pull-over sweater, a buttoned-down-collar shirt, and a pair of un-creased pants that I try to pass off as slacks. In this situation, I am easily out-classed by everyone in the room, including Sissy's teenage-brother, Beau, who is sporting a conservative tie and navy-blazer *(for God's sake),* with the family 'Crest' embroidered on the chest pocket! Even if I was warned ahead of time, which I wasn't, it wouldn't have made any difference. At this point in my life, I don't even own a sport coat, let alone a decent pair of slacks. To say that I am a little intimidated by this unabashed display of Southern high-society, would be putting it mildly.

Sissy and her cute younger sisters, Annabelle and Kizzy, eagerly show me around their sprawling plantation. And when I say 'plantation,' I mean full-blown, working, sugar-cane estate, dripping with moss-covered live-oak trees; looking to be hundreds of years old, a huge, spring-fed swimming pool, with lots of spooky swamp-land bordered by manicured lawns that look like putting greens. There are horticultural-gardens everywhere, horse stables and a fabulous, antebellum mansion-of-a-house… that kind of plantation! They actually have 'hired help,' consisting of a middle-age couple, who live in one of the quaint, remodeled out-buildings on the property. The wife serves as the starched and uniformed 'maid,' and the husband, the formal-dressed 'butler,' who doubles as the family's 'private chef.' Together, they dutifully 'keep the place,' preparing and presenting each formal meal with precision and panache.

Most of the trees, and many of the structures, are older than the "United States" itself! (or "The Union," as they solemnly referred to it). The place even has a name… its own name, out of respect for the land's ancient heritage and unique personality. It's called "Neeka," a derivative of the indigenous Chitimacha-Indian name for "Spirit," which I suppose is just as good as "Tara" in 'Gone With The Wind' or "Shilo," from the 'Big Valley' television series. Perhaps, when and if, I get out of this experience alive, my brother and I should re-name our one-lung, L.A. 'walk-up' something romantic like, "Windsong" or "Starblanket." Why not, we've got a shaggy lemon tree growing in the parking-strip out front. This whole 'Scarlett O'Hara/Rhett Butler-thing' is like a stealthy dream or some 'life-test' that, somehow, paradoxically, I don't want to fail.

The formal family-dinner (which, for some reason, is being held in my honor) seems to be going well… at least through the initial, sumptuous courses of shrimp-gumbo, wilted-lettuce-salad, rack-of-lamb, au-gratin potatoes, asparagus with cream sauce, and a few southern side-dishes that aren't adequately explained to me. Each course is generously slaked with goblets of expensive wine, which are being constantly refilled from somewhere over my right shoulder. Man, I am in hog-heaven! My culinary-deprived bachelor stomach is singing the "Hallelujah Chorus" at these rich and previously undiscovered gastronomic indulgences. As the table candles begin to blur, someone starts a round of formal toasts, accompanied by a separate after-dinner liqueur served in large brandy snifters. At this point, I am feeling no pain and happily join in with the numerous celebratory salutations, as each family member extemporaneously recites a short homily appropriate to the apparently auspicious occasion. Each clink of my glass, and subsequent sip of agreement, further warms my blood and flushes my cheeks with familial feelings of well-being, which I have not felt in years.

When it finally falls to me to deliver an appropriate toast, I feel as good as any young man can, without having to apologize afterward. So, I rise, rather cautiously under the circumstances, and instinctively perceive through my lubricated senses that the room's informal chatter has fallen to a solemn hush. The family's sudden, undivided attention throws me a bit off stride, as I steady myself against the table for an impromptu presentation. Then, and might I say rather verbosely, I formally express my sincerest gratitude to my gracious hosts: Sissy.... her parents... her brothers and sisters, the hired-help, the cat, the dog... and I would have thanked the fichus tree in the corner had my sorely over-worked guardian-angel not charitably interceded at the last, face-saving moment. I conclude my rambling discourse with a sappy attempt at scripture, which came out instead as a queer paraphrase of "Tiny Tim," from Charles Dickens' "A Christmas Carol."

"And God bless all... Amen!"

Feeling quite satisfied with my unrehearsed performance, and basically feeling good in general, I plop down and roll a goofy glance in Sissy's direction, anticipating her glowing approval. Instead, I see her sheepishly gazing at her asparagus, avoiding eye-contact with everyone. My last gulp of brandy hits me precisely at the same moment that a fevered spike of my heart-rate informs me: 'something is definitely amiss in paradise!' A blatant lull in the festivities becomes apparent for no perceptible reason. I self-consciously direct my own gaze to the empty plate before me, and attempt to become inconspicuous as possible, until this unnamed hurricane blows over. My bloodshot eyes dart to and fro, trying to assess the social climate around the table. Eventually, the not-so-golden silence is mercifully broken by the chef's timely entrance, bearing the evening's decadent desert; a flaming 'bananas-foster,' fully ablaze and marinating in sweet-smelling, dark rum.

Much later in the evening, when Sissy and I are finally allowed some unchaperoned time alone, I discover the reason for her families' cool reception at my casual dinner toast. It seems that Sissy may have slightly embellished the attendant facts surrounding her and my long-distance relationship, which I had no idea even existed, in a calculated ploy to prompt her father's generosity in enticing me to be her Mardi Gras escort. Sissy awkwardly explains her family probably, may have anticipated, that I'd be announcing my intention to... well, you know... announce our engagement?

Picking my jaw up off the floor, I think to myself. *Wow! I saw this on a "Twilight Zone" episode*; where the hip bachelor wakes to find he is married, his wife is nine months pregnant, and his hopes of living a glorious, carefree life are dashed in the time it takes to sandwich a thin plot between multiple prime-time commercials. Having no idea that Sissy's innocent invitation came with so many strings attached, I instantly feel flattered, hornswoggled and mind-blown, all at the same time.

"Engaged?" I blurt out before Sissy's hand quickly muffles my unbelieving lips. "I had no idea! I mean, not that, you know, under the right circumstances!" Sissy starts tearing up and begins to apologize for placing me in such a precarious position. I chivalrously whip out my handkerchief, as she adamantly pledges to set things right with her father, which, in keeping with time-honored Southern tradition, would obligatorily trickle down to the rest of the family, confirming my status as an innocent, naïve, Yankee with no clue as to how things are done down in Dixie. Sissy also agrees to let things between us take their natural course, promising I will be more than impressed with the upcoming week of Mardi Gras festivities, and perhaps, who knows... I may even want to visit again.

Well, if she puts it that way, in such casual, non-committed, semi-commitment language, I think to myself, *Hell... I can live with that!* "But please!" I plead. "No more potentially life-changing surprises. I don't think my heart can take it!" Sissy's moist, starry-blue, eyes assure me of her good intentions. And so, of course, I forgive our initial, slightly bumpy, re-introduction.

Thus, my first excursion into the wild-world of Mardi Gras, and New Orleans, and its southern-style, French-Creole tradition, takes on the distinct aura of 'baptism-by-fire!' Every day, it's up at the crack of dawn, which cracks a lot earlier in the French Quarter than it does in L.A. Actually dawn doesn't crack in New Orleans, it yawns slowly, stretching out the kinks from the anonymous excesses of the previous evening; stirring from its brief cat-nap, somewhere between four-fifteen and five a.m. I thought I was up to anyone's festive challenge, being in what I consider the prime of my life. But, this fast-paced, twenty-four-hour lifestyle, with its boundless assaults to the senses takes a little getting used to; like foolishly trying to navigate a never-ending, mad, merry-go-round, while stubbornly attempting to walk a straight line. Just before you think you're going to pass out, it's back in the limo again, sleepless in paradise, off to some traditional breakfast spot, in the Quarter or outlying Metairie or Abita Springs, to chew on some 'Noowahlins'-style, chicory-blend coffee, dunked liberally with deep-fried, sugar-coated 'beignets,' to gather enough strength for the next jam-packed, moon-loop of grueling pomp-and-circumstance.

As the official escort to the Queen of a major Mardi Gras Ball, I feel like Prince Philip dutifully accompanying the Queen of England on her official duties. And given that the most formal event I've previously attended was the Bar Mitzvah of a school-chum *(which was indeed a wild time)*, the nimble circuits of my normally sensible brain have become as taut and brittle as a blackened, Cajun fish.

Eventually, finding myself comatose in the backseat of the family limousine, on the way to the big event; the 'Krewe of Olympus' Mardi Gras Ball,' or traditionally stated, "The Olympus Ball," I attempt to pace myself for what has been touted as the grand climax to the entire week of 'Fat Tuesday' festivities, at least as far as my meager involvement is concerned. I am definitely calling in sick when I get back home; to dry out from this continuous, high-octane, stupor I've so willingly participated in over the past nine days. It definitely wouldn't do for "Shaker the Country Bear" to spontaneously combust, the first time someone struck a match in my general vicinity.

Just as the cobwebs in my brain begin to clear from the previous evening's raucous madness, there's another royal reception, special event or other convenient excuse to indulge in the best food and drink on the planet. I've had to let my tuxedo-pants out twice, just to accommodate my accumulated indulgences. I can't imagine what I'd look like if I lived, full-time, in such high-society, southern privilege. I'd have to go into penitent hibernation for the entire Lenten season, just to maintain the functionality of my wardrobe. Either that, or frequent the local 'Large-and-Husky' for monthly fashion reinforcements!

Suddenly, I awake to the distinct sound of someone thumping on a watermelon. Then, I realize it is Sissy's youngest brother, persistently tapping me on the head that incidentally, feels as large as a basketball. Embarrassingly, I find I've been slobbering on Beau's shoulder for, I don't how long; having passed out again.

Focusing my inadvertent gaze, through the limo's tinted side-window, it becomes apparent that we are here... at the famed "Olympus Ball Room; parked discretely at the back entrance to the hallowed citadel that historically epitomizes both 'Southern' and 'Traditional' (any imitation of which, pales in comparison). I muster a quivering smile at my naiveté, thinking I had previously broached the outer-limits of 'socially-deviant-behavior' back at ole' Wazzu. These southern aristocrats could kill a person with their never-ending zest for showing an outsider a good time. I am so grateful to have the lovely Sissy, "Queen of the Ball," to focus on. If it not for her guiding restraint and constant encouragement, I'd hate to think what back-alley, French Quarter, dumpster they'd find me in... or under.

Its 6:00pm and already dark; the winter solstice showing its full effect with shorter days and longer nights. My earlier head-banging hang-over has mellowed to a dull roar, thank God. The lovely Sissy is ensconced at the historic Hotel Monteleone in a private suite of rooms, which serve as the families' Mardi Gras headquarters, where she is being primped, pampered and coiffed for her once-in-a-lifetime role as "Queen of the Ball!" By the telling smirks and winks I am catching from Sissy's older brothers, and the blushing nods of her younger sisters, I'm afraid (as I've been warned) that I am in for the night of my life!

By now, my sorely stretched imagination has been tested beyond all rational limits. Sissy's father, the staid southern-gentleman that he is, finally takes pity on my feeble attempts to extricate myself from the limousine. And in what I unexpectedly perceive to be a charitable display of paternal affection, he grabs my arm in firm assistance. Propping me against the limo, he places a comforting arm around my slumping shoulders to steady me for the short, fateful, walk to the back door of the ballroom. But first, as if to commemorate this auspicious moment, I find myself surrounded by Sissy's three brothers and their father, in a mental snapshot of male camaraderie, forever to hang in the hallowed halls of my mind. Without a word, I sense the sweet aroma of their acceptance and approval, which, apparently, I have earned by humbly surviving whatever they threw at me during the past week of non-stop, bawdy, but tasteful, hazing. With an informal show of solidarity, the brothers stretch their arms forth, three-musketeers-style, grabbing my hand in theirs, waiting with steady eyes for their father's tentative seal of approval. Then, as if marking some time-honored mystical rite, Sissy's father places his palm on top of ours and solemnly intones, "All for One...?" And the brothers respond in unrehearsed unison, "One for All!," with me verbally rushing to join in. I then see my hand fly high into the air and experience a strange, ecstatic, feeling of significance. The sacred streets of the French Quarter echo with slaps to my back, and an ego boost rivaling any adrenaline rush I've ever known. I get the feeling they had each placed bets on how long I would last, before frantically fleeing to the airport in defeat. But now, in this farewell of sorts, before I leave their magical 'Land of Oz,' with its mystic wizardry and periodic, meaningful, life-lessons, I sense they are truly sad to see me go. The family patriarch; the real-life Wizard behind this constantly shifting Creole-curtain, then winks at me, as if to provide some glimmer of hope for any future desires I may have for his eldest daughter. Sensing his acceptance and the warm support of Sissy's brothers, I respond with a grateful grin.

It's then that I realize, for the first time, that this stately southern gentleman, could someday, given the right circumstances, become my father-in-law! His clear, blue eyes penetrate mine, just as Sissy's can, and a knowing smile spreads across his face. He pats my cheek, godfather-style and softly intones, "You've done well son." And in a moment thoroughly memorialized in each of our hearts, we move in a group-embrace to the door of the ballroom.

"Now, let's get you a drink," I hear the Wizard say.

Chapter 12

'FEAR AND LOATHING' IN THE FRENCH QUARTER

The rest of the long and impressive evening is a blur of high-society pomp and circumstance, the likes of which, no Yankee from my neck of the woods has ever known. To paraphrase the great, gonzo-journalist, Hunter S. Thompson, "The Olympus Ball is exactly what every hip American would be doing on Saturday nights if the 'Rebs' had won the war...'" The madness begins, and is lavishly sustained, by endless bottles, flasks and decanters of nothing but Dixie's finest medicinal spirits. Masterfully prepared Southern-style cuisine, ala Cajun Chef, Paul Prudhomme, is continuously and liberally dispensed by tuxedo-clad black-men, whom I've been told have faithfully provided impeccable service and assistance to the Olympus Krewe for more generations than anyone can recall.

Not accustomed to having another man assist me in getting dressed, I am ill-prepared to deal with the intimate details of how my evening's "Costuming" is to be accomplished. Fortunately, my personally assigned wardrobe assistant; a petite gentleman named "Charles" (perhaps in his sixties, with tightly quaffed salt-and-pepper hair), takes me in his charge and routinely begins the process of stripping me down from my tuxedo and re-wardrobing my limp and non-responsive body, with the appropriate, garish, outfit that seems to have been picked out for me. Given my current reality-distorting blood-alcohol-level, and the distinct impression that Charles wishes to get this affair over with as judiciously as I do, I relinquish my near naked personage to him, lock, stock and barrel, which of course, is all I am capable of doing at the moment.

Now, when I say "costuming," I mean full-blown, pastel colored, satin-and-lace, 'jester's suit,' with a towering peacock-feathered headdress, thigh-high white-tights and multi-colored elfin slippers that curl at the toes. By the time Charles has me properly attired and propped to my feet, I look like a flaming version of a "Ralph

Steadman," caricature from some Mardi Gras nightmare I cannot awake up from. The only thing saving me from a full-on, raging panic-attack is that, mercifully, my true identity is hidden behind an ornate and surreal Mardi Gras mask, which thankfully covers my face, replete with shiny sequins and a small veil (yes, I said veil) extending just below my quivering chin. Later, to my apoplectic consternation, I find a detailed description of myself as the Queen's 'jester-suited' escort, including my full name and a short pedigree (in my case, very short), prominently displayed in the evening's program. Thus, being stripped of any dignity I naively hoped to preserve, I resign myself to my current depraved condition; being thoroughly intoxicated, dressed like a strutting medieval-harlequin, attempting to negotiate a massive, unreachable wedgie, frantically trying to learn my 'lines' from a 'script' that someone hastily thrust into my sweaty, trembling hands (the text of which, keeps fading from focus as I try to read it). I barely catch someone's off-handed remark about the evening's upcoming "Tableau" performance, where the "Jester" has a time-honored and significant role to play, as my addled mind scurries up through endless levels of pseudo-reality, trying to wake from this freakish, fear-and-loathing nightmare, while at the same time keep from falling into the bottomless pit of delirious insanity. Suddenly, serenely, I find myself out of my body, perhaps through some psychotic defense mechanism, looking like a retro-image of Jacob Marley's ghost in the thralls of a hypoglycemic stupor, dragging my massive chain of penitence through Hades, each link representing a wrong turn taken at some forgotten fork in the road of my miserable existence. Thus, rationalizing my situation in vain, I postulate that this entire, twisted experience is destined to become a featured masterpiece in the ongoing, episodic series of my worst reoccurring nightmares.

 I would love to read the "huntersthompsonian" account that the good doctor of journalism could elucidate, while similarly over-medicated; derailing the opulent decadence and underlying psychosis at play in this inner-sanctum of 'Hell-gone-mad,' or as he might have termed it, "'another glorious, already-crested, high-water-mark of the swiftly fading American Dream.'"

Fortunately, my momentary depression is buoyed by the sudden appearance of Sissy's gregarious brothers, each outrageously costumed in outfits approximating "The Three Musketeers," in drag. Sissy's father soon joins us in his own regalia, generally resembling a sinister "Captain Hook" on steroids (having been electrocuted by a thousand volts). Periodically, we find it necessary to peek from under our sequined masks to remind each other who the hell we are. Unabashedly, we boldly re-enact our Musketeer pledge; "All for One, and One for All!" to the general bemusement of the other outlandishly-clad southern-aristocrats mingling amongst us.

If gazed upon at askance, the entire scene could qualify for a limited-edition anthology of Mr. Steadman's shape-shifted characatures from the further adventures of Thompson's drug-addled journal, posthumously entitled "Fear and Loathing in the French Quarter." I humor myself with the 'gonzoesque' irony that, if I'm lucky, I won't remember any of this by morning. "Ho, ho, Mahalo…& Res ipsa loquitur." (HST).

The balance of the evening remains hazy at best. Stumbling around the lavishly decorated antebellum ballroom, dutifully shadowing my newly-adopted 'Brothers-of-the-Realm' and their doting father, I am introduced to a never-ending kaleidoscope of strange characters whom, seemingly, narrowly escaped Alice's rabbit hole, only partially unscathed. Sweating profusely beneath the hot klieg-lights, which grotesquely, then sublimely, highlight the outlandishly costumed men and tightly-cleavaged women in their 'Gone With the Wind' gowns, I struggle to ignore my bodies' nervous, 'Johnny-Depp-ian' reaction to the stress it's being put through.

In my thoroughly inebriated state, each pure-white dress blossoms before me in hoops and bustles and petticoats, rustling and flowing in spiraling circles upon sparkling slippers that glide in three-quarter-time across the floor. It's all reminiscent of the 1938 black and white film "Jezebel," directed by William Wyler, starring Betty Davis and Henry Fonda. And in reality, the 1952 debutante ball depicted in that memorable Warner Brothers' picture is based on this very same, famous and incomparable, "Olympus Ball." However, given my depraved condition, the entire scene takes on a more bizarre, Maurice 'Sendak'ian' tone.

Fortunately, my dance-card, which is tucked away in the gold-lame pouch dangling at my wrist, is seldom needed to determine whom I should dance with next. During the next few hours of my intimate social interaction with the blue-blood stock of New Orleans' high society, I find I have been strategically, successively, paired with each blushing debutante in Sissy's "Royal Court." Each of them seem to know who I am, despite, or most likely because of, my outrageous costume and my repeated attempts to become a wall-flower between dances. No doubt they've been instructed to keep me out of trouble, and otherwise fully occupied, until the waning hours of the evening, or realistically, the wee, small hours of the morning, at which time, I am finally scheduled to dance with the young and beautiful (and I might add, tightly cleavaged herself) Sissy.

Speaking of whom, I can hardly capture in words, the rich, sensual, experience I am confronted with, when gazing upon Sissy's voluptuous figure at such a regal event. My fully lubricated senses are completely receptive to her every move, having been so craftily titillated as the evening progressed, layer upon layer, toward the final culmination and Sissy's official crowning as "Queen of the Ball!" Being young, and in what most would consider the prime of my life, having survived the previous week's southern-style boot-camp, my tweaked and frazzled hormones are fully-raging and ready for anything. Stewing in my own juices, my brain salivates, as I count down the minutes before I can be with her; before I can hold Sissy's slim, curvaceous body in my arms, and press my flushed cheeks to hers, moving and swaying with the music. The food, the drink, the orchestra, the wafting pheromones, all provide a splendid, mind-altering experience, as the centuries-old southern-rite-of-passage from nubile innocence to full bloom womanhood is sumptuously celebrated with glorious aplomb.

Periodically, through the crowd of bodies and the haze of sweet-smelling cigars, I catch a glimpse of Sissy's delicate frame seated on the stage, high on her regal throne. Her bare-shouldered, white gown sparkles with a thousand points of lights, which emanate from the innumerable beads and sequins and precious stones that adorn its classic antebellum design. She sits delicately with perfect posture, scepter in hand, framed in a luxurious white robe, extending to a twenty-five-foot, ermine-trimmed train. But, by far, the most striking aspect of her regal attire is the exquisitely designed and elegantly bejeweled, tiara-style, high-back collar that blooms stately from her delicate shoulders. The entire affair semi-encircles her head like the gilded petals of a graceful rose, the effect of which presents her stunning countenance as a glowing centerpiece, radiant as she surveys the admiring subjects of her magical realm.

Admiring Sissy from various locations on the dance floor, it suddenly dawns on me with frightening, almost sobering, clarity that Sissy could be my 'One and Only'… the soul-mate I've so cautiously been searching for. Her gorgeous frame and classic features, her luxurious, raven hair, symmetrically highlighting her indescribable face… everything about her pulls my fear-ridden, conflicted-self into one coherent whole. What a feeling to have for the first time in one's life; impossible to explain, unless you've held it in your own heart. *So, this is what love is all about.*

Suddenly, an odd thought occurs to me while dancing with the last, comely, Princess in Sissy's debutante court. I need to thank my mother for making me dance with her on the kitchen linoleum as a youngster. Inadvertently, and more likely intuitively, she was preparing me for this very moment. If she could see me now. *Actually, given my outlandish attire, I'm glad she can't.* This last young lady is larger than the rest, but graceful, and most complementary in her demeanor, making for a pleasant partner to chat with as we swirl to the music. When the number ends, I bow to her buxom curtsey and thank her for the honor; a social grace I quickly picked up observing the seasoned veterans around me.

"And now," the young woman whispers, blushing over the tip of her hand-held fan. "It's time for you to dance with the Queen!"

I will remember those bubbly, confirming words for the rest of my life. Then, with the opening fanfare of a Hollywood musical, I turn to see the dance floor clearing before me. Beautiful, costumed, couples glide back and away, creating a ceremonial corridor extending from myself to the lavish stage, where I see my beloved Sissy now standing, scepter in hand, awaiting my approach. Being clueless as to the required formalities, I stand there with my mouth gaping open, taking in Sissy's Queenly beauty and the majesty of the moment. Fortunately, the satin veil of my harlequin mask covers my awkward stupor. Then, like the magical appearance of 'Glinda,' 'The Good Witch of the North,' in "The Wizard of Oz," all eyes are drawn to Sissy's stately splendor, as she floats to the edge of the stage. This is the appointed time when the Queen descends from her throne to greet her adoring subjects and dance with a small, select cadre consisting of her royal counterpart, the venerated 'King of the Ball' (an annually selected pillar of community), then her own, and highly-regarded, 'Father-of-the-Queen,' followed by various well-placed aristocrats, each waiting to confer their ceremonial blessings on Sissy as the newly crowned "Queen of the Olympus Ball."

But first, as I quickly surmise, it is my privileged duty, as the Queen's 'Official Escort,' to take Sissy's royal hand and lead her down the ceremonial stairway for her first official dance as Queen. And since I've been mentally 'winging it' this entire evening, my anticipatory senses are exhausted and a bit slow on the uptake. It takes a not-so-subtle fan-rap to my shoulder, from my full-figured dance partner, to snap me out of my daze of admiration. Then, humorously, and causing a measured twitter from the crowd, the heavy-set maid cattle prods me with her fan, goading me, toward the stage saying, "Take your mask off and go get her!"

Without warning, I suddenly find myself blinded in the center of a white-hot spot-light, stunned like an alien abductee in the paralyzing ray of a UFO. I force myself to stagger, unmasked, toward the proscenium, blanching in the fiery reflection of the beads and bangles of my own, hideous costume. With my last hope of anonymity now an historical footnote, I blink against the dancing lights, trying not to trip over my ridiculous elfin slippers. Squinting into the dazzling haze, all I can see, and the only thing I allow myself to concentrate on, is Sissy's brilliant, glowing beauty, waiting, hovering, like the shining sun, shimmering with grace and beckoning my approach. Sissy is surreal and seems unattainable. But, she beckons me on. I don't remember ascending the stairs. My first real sensation is the anchoring of her hand in mine, lifting it high, leading her down to the ballroom floor. Her nubile attendants expertly unhook her royal train from her perfect shoulders as my arm instinctively flows to the small of her back, pulling Sissy's regal countenance to me. And then, time becomes lost....

Without thinking, we move together, effortlessly, to the same traditional waltz that has played for hundreds of years, generation upon generation, in this very place, at this exact moment. As if we were born for this very moment, Sissy and I hold tight to each other, swaying and swirling in the hypnotizing spotlight, every eye fixed upon us, playing out every dream ever dreamt about this remarkable evening.

Then, in the blink of an eye, Sissy's wondrous face transforms into the beautiful image of Jan Flannery dancing in my arms to the same orchestrated waltz, back in the Ballroom at the Grand Hotel! Victorian costumed guests swirl gracefully around us, as Jan continues an ongoing conversation, that somehow, we are fully engaged in.

"Tell me about your children again," says Jan, gazing at me with those same sparkling blue eyes that, a moment ago, had been young Sissy's.

Seamlessly, and surprisingly, without too much mental anguish, I engage the alluring Jan Flannery in mid-thought, attempting to maintain a conversational tone despite my middle-aged huffing and puffing.

"The oldest, just graduated from college, and is thoroughly enjoying being grown up, spending every dime she earns. Then there's the artistic one, blossoming into a beautiful young woman; a budding writer I think. Then our super-model-soccer-star, still enjoying the thrill of competition. But, her good looks are quickly catching up to her. And the youngest, the only boy, is just growing into his own. He'll most likely be taller and lankier than his Dad, and better-looking, thank God."

Just how long Jan and I have been intimately dancing and conversing is totally lost to my current recollection. I count myself fortunate to have seamlessly flowed from my dream-like reverie with Sissy, to dancing with Jan again, after all these years.

Just then, the doctors, David and Amanda Johns, glide up to us, matching our steps and, seemingly, assessing our psychological compatibility.

"You two make a lovely couple," Amanda provocatively states, still incongruously petite in the rangy arms of the towering Dr. David.

Jan blushes appropriately, and I smile without saying anything.

"Indeed," Dr. David adds dryly, "Your individual auras seem to complement one another." Both of them display the glowing effects of the evening's free-flowing champagne.

"We'll take that as the highest compliment," I finally say with a responsive bow, "coming from such eminent scholars as yourselves."

"Perhaps you've been here before," Amanda mysteriously adds without explanation, despite the obvious; this being the Somewhere in Time weekend. Her off-the-cuff statement creates a natural pause in the conversation.

"Indeed, we have!" I say looking at Jan, side-stepping Amanda's metaphysical undertone.

"Would you two like to join us for a cocktail in the Cupola Bar at the top of the hotel?" Amanda asks, surreptitiously including Jan in her invitation.

Waiting for Jan's reply, I quickly confirm my own availability, "I have officially extended my personal curfew for the entire weekend."

"I'm afraid I'll have to take a rain check." Jan says. "I have to be up early, to make sure the morning activities start on time." Then surprisingly, she adds, "Perhaps tomorrow night? That would be fun."

"Of course," Amanda says, beaming with a satisfied smile.

"Yes," I add, sealing the deal. "That will be great!"

"Indeed..." David confirms.

"Well, perhaps we'll see you later then..." Amanda says, re-affirming her invitation for me to join them later. She and David then whirl off together, unconcerned as to my actual answer.

"*As time allows...*" David mouths over his shoulder, gliding away.

Thoughts and emotions, both good and perhaps questionable, flood my heart, as it pumps in time with the music, dancing and flowing with the lovely Jan Flannery, my old friend... my beautiful friend. We smile and hold each other firmly, exploring the rhythm of this haunting tune... with its strange, familiar melody.

Chapter 13

YOUR LOCAL SIDEREAL BAR

On the way to my room, I decide to check out the fabled view from the "Cupola Bar." The elevator slides open at the Hotel's top level, and I climb the final flight of stairs to the club level. *Wow, what a view!* The scene is breath-taking, even at night. Especially at night! From horizon to horizon, there is a panoramic view of Lake Huron, the Straits of Mackinac, and the entire span of Mackinac Bridge, spreading like an elegant string of pearls, with the expansive blackness of the lake beneath a canopy of sparkling stars. The bar itself is generously populated at this late hour with all manner of 'characters' and 'likely suspects,' each basking in the smoky haze of 'intrigue' and 'plot twists' everywhere you look. It's like walking into the gritty blend of a J.A. Jance detective novel with the romance and allure of expatriate France or Algiers; one of those smoky gin-joints where everyone has a story to tell, and apparently enough time on their hands to tell it.

A smooth-jazz trio of tuxedoed brothers play lazily at the end of the bar, wasting their lives away, seemingly, loving it. Their front man, a thin Sinatra-style crooner with slicked-back hair and 'suave' written all over him, winks me in as the newest arrival to this hazy nether-world; this 'whatever you want it to be' world, where everyone plays out their fantasies, watching the regulars and the nightlife newbies playing out theirs.

"Michael!" I hear someone call my name from the opposite end of the dimly lit lounge. Visually picking my way through the various clandestine conversations, I recognize David and Amanda occupying a cushy window-table next to the band, enjoying the spacious view of the lake below. Theirs's is the spot I imagine Humphrey Bogart would sit, trading sharp-toned barbs with the alluring Ingrid Bergman in "Casablanca;" that 1943 classic picture of romance and intrigue. I sidle their way with one hand in my tuxedo pocket, like Bogie's character, Rick Blaine.

"Well," I say, in a sloppy paraphrase of 'Bogey' himself, "'Of all the gin joints, in all the towns, in all the world... and I walk into yours.'" Amanda laughs, instantly recognizing my weak 'Bogart' imitation, and my loose interpretation of Rick Blaine's famous line in the movie. *Once a tour-guide, always a tour-guide,* I glibly think to myself.

Amanda then chimes in, imitating Ingrid Bergman, as "Ilsa Lund," without skipping a beat, "Play it once, Sam. For old time's sake."

The jazz brother at the piano picks up on Amanda's impromptu remark and nonchalantly segues into "As Time Goes By." The suave one picks up the cue and croons into his vintage 1940's microphone: "Da-dy-da-dy-da-dum... Da dy da dee da dum," while brother number three falls in with a hypnotic back-beat on his stand-up bass.

"I thought I might still find you here," I say. "Enjoying the view?"

"Of course," David says, raising a welcoming glass of wine.

""I wasn't sure it was you," Amanda says, with another Bergman paraphrase from Ilsa Lund.

"I had to check out the world-famous view from the Cupola Bar, and it's urbane, ex-patriate atmosphere, before turning in for the night. And look at you two," I remark. "Still going strong into the wee hours of the morning!"

"Yes, well, with no kids to put to bed, and no clients to see in the morning, David and I take advantage of whatever time we can to spend together."

"Well, don't let me interrupt."

"No, no, please... we've had enough 'alone-time' for one evening... haven't we dear?" Amanda fawns in David's direction.

David responds with dramatic flair: "'We'll always have Paris. We didn't have. We lost it until you came to Mackinac Island.'" He lifts his glass again, playing the romantic Casablanca allegory to the hilt.

"Oh, please..." Amanda returns to David. "Sit down Michael, and relax," she continues, inviting me to join them.

"Please do," David agrees, pulling out the Art Nouveau chair next to him.

At their insistence, I take the seat with a bird's-eye view of the lake; David on my right and Amanda's small frame perched across from me on the cushioned bench that rings the semi-circle of the large picture window behind her. Still wearing our formal evening-attire, and as Rick Blaine might say: "David wore gray... Amanda wore blue...." with the jazz boys dressed in their white dinner-jackets, along with the other exotic-looking night-life, the place resembles a scene from "Rick's Café Américain," French Morocco, December 1941.

"Thanks," I say, taking the opportunity to relax after a full day of Somewhere in Time activities. "I don't think I could sleep anyway. I seem to be energized or something; probably the excitement or the champagne."

"Perhaps kismet or some unseen force!" David adds, with verve and punctuation, drawing me into their obviously high-brow conversation. Then, with a penetrating stare, and another salute of his glass, he tips the wine to his lips.

"Oh stop David!" Amanda interjects apologetically, providing temperance to David's sometimes quirky veneer. "The poor fellow hardly knows us," she continues. "Not that it would make a difference; when it comes to knowing David." she adds, in jest for my benefit.

"Alright," David responds. "'I ain't sleepy either,' as the piano man, Sam, would say. So, have a glass of our favorite cabernet sauvignon and enjoy your space."

"My space?" I reply, as David reaches for the open bottle on the table between us.

"Yes, your space, our space. There's so much more going on around us than you'll ever know. It's difficult to comprehend actually," David continues, with an enthusiasm that belays the lateness of the hour. "But, if you know where to look... and what to expect... you'd be amazed at what you might find. Or, perhaps, what finds you."

I unbutton my tuxedo jacket, loosen my tie and sit back to enjoy some good conversation, good wine, and the musical stylings of the 'Jazz Boys' augmenting the mood just beyond our elbows. I quickly surmise that David and Amanda are emerged in a mind-altering buzz, which is a level or two above mine. So, and since I'm not driving, I decide to catch up, to stay in their conversational league.

"What kind of wine is this?" I ask.

"Do you have a couple hours?" Amanda warns me, rolling her eyes in acquiescence; indicating I have tread upon one of David's favorite subjects. "Not tonight David," she pleads, with another of Ilsa's classic lines from Casablanca.

"Oh, 'especially tonight!'" counters David, imitating Rick Blaine with a slight Bogart lisp. "This is serious business, and not a frivolous waste of anyone's time, or space," David says, seriously. He then turns to engage me, "This, my good man, is the remarkable 'Bergevin Lane' Cabernet Sauvignon." His impeccable French pronunciation flows effortlessly from his tongue, testifying to the fact that his intellect has not diminished one scintilla, despite the copious quantities of champagne they have already consumed, and now this bottle of his favorite wine.

"What's that again?" I ask, as David pours a tasteful third-of-a-glass into an empty goblet that seems to have been waiting for me.

"Here's the story... and it's a good story, one with a "wild finish," as Bogie would say. And a tale you'll especially appreciate, being a fellow Washingtonian and most likely a connoisseur of the perennial conflict between true-love and virtue. Salute!" David says, interrupting himself, and encouraging me to taste the deep, ruby-red cabernet.

"As it turns out," David continues, not waiting for my anticipated reaction, "the rich, fertile valleys of southeastern Washington State are located at the same optimal grape-growing latitude as the legendary Bordeaux and Burgundy regions of France. And this particular 'fruit forward, easy drinking Cabernet offers a suave nose and palate of blackberries, sweet dark cherry, vanilla and hints of chocolate and cassis.'" David finally pauses, to study my response. I pause, while the jazz-boys play on, acknowledging David's poetic characterization of the wine's superior qualities.

"I'm impressed! How do you know so much about wine?"

Sarcastically, Amanda answers for him, "He memorizes the Winemaker's Notes off their website."

"That, and the fact it's printed here on the label." David admits with a grin.

"Oh, that *is* good!" I comment, rather naively I'm sure, but with genuine enthusiasm, upon taking my first sip. "I don't know much about wine. But, when it comes to eating and drinking, I know what I like."

"And that, my friend, is the secret to life." David says, relishing another sip and leaning back with full satisfaction.

"What?" I ask in jest, "eating or drinking?"

"No. Well, both, and knowing what you like." he continues, with a measured self-indulgence, letting the smooth notes of the cabernet linger on his palate and merge with the musical emanations of the jazz trio.

I nod in agreement, letting the wine's rich flavors and subtle impressions flood my senses.

"And now you know," Amanda says, in her own satiated sigh of self-reflection. She places her empty glass on the table and waves off David's dutiful attempt to refill it. David puts the more-than-half-full bottle back in its place of honor on the table and continues his rambling narrative, apparently, not ready to call it an evening.

"The fascinating part is... it's not only the similar earth latitude... but more importantly, it's the astonishingly similar effect of the cosmic sidereal rays!"

"O.K., that does it for me." Amanda interjects. "I've reached my own cosmic limit," she says, surrendering to David's conversational segue.

I suspect Amanda is all too familiar with her life-mate's propensity for the bizarre and eclectic, and relationship-wise, she can probably take only so much, having reached her limit long before the 'earth's latitude' and 'cosmic sidereal day' became relevant topics of discussion.

David and I politely say our good-evenings to Amanda, who assuredly insists…

"No, no. You boys stay as long as you want. I'm going straight to dreamland as soon as my head hits the pillow."

David gratuitously kisses her hand, silently apologizing for any insensitivity on his part.

"I wish I didn't love you so much." Amanda sighs to David, parroting another Ingrid Bergman line to Humphrey Bogart.

Then, seamlessly, the band segues into the Casablanca theme song, matching the mood of Amanda's exit:

> "It's still the same old story
> A fight for love and glory
> A case of do or die.
> The world will always welcome lovers
> As time goes by...."

(Words and music by Herman Hupfeld, ©1931 Warner Bros. Music Corporation, ASCAP)

"Great woman..." David says, regaining his chair and regarding Amanda's seductive figure, weaving through the tables. Saluting her departure, he lifts his glass in contemplative reflection.

"You're a lucky man," I say, admiringly, enjoying the cabernet slowly circling in my glass.

"Indeed," David says. Then, in a strikingly good Bogart paraphrase, he adds, "'That's the way it goes... one in and one out....'" "Now, where were we?" he continues, in his Pavlovian voice, re-engaging like an absent-minded professor. "Ah, yes, 'the cosmic sidereal day!' That's s-i-d-e-r-e-a-l and pronounced, 'sy-dear-ee-ill.' It means, 'having to do with the stars."

I settle into my chair; "my space," as David characterizes it, and sip my Bergevin Lane, fully content with myself, and ready to enjoy the good doctor's informal lecture. Suddenly, it dawns on me that my flush of satisfaction doesn't even depend on the subject matter of the conversation, but rather, the good wine, the interesting company and just being present in the moment. If nothing else, I'll relish this simple gift that has found me on this late, October evening at the Cupola Bar on Mackinac Island.

David refills our glasses and continues preaching to the choir of one.

"The important thing to remember is, everything is energy! I mean everything; molecules, people, rocks, the spaces between spaces, even your thoughts... eh?, and my thoughts... everything! All this energy is constantly moving and vibrating, each particle, at its own specific frequency. Like Nikola Tesla said, "If you want to find the secrets of the Universe, think in terms of energy, frequency and vibration."

I feel my mind expanding and tightening in my skull, as I attempt to follow David's free-flow line of thinking. It's a good thing I've read some Shirley MacLaine lately... but obviously not nearly enough. I attempt to concentrate through the warming glow of the wine and the pull of the late hour, to focus on what David is saying.

"Let's say the dome ceiling here at the Cupola Bar is pointing straight out into space, which it is. And, since we are currently situated at approximately the earth's 45th parallel, which is the horizontal line half-way between the equator and the North Pole..." David pauses to grab an orange from a nearby fruit basket for illustration purposes.

"We are currently forty-five degrees, fifty-one minutes, and two seconds, north of the equator to be precise. I checked it on the internet. And the Grand Hotel is located, right about here." He marks the orange by poking a fringy, cellophane-tipped, tooth-pick into it, as if planting a flag in the corresponding location.

"Now, let's not forget the earth is tilted on its axis about twenty-seven degrees in relation to the galactic plane. So. Isn't this amazing? Since we are sitting at forty-five degrees latitude and tilted another twenty-seven degrees, that totals seventy-two degrees in relation to the ninety-degree, horizontal, plane running through the center of the galaxy!"

I fight to keep my eyes from glazing over, trying earnestly to focus on the tip of the tooth-pick protruding from the side of David's miniature earth. David then manipulates the orange in his hand, causing it to rotate with his fingers.

"Now here's the really 'wild part,' to paraphrase Bogey," David continues, "Since the earth is located just slightly above the center line of the seven-thousand light-year-thick Milky Way Galaxy, traveling at approximately 230 kilometers per second, guess where the roof of the Cupola Bar is pointed, once every twenty-four hours, minus approximately 4 minutes per day?" My eyes are watering, trying to track David's detailed and enthusiastic presentation. I blink, and let the massive freight train of David's superior knowledge Doppler pass me, as if I am standing still. Mercifully, David answers his rhetorical question.

"At the exact center of the frickin' galaxy! Give or take 'three-one-thousandths' of a percentage point either way. And since the earth is over twenty-six thousand light-years from the center of the galaxy, it hardly makes a difference!" David pauses for dramatic effect, which sadly, does not immediately register with me, as I pretend to contemplate the cosmic proportions of David's obviously well thought out dissertation. "Wow..." I say, in obvious understatement, forcing David to clarify further.

"Don't you see?" he implores. "At certain times during the year, the forty-fifth parallel, at specific locations around the planet, lines up in a straight shot to the center of the Milky Way!" David chuckles at the shear audacity of it all, and takes a quick gulp of wine. "And guess what time of year this all takes place?" he asks, hopefully rhetorically again, as I have no clue as to David's latest "double-jeopardy" brain-buster. "Grape growing season in Bordeaux, France and the Walla Walla valley!" he announces triumphantly. "Both of which are situated at the same approximate earth's latitude! And more importantly." he adds, "during the crucial peak of the earth's annual grape-growing season, Bordeaux and Walla Walla are at the same sidereal-angle in relation to the center of the galaxy!"

David then raises his glass and reclines in full satisfaction, as if he just delivered the mother-lode of all scientific punch lines... and knows it. Unfortunately, his major point just went over my head and soared out the window of the Cupola Bar. With only a vague understanding of David's belabored point, I employ whatever rudimentary 'active-listening' skills I can muster from my mediation training, to acknowledge the gist of what I think his hypothesis really means.

"So..." I say, taking it one sound-bite at a time, "Once every twenty-four hours... at certain times during the year... the roof of the Cupola Bar... the Bordeaux region of France... and the Walla Walla Valley... are pointing towards the exact center of the Milky Way galaxy?"

"Precisely," David says with a triumphant nod of his head.

"Well, that is something!" I say, still not understanding the full implication of my own words. "You should tell somebody about that." I say. "They could extend Happy Hour or something, or rename the place. The uh... 'Straight-Shot Sidereal Bar!'" I chuckle and take another sip of wine, reveling in my witty response, thinking I've heard the whole story.

"No, no, no... don't you see?" David half-whispers, trying to keep from becoming exasperated at my simple-minded analysis. "Wait a minute!" he says. "What am I thinking? It's not your fault. I forgot the best and most unbelievable part, the really wild finish!"

"What?" I ask, pensively, while David leans in closer, to deliver the kill-shot for his cosmic narrative. Instinctively, I wonder whether I really want to know what's coming next.

"Do you know what is located at the center of our galaxy? The exact, freakin' center of the Milky Way? David stares into my eyes, uncomfortably close, accompanied by the Jazz boy's collective gaze, as they wait for David's climatic answer.

"No, what...?" I whisper, apologetically.

"A massive, but nano-sized, swirling, mega-death of a black hole, slurping up every goddamn thing in sight!" The 'slurping up' part of David's unexpected brain-fart is strategically poised at a ramp-up in volume that causes an immediate reaction from the neighboring sidereal night-owls, and a synchronistic grace note from the 'Jazz Brothers,' who are frozen, statue-like, leaning in our direction. My blood-shot eyes slide sideways behind the upturned glass at my lips, where David's verbal-aneurysm had caught me in mid-gulp. I smile sheepishly at the prying eyes and timidly mime a toast to the crowd, to punctuate David's ultimate point. The collective retard from the Boys in the Band eventually fades into the local sidereal sunset, as the Band continues their musical ramblings, and the earth starts revolving again at the Cupola Bar.

"Wow." I say.

"Yes." David says, in complete satisfaction. "And at the center of that massive black hole there is so much pure energy streaming out, in a reverse-blast, that it's totally immeasurable! More power than you could ever dream of or imagine. And it's bombarding every living, vibrating thing in the galaxy at all frequencies, including yours and mine and every one of those succulent grapes that went into this extraordinary Bergevin Lane Cabernet Sauvignon!"

"And, believe it or not, for the next twenty minutes or so, you and I are poised at the apex of today's 'local sidereal burst,' coming straight at us from the center of the Milky Way." David studies his wrist watch, as if counting down the minutes.

"Local sidereal time for our exact location here at the Cupola Bar on Mackinac Island, and its corresponding twenty-minutes of peak reception from the center of the galaxy, starts right, about… now!" David marks the precise moment by thrusting the orange's antennae-like toothpick straight up to the ceiling in a dramatic, sidereal salute. The piano-man punctuates David's gesture by jumping to the top of a rolling arpeggio with the patriotic bounce of Branson's "Dino" on the Fourth of July. The brother on the stand-up bass marks the moment with a bone-conducting slide of his 'D' string that shoots straight through the roof. I follow the toothpick's trajectory with my flabbergasted imagination, up and out, twenty-six-thousand-light-years, to the very core of the unfathomable black hole at the center of the galaxy, as David lifts his glass for one last toast. I clink mine to his and sit up in my chair.

"To 'The Force!'" David implores.

"'The Force!'" I repeat.

Then, David adds by way of benediction, "As time allows."

"Amen!" I intone, as the 'Jazz Boys' swirl and sway to some cosmic tune, with haunting vocals that sound like something from "Star Trek."

"'So, if it's December 1941 in Casablanca, what 'sidereal' time is it in New York?'" I say, unabashedly showing my mental exhaustion with another, seemingly appropriate quote from Casablanca.

"'They're asleep in New York,'" David says, in his best 'Bogie' imitation. "'They're asleep all over America...'" he adds, finishing Rick Blaine's famous line. Then, as himself and more soberly, "At this very moment, you and I are the only insignificant souls on this puny little planet who are truly awake and contemplating the real meaning of it all. Can you feel the power? Seeping into your bones from the very heart of the galaxy? Let's bask in it, shall we?"

David leans back; closing his eyes and lifts his face to the ceiling, as if lying on some celestial beach on some far-point station, soaking in the sidereal stardust from the center of the Milky Way. I wisely follow my inclination not to ruin the moment by saying anything. Instead, I take a long sip of cabernet and lose myself in the Jazz Boys' ethereal music radiating in the sidereal moonshine, while the bass-man stretches time with soft, back-phrasing bass notes... from eternity.

"And speaking of Basques," David adds after a long, therapeutic silence, either totally out of context or intentionally making a bad pun on 'basking' in the sidereal surge.

"You know, those mysterious, indigenous, peoples of Europe, in the Pyrenees Mountains, between France and Spain? Their ancestral homeland is centered on the 45th parallel, along with the Languedoc Roussillon region of France, which is the birthplace of the Knights Templar, and the rumored exile of Mary Magdalene after the crucifixion of Jesus."

"Oh, Great!" I think to myself. *"Now my mind is reeling."* It just so happens that my wife is Basque; third generation from Bizkaia, Spain. And my father and grandfather were both Masons. I've always had a strange fascination with secret societies, especially the Knights

Templar. But, even freakier, and it now just hits me... I was born in Walla Walla, and my mother's maiden-name is 'LePage,' which is French!

"*Oh... my... God!*" I try to conceal a bone-chilling shiver that shoots up my spine and ends in the short hairs at the back of my neck. David continues...

"They've done scientific studies on the unknown energy that bathes the earth during the height of each sidereal day. It started back in 1931 when a radio astronomer at Bell Labs named Karl Jansky was trying to identify the unknown radio interference that was constantly affecting shortwave radio transmissions. Since he couldn't find any earthly origin for the mysterious static, he finally realized it was emanating from the center of the galaxy!"

"Oh, man!" I say, pounding back another gulp of Bergevin Lane, finally catching onto David's fantastic tale.

"Yeah, but wait!" says David, grabbing the wine bottle and refilling our glasses. "Another scientist, James Spottiswood, a physicist, has recently found a remarkable correlation between the peak point of each Sidereal Day and spontaneous "Anomalous Cognition!"

"No shit!" I respond, now fully engrossed in David's incredible story, but having no idea what the hell 'spontaneous anomalous cognition' is. "So, what's 'spontameous anomonous cog-dition?'" I ask, stumbling over each word, confirming I have had way too much to drink, at least to carry on a decent conversation with a PhD-social scientist.

"Spontaneous Anomalous Cognition is extra sensory perception... E.S.P!" David whispers, for no apparent reason.

"Oh man! I knew it!" I say, in a clandestine voice. "Those damn aliens have been reading our minds from Mars for millennia! Richard C. Hoagland knows all about this stuff" David glances at me sideways through his glass, satisfied at least that he's got my full attention. But, probably wondering, what the hell I am talking about. He then summarizes:

"So, the bottom line is, for approximately twenty minutes every day, focused around thirteen-thirty local sidereal time, the earth and everything on it is bathed in a mysterious, incalculably powerful force, emanating from the center of the galaxy."

I pull my great-grandfather's pocket-watch from my vest. "But, it's way past one-thirty in the afternoon?" I say, with thick lips and a slack jaw.

"Yes, but local sidereal time advances four minutes every twenty-four hours throughout the year. Due to the earth's rotation, and the wobble of its precession, and our path around the sun, peak sidereal time can theoretically happen at any time, day or night. Tonight, it just so happens we are still within the peak twenty-minute window. Can you feel it? Isn't it wonderful?"

"I feel something." I say. "I'm afraid my senses are a bit dull to be feeling much of anything, especially the source or 'The Force' of the Milky Way. Hey, get it? The source of the Milky Way? Moo...!" I chuckle again, far beyond caring that my jocular humor is juvenile at best, even taking into account my inebriated condition. David, however, doesn't seem to mind, having fulfilled a deep-seeded, personal need to relate his esoteric theory to anyone with the I.Q. over a sea anemolee. *"Damn... I can't even pronounce "sea anemone" in my head! I'd better call it a night, before I make a complete fool of myself."*

"Well, David old friend..." I say. "I believe I'll call it quits and leave you to bask in the local sidereal sunset. Get it? Basque? Forty-fifth parallel?" I laugh a completely stupid laugh and don't even care.

David raises his glass while I attempt to stand, but plop down again to gather my equilibrium.

"Whoa... watch that backwash from Jupiter's rings," David says, circling his wine in a slow, undulating vortex.

"Before you go," he adds, "I have a short Sonnet that may have meaning for you, now that you've been enlightened, as it were. An 'Ode' to Lewis Carroll, the author of "Alice in Wonderland.""

"Alright... I'm ready." I acquiesce, bracing myself with both hands on the table while the musical 'Brothers-Three' anticipate David's recitation by breaking into some local sidereal tune, the mic-man softly humming in the background.

Twas brillig still
Where wumbles wove
As wumbles will
With slithy toves.

And you my precious
One must bow
Again, again…
As time allows.

But, wake now know
Like diving grebes
Who deep do swim
Their wuthering needs.

And don't be shy
Nor briney flow
As yours is now
And now is ho.

You the like
May never know
Not how the burble
Warbling goes.

And time is send
When you are here
Go summit now
And slumber fear.

For blessings kill
With regal boughs
So brillig still
As time allows.

"Oh Wow! Very good!" I applaud with heavy hands, expressing my approval to David and the Band for what has definitely been an extraordinary evening. "I don't know what the hell it means," I say. "But, it is really deep." David and the Jazz Boys accept my sloppy accolades with humility. David salutes my, no doubt, minimal retention of what he has so generously poured into my aching brain this evening. I stand, purposefully, to say farewell, feeling no pain whatever, and wishing none to no man, or woman, if the truth be known. *Where the hell did that come from?*

"Well..." I say. "As the sidereal source sinks slowly in the west, no strike that, straight over head, I bid you adieu kind Sir, and thy 'Brothers-Three,'" I add, bowing to the band. "Until the morrow then." I profess to all, in a shoddy attempt at theatricalness.

"As time allows," David slips in, with a parting smile.

"Indeed," I say, vaguely reaching out to shake his hand, "As local sidereal time goes by!"

I then point myself in the general direction of the descending stairwell and attempt to navigate my exit as the Jazz Boys resurrect the Casablanca theme song as a parting gesture.

> You must remember this
> A kiss is just a kiss, a sigh is just a sigh...
> The fundamental things apply
> As time goes by...

I pause at the head of the stairs, remembering one final scene from Casablanca; when Humphrey Bogart gives his send-off speech to Ingrid Bergman as she boards the plane to Lisbon and freedom with her resistance-leader/husband, Victor Lazlo, when Bogie tells her, *"... the problems of three little people don't amount to a hill of beans in this crazy world."* And then, at the end of the film, when Bogey strolls off into the fog with Claude Rains, the corrupt Captain Renault, and says, which I throw back to David:

"'I think this is the beginning of a beautiful friendship....'"

"'Here's looking at you kid,'" is the last thing I hear, as I stumble down the stairs.

("As Times Goes By," words and music by Herman Hupfeld, ©1931 Warner Bros. Music Corporation, ASCAP)

Chapter 14

CONTEMPLATING THE RABBIT HOLE...

Back in my hotel room, I take my time getting ready for bed, wallowing in the reflective effects of the evening's blend of champagne and cabernet sauvignon. The former, I toasted with the beautiful Jan Flannery, as we said our hesitant goodnights. Suddenly, I remember with pleasure that I have secured an early-morning breakfast-date with Jan in the hotel dining room. Thus, as I recount the evening's lingering moments, I savor the anticipation of our meeting tomorrow. Perhaps, it's the wine loosening the memories that I so flirtatiously entertained as a young man, and thought I had long forgotten, but I haven't felt this excited in ages. Like being a school kid again; not wanting to go to bed and, alternatively, wishing the morning would come quickly. I then ponder whether it's a good thing that I haven't been this excited for so long.

What the hell... I chide myself. *'Mid-life' means you've got as much to look forward to, as you have to remember, right?* My mind runs wild with the possibilities.

Rich, soothing shadows emanate from the desk lamp in front of the window, casting a warm glow about the room. The lake is dark and quiet beyond the lace curtains. Methodically, I disrobe, placing each article of clothing into the hanging-bag. I turn down the fresh sheets of the plush queen-bed, brush my teeth, and take one last look at my aging, rosy-cheeked face in the bathroom mirror.

I wonder what Jan thought, seeing me after all these years?

She really hasn't changed a bit, still so gorgeous, with an ageless essence that shines through every pore of her bright, vivacious body. I, of course, have definitely changed. It seems more than a lifetime ago that Jan and I shared our sun-drenched summer together. Walking and talking, and sharing our hopes and dreams for the future. Ours was a purely platonic relationship, as many of the truly great ones are. But, oh so splendid and admirable, especially by today's standards. She was married, and I was recovering from my long-distance relationship with Sissy, the beautiful Southern Belle. (*Why Sissy and I never married, and had lots of rambunctious, southern-fried children, I'll never know. God knows, we both gave it our best shot*).

Jan and I, on the other hand, fit together like old friends from the moment we met on the Somewhere in Time movie set. It's as if, we picked up where we left off, from some elusive point in time that neither of us could put our finger on. And in a strange, familiar way, it was fulfilling just to be with one another. Sensing a shared foundation we both wished to extend as far as our fates would allow.

While Jan is still the figure of a 'Sophia'-like Goddess, exuding beauty and wisdom, I definitely have put on a few pounds, since we last held each other's gaze. The only 'thin-thing' about me now is my hair. Thank God I haven't succumbed to one of those stealthy comb-overs. Even though I'm relegated to carrying my once-svelte, Corinthian-leather-briefcase-self around in a bulging archive-box on a rolling document dolly, what the heck! All in all, I'm still not a bad catch, if you take into consideration the whole package.

Standing before the bureau mirror in my one-size-fits-all (but-this-size-barely-fits-me) Grand Hotel terry-cloth robe, with its thick embroidered crest, I examine myself, amused and a bit shocked to discover I am developing a healthy, 'Nixon-esque' set of jowls, reminiscent of my grandfather! *God certainly has a sense of humor.*

I was much better looking in the summer of nineteen-seventy-nine. But then, who wasn't? I have developed a noticeable bulge where my slim chin once met a classic jaw line, reminiscent of, well, me, as a much younger man. But, despite the minor imperfections, there is still something in those aging eyes. Something both ageless and timeless, that belays the wuthering of time. There is a stately presence. And if gazed upon closely, perhaps intuitively, the true essence of who I really am can be seen in this full-featured face, like a timeless aura that won't be denied. Despite the belly-warming glow of the wine, or perhaps because of it, I can see it, even feel it, through the graying sideburns, baggy eyes, and the plump, but kind, countenance.

I allow myself a final, reflective moment to consider whether Jan could perceive my true essence as well. Not with her eyes of course, but perhaps, with her heart. Then again, I wonder why I even care what she sees in me, or feels about me. *What the hell am I thinking?*

Why am I here anyway? Alone, on this late October evening at the Grand Hotel? The latent effects of the Bergevin Lane are wearing off, as reality creeps in like a smashed pumpkin at the stroke of midnight. Speaking of midnight, I glance at my pocket-watch on the bureau and note that it is well past the witching hour. And tomorrow promises to be another full and stimulating day, filled with Somewhere in Time activities.

Finding it hard to forsake the therapeutic reverie I have so painstakingly worked myself into, I finally slip under the cool, crisp covers, pulling them high over my still-robed self, and lay quietly, welcoming the sleep as it comes. In the slanting moonlight, the digital clock reads *"1:27am."* I've set my alarm for *"6:30 am,"* to give myself plenty of time to shower and shave and dress for my 'breakfast date' with Jan. I position the hotel pillow just the way I like it, propped up, but not too high. I reach for the nose-mask of my CPAP machine and turn on its soothing positive-air-flow, to prevent my legendary snoring from waking everyone on my floor. Then, to complete my routine, I don the ear buds of my iPod, a habit I've recently gotten into; falling asleep to Hemi-Sync® white-noise, in an attempt to sharpen my mind and facilitate communication between both sides of my brain. Something I've found waning lately, as I slide down the far side of these fifty-odd years. Actually, I find the soft, white-noise quite relaxing. I bought a series of relaxation tapes at one of those holistic health-fairs a while back. Dr. Nick Begich was giving a lecture on the Hemi-Sync® theories of Robert Monroe and his famous 'Monroe Institute.'

"Hemi-Sync®" is an audio-guidance process that works through the generation of complex, multilayered audio signals, which act together to create a resonance that is reflected in unique brain-wave forms characteristic of specific states of consciousness. The result is a focused, whole-brain state known as hemispheric synchronization, or "Hemi-Sync®," where the left and right hemispheres are working together in a state of coherence." Which is touted to, "help you experience enhanced mental, physical, and emotional states," or so says Dr. Begich's website.

Indeed, ever since I was diagnosed with sleep apnea, I've come to appreciate how important proper sleep-patterns can be for a healthy, waking reality. Tonight, however, it won't take much to get me to that deep R.E.M. sleep I crave so much. Soon, the dreams will come. And I'll be there in the midst of them. Enjoying and experiencing every moment. Perhaps, I'll dream of that long ago summer, of the beautiful Jan Flannery; my innocent, summertime infatuation. Such a fond memory... untouchable, yet unforgettable. Drifting, a beautiful harvest-moon hovers over the lake. What a perfect ending to a perfectly wonderful day....

Chapter 15

WAKE UP CALL

It seems that only minutes pass in a dreamless state of bliss, when suddenly, I am shocked awake by the door of my room bursting open, and the harsh light of the hallway throwing shadows around my darkened room. Startled to semi-consciousness, grasping for reality, I fall on the floor next to my bed hopelessly tangled in the bed covers, flopping like a fish out of water, frantically trying to defend myself against some unknown intruder. Despite my pounding heart, I hold my breath and attempt to determine which 'flight or fight' response my fully-firing instincts deem appropriate. Just then, my swiftly peaking panic-attack is interrupted by a strange, almost recognizable, commanding statement:

"Wake up man, you're late!"

My brain blasts into defrag-mode, attempting to cross-reference this strange 'impression' against the terabytes of back-up data I have hastily stashed away for potential use at a moment like this. There is definitely someone in my room, dashing about, to and fro, making himself at home, and continuing to address my general direction with odd statements, as if I have slipped into some parallel universe or different dimension. Just as my brain is about to freeze-up like a cheap laptop, I perceive a familiar, exasperated voice.

"Bro,' didn't you set your alarm? I've been up for an hour already. Get it your butt in gear!"

Just then, the shocking scene before me is blindingly lit by the light being switched on with authority. Squinting through puffy eyes and peeking over the side of the bed, I am totally astonished to see my brother, Greggy, seemingly in the flesh. But also, impossibly younger than he should be, unloading his burden-filled arms in an all-too-familiar, frenetic pace. If this is a dream, it's definitely the most realistic dream I've ever had! Transfixed by the strange scene unfolding before me, I carefully retrieve myself from the floor and stand dumbfounded, like a discarnate entity, taking in this separate reality that I suddenly find myself in the midst of.

"Greggy...?" I hear myself say, faintly, to my brother's shocking vision before me.

Pausing, momentarily, from his flurry of activity, the spirit turns to address me, providing my first good look at this youthful version of my own brother, appearing to be in his mid-twenties again.

"Well, get moving shit-head! Get showered and shaved!" he admonishes, throwing a fully loaded garment bag onto my bed. The bag flops down with a rush of air that startles me further awake. I step back to steady myself, and wipe the sleep from my eyes, still not fully comprehending what is happening.

"Greggy?" I force myself to say again, waffling somewhere between a statement and a question.

"There's no time to talk," he retorts, rushing into the bathroom and splashing cold water on his face. Drying off with a towel, he reemerges and throws it in my face.

"You missed one hell of a party last night. Where the hell were you? I only hope Chris and Jane can make their five-thirty call this morning. I'll tell you all about it later. It was unbelievable!"

I can't believe my brother's hand-towel actually hit me in the face. This isn't like any dream I've ever had! I instinctively catch the towel as it falls into my hands. I look at it, then back at my animated brother, as he continues his excited narrative, unpacking the garment bag on my bed.

"Chris flew Jane, Jan Flannery and I to the mainland in the plane that he stashed at the airport. Nobody's supposed to know, because of the studio liability-thing. Chris needed the flying time to keep his instrument rating. We went bowling, ate pizza, and did up the town. Although I couldn't tell you which town. Those 'Yoopers' couldn't believe that 'Superman' just dropped out of the sky into their little berg in the middle of nowhere. Yoopers, that's what they call the locals on the Upper Peninsula; the 'U.P.' We got back at two this morning! Geez, I'm gonna pay for it today!"

I take a tentative step forward to get a better look at my vivacious younger brother, just as I remember him; continually in a full-tilt boogie. I attempt to lock into this jolting reality long enough to say something and clear the sleep from my throat.

"What's all this stuff?" I say, shocked to hear my words sounding different somehow.

"This is your big acting debut buddy!" Greggy says, throwing a pair of new old-fashion lace-up boots on the bed in front of me. I feel numb, watching him move in cartoon-like fast-motion around the room.

"Maybe those acting class love-scenes with Rae Dawn Chong will finally pay off. God knows, none of your screen-plays did shit!"

Suddenly, and characteristically, my brother stops in mid-thought and looks at me with that familiar look. Then, he deftly smacks me with a pillow and laughingly blurts out...

"Are you just going to stand there or what?"

Catching the pillow, I see my fuzzy reflection in the bureau mirror, as my brother bends over to continue unpacking the garment bag. I glance to the lamp-stand for my glasses, but don't see them. My iPod is still in the chest pocket of my robe, with the ear buds dangling over my shoulders behind me. My terry-cloth robe seems bigger than I remember. Stretching out the kinks from my evidently short-term slumber, I think to myself, *"I'm going to wake up any minute now."*

That's funny. In this dream, my normally-stiff-in-the-morning, carpel-tunnel, wrist doesn't even hurt. That chronic, restricted, motion is gone. And speaking of stiff... that hasn't happened in a while. I attempt to focus on my reflection in the bureau mirror, zeroing in through my fuzzy astigmatism. Suddenly, gasping in disbelief, I cover my mouth, in a poor imitation of a muffled 'B-movie' horror scream. Greggy jumps at my unexpected panic and quickly looks around. Assuming that his shock will be as great as mine, I wait for his reaction, as he follows my gaze to the mirror. Evidently seeing nothing alarming, he falls back into character with a smirk.

"You idiot! You scared the shit out of me. I haven't had much sleep you know. Now, hurry and get shaved. By the way, I saved the best costume for you. Other than the custom job Jean-Pierre designed for Chris. You owe me big-time... Erik Estrada!"

As Greggy rambles on, I finally realize, that staring back at me in the mirror, is my old, or rather, previously younger, self! In my mid-twenties again, with plenty of brown, disheveled, hair, where moments before it was thinning and graying! I rush into the bathroom to take a closer look, slapping cold water on my face. I quickly dry off with a hand-towel, lifting my head slowly in the light of the bathroom mirror.

Oh... my... God! I'm young again! And better-looking than ever! I am myself as a younger man, seemingly alive and in the flesh!

As this reality registers with both hemispheres of my still middle-aged brain, I slap myself hard, feeling my eyeballs shake, confirming, somehow, that I am totally awake and breathing... yet, with all the memories of my old middle-aged self?

What a concept!

I straighten up to take in as much of myself as I can see in the bathroom mirror. I glance down in shock, and find that a major part of me, my familial, substantial belly, is gone! *Holy Shit!* I quickly open my robe and am similarly stunned to see my entire body, from chest to toes; everything, without the obligatory obstruction of my middle-aged gut. And speaking of everything! *"Sweet Jesus!"* Decadent thoughts of youth, rush to my reeling brain.

I cover up and burst from the bathroom with youthful exuberance to confront my brother.

"Greggy, I can't believe I'm really here...!" I spin him around and feel the reality of his youthful shoulders. Uncharacteristically, I give him a hug. He blanches at my sudden enthusiasm, wondering what the hell has come over his usually subdued older brother.

"Yeah, I can't believe it either..." he says, giving me a sideways look. "Don't get misty on me, or I'll have to deck ya. I'm supposed to be the crazy one, remember?"

Intuitively, I bring it down a notch to match the tempo of this amazing, new reality. Then, and still not completely understanding what has actually happened, but totally committed to making the most of it while it lasts, I quickly assume my role as a twenty-six-year-old older-brother, miraculously back on Mackinac Island again, in what looks to be the Summer of 1979, during the filming of "Somewhere In Time!"

Man, what a head-trip! I think to myself, as I dash back into the bathroom, following Greggy's admonishment to get myself in gear. Next to the sink, I immediately recognize my old, 70's era, saving-kit and my crusty contact-lens. Automatically, I begin the process of getting ready for whatever's going to happen next. I wonder, whether someone slipped something into my drink last night.

But, this is way too real. This is one of those magical things you read about, or see in the movies, but not movies you're actually in!

I can't get over seeing myself young again, and good-looking as well.

Incredible!

I nick myself shaving and quickly realize these old blades are nowhere near the quality I've gotten used to in my old-age. Then, it hits me. I wipe the small drop of blood from my side-burn and stare at it on the tip of my finger, working it around with my thumb.

This is real. I am really here!

And I'm young again, with no aches or pains! Even that ugly mole on the side of my neck is gone. And wait....

Holy shit!

It suddenly dawns on me. In 1979... *I'm not married yet!*

There's no ring on my finger! None of my four kids are born yet! I haven't even met my lovely wife-to-be! *Oh man.... I mean, Oh man!*

What starts deep in my chest as the beginnings of a full-blown mind-freaking panic-attack, suddenly blooms into a personal declaration of ultimate, transcendental amnesty!

"Yes!" I declare with a shout, not caring whether my brother, or anyone else, thinks I'm crazy this early in the morning. Besides, my brother would confirm my mental instability in a second.

"Yeah, yeah," I hear him remark from the other room. "Hurry up!" he says, continuing his multi-tasking.

It is with sobering hindsight that I remember this period of my life as being my 'Last Great Hurrah,' the best, most amazing, summer of my single life. And now, as I stand here, contemplating the unimaginable, I wonder....

Is it really possible, to alter what has already taken place, to make different decisions and follow another path?

Not that I would want to. But, the possibilities are intoxicating. The exuberance, and the reticence of it all, effervesces within me.

It must be those damn Hemi-Sync® tapes I've been listening to....

I thought something was different these past few weeks, ever since I started using those white-noise, relaxation tapes. Periodically, incongruent realities would pop into my brain, like hypoglycemic, low blood-sugar, flashes. At the time, I attributed it to becoming more creative; using both sides of my brain more effectively. *Perhaps, that is what is actually happening!* Or there's the parallel universe thing; some Michio Kaku string-theory deal. Or maybe I've just been listening to too much late-night-talk-radio.

Finishing a quick shower, I rinse the conditioner from my hair and open my eyes, looking down to confirm my still youthful body, and the washboard stomach I had completely forgotten about.

I can't believe this! What a miracle! What an opportunity.

I towel off quicker than normal, having much less body to dry off than before. I easily wrap the towel around my waist, something I haven't been able to do for decades. Then, finding it hard to curb my excitement; longing to re-engage in the familiar sibling-banter I used to enjoy so much, I open the bathroom door to throw Greggy a choice insult, only to be shocked out of my head, again, in the blink of an eye! There, sitting on the bed, is a portly, middle-aged couple, in turn of the century wedding garb, locked in a passionate embrace, in the preliminary stages of what appears to be their wedding night! I quickly ease the door closed, without interrupting their passionate mutterings.

What the hell…? This is crazy! What is happening to me? Oh no… Oh my God! What if I've died and gone to Hell? That's it! Hell is living your shitty life over and over again, to witness what a sinful jerk I've been. No, no, really, I can't handle this! I'm soooo sorry, Lord?

I glance at my still flat stomach and confirm that, physically at least, I haven't changed. Desperately, I stare at my face in the bathroom mirror. I feel my blood-pressure pounding in my ears, like an oncoming aneurysm approaching at zephyr speed. I stand, panicked and frozen, with nothing between me and this other reality, but a bathroom door and a terry-cloth towel.

I've got to think quick! What do I do? What would the suave and erudite Dr. David Johns do? Hell, what would Jesus do? I have no idea....

I crouch down to peek through the old-fashioned keyhole. The rotund bride and groom are fumbling to remove each other's garments without much immediate success. Indeed, the eager groom is a bit flummoxed, attempting to navigate the fluff and folds of his plump bride's voluminous wedding gown. And my damn brother is nowhere in sight! Neither are my things, which only moments ago were liberally strewn around the room.

I must have side-slipped into another reality, again! Either that, or I'm still dreaming, or time-traveling, or God knows what?

Fighting to fend off another oncoming panic-attack, I look in the mirror again and see the perspiration beading up on my lineless brow. My heart feels like it's going to pound through my chest. I slap cold water on my face and towel off again, hoping that will do the trick, and bring me back to 1979 or 2005. *At this point I don't care which!*

I peek through the keyhole again and sure enough, both hefty newly-weds are under the bed sheets. For a crazed moment, I think of making a break for it and escaping into the hallway. Then, I quickly dismiss the idea, as I can just picture myself scampering down the hallway of the Grand Hotel with nothing on but a wet towel and a frantic look on my face.

Then, it dawns on me.... This whole disastrous time-travel-thing must be connected to the hemi-sync process somehow. I grab my iPod from the pocket of my robe and plop down on lid of the toilet. I jam the ear buds into my ears, frantically fidgeting with the digital controls, praying like a monk that the batteries aren't dead, trying to remember when I charged them last. *O.K., O.K. This'll do it! Come on....*

I try to remember which Hemi-Sync track I used last night.

I think I started at the beginning of track one, and just let it run. Or did I. It could be any one of the fifty tracks I transferred to my iPod. And God knows how long I can hide out in this bathroom before one of the newly-weds needs to use the facilities?

Glancing nervously around, I realize there is no place to hide, except the shower. But, even with its textured glass and my newly svelte body, I wouldn't be invisible enough to go unnoticed.

What kind of half-assed explanation could I give?

"What in the blue-blazes are you doing in our wedding boudoir?" *I can hear him say.* "The audacity!"

"I am so sorry Sir... No, really, I must have been sleep-walking again. I'll just let myself out." *or* "What do you mean your boudoir? I'm calling the hotel manager!"

Damn you Steve Jobs! I'll never trust technology again.

I hum nervously to myself, rocking back and forth with my eyes tightly shut, drinking in the white-noise streaming from my iPod. I turn up the volume to the max and stare at the battery indicator, which only shows one bar left.

I need to get back to 2005! The battery's going to die sooner or later anyway. And then where will I be? How will I ever get back?

Suddenly, a shaft of golden sunlight streams in through the bathroom window, hitting me in the face. Something feels different; stronger and brighter, like a summer sunrise. I lunge to the key hole. Holding my breath and wiping the sweat from my eyes, trying to focus. I can't see a thing! Only a dark, bluish color filling my field of view. Then abruptly there's movement! My brain grasps for some kind of logic, trying to process what I am seeing.

Yes! Oh, thank God!

I've never been so ecstatic to see my brother's blue-jeaned butt mooning me, as he picks something up in front of the bathroom door.

I wait for a moment, to gather myself, and confirm that it's really him. Then, shaking my head, I grab my chest, take a deep breath, and open the door.

I must look pretty 'spent,' as I timidly emerge from the bathroom and back into our hotel room in 1979.

What a relief to be back with 'Greggy' again. I swear, I'm not letting him out of my sight. I may be youthful in body, but my middle-aged nervous system is shot to hell! And speaking of Hell...! *Thank you Lord! No, really... Thank You!*

I must have aged an additional ten-years in the last few minutes. My brother looks up from his chores just long enough to give me another sarcastic barb.

"Man, you look like shit?" he says, trying to hide his genuine sibling concern. "Don't worry, they'll put some color in your face over in make-up. Oh yeah, and they're probably gonna cut your 'doo' too, and maybe nix the mustache. That 'seventies-look' ain't gonna cut it. Get it? 'Cut it?'"

Greggy snickers to himself and continues preparing, as I take in another calming breath of gratitude. Relieved to be back somewhere familiar again, I notice the mid-summer sun rising over the lake.

"O.K., this is what I've put together!" Greggy says, sliding a handsome, old-fashioned, three-piece, suit out of the garment bag on the bed.

"This cream-colored-number will make you stand out like a beacon, day or night."

"Very nice," I say, genuinely impressed and, of course, grateful to be back, wherever 'back' is. "No, really, it's beautiful!"

As my brother continues his proud explanation, I content myself to just enjoy the moment, again. It's amazing how quickly one can adjust to this crazy time-travel-parallel-universe thing. I watch my brother with a whole, new perspective than when we were originally this age... doing this exact same thing. I remember thinking how fascinating he was, when we were growing up. Even if he wasn't my brother, I'd still think so.

Then, a few classic quotes from the great New York Yankee "Hall of Famer," Yogi Berra, flash through my brain:

"This is like déjà vu all over again." or

"If you don't know where you are going, you will wind up somewhere else." And my favorite:

"If you come to a fork in the road, take it."

I watch my brother as he demonstrates how to don the ensemble in the proper order, and I remember this moment as if it were yesterday. And here I am, living it all over again. But, this time, with the sobering perspective of time. Suddenly, I realize this current 'here-and-now' is only a few short years before my brother's tragic 'accident,' or his first suicide attempt, depending on who you talk to, and just prior to him being diagnosed as bi-polar. It's also a full decade before I had to yank his poor, chemically-imbalanced, butt off Arnold Swarzennegger's "Terminator 2" movie set, and slap him into the psych-unit, to get his meds straightened out. If I didn't know that everything eventually turns out O.K. in the end; that he's still alive, and still my crazy little brother, I'd be a little depressed right now. For a moment, I wonder whether I should, or could, do anything to keep him from going through all that hell. But then, these sorts of heavy thoughts are way beyond my current, diminished mental capacity.

I better just take it one fork at a time.

Chapter 16

TAKING THAT FORK IN THE ROAD

Greggy introduces me to the 'second-assistant-director' in charge of 'atmosphere personnel,' who sends me to the make-up trailer for a drastic overhaul, and to put some color back into my cheeks.

"Everything washes out on camera," I hear one of the make-up babes telling another extra.

Eventually, I find myself milling around with a small cast of freshly costumed, and seemingly overly made-up, 'extras' at one end of the Grand Hotel's fabulously long front-porch, watching the warm July sun climb into the blue sky at the east end of the lake.

It's then that I see the beautiful Jan Flannery for the first time... again. This time, as a young woman again. It's hard getting use to doing things for the first time, again. Déjàvu is a strange thing when it becomes routine. It's like living your life knowing all the punch lines, even when the jokes are being told with fresh enthusiasm. The tight rope that your brain must traverse can be exhausting. Fortunately for me, and I never thought I'd say this, even though I seem to have retained all the raw data from my 53 year old brain, I've also retained my middle-aged tendency to forget certain details. Thus, even though I've lived this entire scene before, albeit a quarter-of-a-century ago, it has a pre-Alzheimer's edge of newness to it, alternatively tempered with a genuine rush of nostalgia and a certain 'gonzo-esque' fear-and-loathing. *"Buy the ticket, take the ride,"* as Hunter S. Thompson would say.

Finally, one of the production company's 'assistant-to-the-associate-somebody-or-other' starts pairing us up, boy-girl-style, and instructing each pair how to 'walk' or more precisely, 'promenade,' as atmospheric-personnel. This, in order that we learn how to lend an air of authenticity to the scenes being filmed later this morning. Here we are, about twenty of us, all different shapes, ages and sizes, dressed 'to-the-tee' in brand new, old-fashioned-style clothing, complete with all the accessories that my brother and his 'female-costumer' counter-parts could muster from their respective mobile costume-trailers.

For years I have enjoyed watching my fastidious brother work on the lower lot in the Wardrobe Department at Universal Studios. I'd visit him on my breaks as a tour guide, and was always impressed by his detailed organization, and how he kept track of everything; from the little 'Battle-Star Galactica' military chest pins, to an entire warehouse of suits and pants and general clothing items, even multiples of the same ripped shirt that Lou Ferrigno would wear in 'The Incredible Hulk.' Every article is cataloged and marked with an identifying code and carefully stored in its place, to be retrieved at a moment's notice or, alternatively, allowed to gather dust for decades in potential anticipation of some future two-hour retro reunion-special.

I really appreciate my brother picking out this classic, 1910-era, cream-colored, suit I am wearing; complete with matching vest and high-collar pleated shirt, with fancy lace-up two-tone, brown boots, just like the ones Chris Reeve wears in the movie. The truth be known, Greggy gave me one of Chris' identical-pair of costume boots, knowing we wear the same size, to save him some time and hassle. Thus, should 'Superman' soil his boots during filming; my crafty brother has a 'replacement pair' close at hand; just a 'brother away.' How I am supposed to 'act' in my stocking feet in such a theatrical emergency he never thoroughly explained. I decide not to ask questions, even though he is my younger brother.

Those of us lucky enough to have landed summer jobs on this small Hollywood picture are a rag-tag, but motivated, bunch. There's a young couple from Seattle; grad-students, who just happened to be in the right place at the right time on a summer vacation. And there's a smattering of locals from the Island and surrounding areas who read the newspaper articles about the filming. But, no matter how we heard about the movie, or where we came from to get here, each of us seems to share the same genuine feeling; that we are participating in something truly special. I remember realizing, even then, that this was one of those 'chances-of-a-lifetime' you occasionally stumble upon, only after taking that pesky 'fork in the road.' How many 'chances-of-a-lifetime' have I missed, by taking the wrong turn?

I received Greggy's initial phone call when I was show-announcing in the Entertainment Center, on the hill, at Universal's Studio Tour. I was back-stage at the 'Wild-West Stunt Show.' My savvy little brother had tracked me down through the studio operator, just moments before I was to burst through the saloon doors and announce to the crowd of tourists, "Ladies and gentlemen! 'Universal's Stunt-Team!'" This, and my other rotating appearances at the 'Animal Actors Stage,' the 'Make-Up Show,' and the ever-popular 'Screen-Test Theatre,' being credited against my lifetime allotment of Andy Warhol's oft-quoted 'fifteen-minutes-of-fame,' accumulating day after day, every hour on the half-hour, from 10am to 7pm, introducing the various post-tour, crowd-pleasing, attractions in the Entertainment Center.

It was fortunate that my brother found me when he did, as it was the last show on that late summer night. I and my buddy, Duke Stevens, (the Tour's 'Incredible Hulk' stunt-double) both had hot-dates with the luscious 'Animal-Actor's Stage,' assistant-trainee, Brenda, (a beautiful blonde with a killer body, who looked like she could handle any uncooperative hundred-and-fifty-pound chimpanzee, as well as an over-zealous 'Show-Announcer' and/or 'The Incredible Hulk'). Neither Greggy nor I could afford an answering-machine in those days, or even a simple pager. So, we became adept at finding each other through the vast network of hidden phones, tucked away in various secret locations around the studio lot. With the competence of a first-assistant-director, we could find each other on a moment's notice in such out of the way places as that dark corner on 'Sound-Stage 39,' where the phone rings silently with the subtle blinking of a small red light, or behind the barn-door of the livery stable in 'Old Western Town,' or the clock-tower in Courthouse Square, or the small bungalow next to the 'Producer's Building' where our friends and fellow 'Brat-Pack' buddies, Barry, Mitch and James, the part-time assistants to 'So-and-So,' (aka, "The Gassy Moles") hang out, on the lower lot. In this fickle 'Business of Show,' you have to be resourceful to compete in the harried world of "there's-always-a-hundred-punks-like-you-kid-(or-better)-waiting-in-the-wings-to-take-your-place," fantasy-land that is Hollywood.

Chapter 17

HOT SOUP FOR 'OL' BLUE EYES'

(**Editor's note**: We apologize preemptively for the occasional expletives that follow, some of which are only partially deleted, and the intermittent spattering of what some would call "coarse language." The author was young, and a slightly randier man, when this unique life-changing experience happened upon him. After considerable debate, the Publisher felt compelled to keep most of the descriptive language intact, for reasons that hopefully will become self-evident).

It's a smoggy, Friday afternoon in May on 'the hill,' at Universal Studios, in the hardened-heart of Hollywood, California. The smell of fame and sweaty spandex wafts up from the producer's building. The tourists are thick as maggots and just as tenacious. The once white handkerchief stuffed into my back-pocket is drenched from sopping the back of my sunburned neck, causing a rather self-conscious wet-spot over my right butt-cheek. Both of my dogs have been barking since noon, and yes, it's quickly becoming self-evident: my studio-tour days are numbered. I can feel it down in my show-announcer bones. I mean, how many times can one decree with charm and conviction: "Ladies and Gentleman... 'Universal's Animal Actors!' or "Universal's Make-Up Team!' to the same madding crowd, day after day, hour after hour, minute by minute, before you yourself become an irrelevant byline on the marquis of life. "Ladies and Gentlemen... 'Universal's Burnt-Out Show Announcer!" (a small spattering of applause... then stone-cold silence).

I've got to do something quick, for my own sanity. I recently survived two years and some change; seven-days-a-week, four-shows-every-two-hours, twelve-hours-a-day, plying my trade as the prestigious (and consequently, minimally-compensated) "Show Announcer," in 'The Entertainment Center' at the world-renowned "Universal Studios Tour." I've done this gig so many times, I know every line that each of the out-of-work, struggling actors use in all four of the Entertainment Center Shows by heart. Of course, I wouldn't admit to it or, no-doubt, I'd be called in off my few-and-far-between days off to fill in for one of the make-up artists, animal-trainers, wild-west stuntmen or screen-test theatre actors, who continually call in sick with their own burnt-out 'fame-and-glory-blues' (but who, in actuality, are attending yet another cattle-call audition, or 'mutilation' as we call them, hoping-against-hope for that long-awaited, semi-reoccurring role on some B-rated day-time 'Soap' that only airs in Japan, at 2:00am, during the Network's summer hiatus).

I've seen the writing on the wall and splashed across the "Hollywood Reporter" in bold print, and it ain't pretty: *"Universal's Show-Announcer goes berserk... sullies himself in front of the 'LTD!" (that's 'Last Tram of the Day,' for the uninitiated).*

"You'll never work in this town again kid!" I hear someone smirk, in a hollow, long-forgotten epitaph, reverberating in my good ear from deep within some sour-smelling, late-night dumpster off Hollywood Blvd.

And so it is, with desperate motivation, I find myself wandering aimlessly around the back-lot, most certainly out-of-my-body, following my frayed instincts and lamenting the fact I did not take that entry-level position in Twin Falls, Idaho, as a cub-reporter for that one-lung excuse of a television station; my one and only post-graduation job-offer, after narrowly escaping with a B.A. in journalism from the "Edward R. Murrow College of Communication."

Previously, I 'served time' as a sluggo tour-guide, leading four-tours-a-day, two-hours-a-tour, 120-twenty-tourists-at-a-time, (most of whom didn't seem to understand English), unconsciously spewing little-known facts and fictitious show-biz trivia into a hand-held mic, sitting next to the hot, diesel-blowing tractor-motor that pulls our packed, three-car tour-tram, which is being driven (if you can call it that) by one of those big-time studio-teamsters, who sit all day recounting the 'inside studio scoop,' while calculating the outside chance they'll ever live to see their pensions, deftly navigating the latest 'oohs-and-aahs' of the studio 'Back-Lot,' as I recite pounds of scripted one-liners and last-minute press-releases, in frantic anticipation of those periodic and inevitable four-alarm, hours-on-end break-downs (usually the tram), stuck with a flat tire in the sweltering, noon-day sun or fending off frigid rain and blinding sleet with my clip-board, dressed in a thin, polyester cardigan, at some boring back-lot location like "Leave It To Beaver" street or half-way between Egypt and 'The Promise-Land' at the bottom of the parting of the 'Red-Sea,' watching it slowly empty and refill around me, over and over, ad infinitum, ad nauseam.

Suffice it to say, at some point in the game, the glamour wears off.

It was in the midst of such a foul and distorted mind-set that I stumbled, almost catatonic, into the non-descript, lower-lot office of my old boss, 'The Jeffster' (a former shell-shocked tour-guide like myself, and the previous show-announcer before me)," now 'sitting pretty' as they say, running the prestigious "Universal Studios Amphitheatre." Uttering something unintelligible, I flailed for his assistance from the industrial-strength, WWII-surplus-gray-steel chair next to his cluttered desk.

Only a few, short, memorable, seasons back, 'good ole' Jeff was the tour-supervisor and I was the Editor of the now defunct, tour-guide-produced, studio "Call Sheet;" that funky, studio-rag that was all the rage with the 'below-the-line' union drones who wanted to stay 'in-the-know' regarding the latest studio scuttle-butt. Written, produced, and solely reported, by us lowly tour-types and edited (using the term loosely) by 'yours truly,' our non-sanctioned, pure-free-speech, back-lot, newspaper could be counted on to deliver the 'real stuff' of Hollywood, along with the 'shear-rumor' and 'underbelly-innuendo' everyone was talking about, but didn't have the guts to print, even in the jaded journals of 'Glitter City.' Small wonder we were eventually 'pulled' by the 'Big Boys' in the 'Black Tower' around our thirteenth edition. But, it wasn't for lack of readership.

As noted, 'The Jeffster,' is now the manager of Universal's "Gibson Amphitheatre" (named for the famed "Gibson Guitar Corporation" out of Nashville), that intensely hip and suave, music venue strategically perched at the crest of the Hollywood Hills, over-looking the studio back-lot and a most incredible view of the glittering lights of San Fernando Valley, in the heart of Universal's famed "City Walk." I had barely planted my sorry ass in Jeff's obviously temporary single-wide, mobile-home office, when, like the gust of a summertime Santa Anna, he grabs my arm and bum-rushes me out the back door, past the security-gate and rows of stretch-limos, like fresh-meat at a soft-porn cattle-call.

"You miserable sonofabitch! This is your lucky day!" Jeff declares, smirking, as we swiftly move through the maze of backstage corridors.

"You just happened to walk into my office at a fortuitous moment! You won't believe what I have for you! And since you won't believe it, I'm going to show it to you myself, up close and personal."

Jeff stops and whips me around, face to face, before taking me into the famed inner-sanctum of the backstage area.

"So, you're looking for something new are you; something not so boring or mundane? Well, you're working for me now! Don't worry, I'll let them know over at the tour office. Your numerous talents are being wasted in that hell-hole anyway. You're gonna love this, man. Your goddamn ship has just come in!"

Yeah, right. That's what he said when I first made it as a tour-guide, and then show-announcer, I sarcastically remind myself.

But, Jeff has definitely peaked my curiosity. I know this guy. He wouldn't mess me over, again. Not him! We've been through thick and thin together, Jeff and I, which of course means absolutely nothing in this town. But what the hell! I'm willing to at least hear the guy out. Maybe he can slide me in as one of those nattily-dressed back-stage guards; those blazer-wearing, tazer-packing, brutes who check in the celebrities at the back-gate. You know the type, walkie-talkie, clipboard, shitty attitude, the whole works. Hell yeah, I could do that. Why not! Lots of famous actors got their start that way, I'll bet. I'm sure I'll think of one. Shit, I wouldn't mind being a lowly usher, helping those touchy-feely, drunken socialites to and from their seats in the dark. All the while, watching the show for free! Man, 'the guys in the band' would be pretty damn impressed! I'm sure I can figure out a way to sneak their sorry asses into a show or two, maybe "The Marshal Tucker Band" or "Santana" or "Linda Ronstadt," or "Willie Nelson." Jeez! All the big acts are scheduled this summer. *I can see us now! The up-and-coming, southern-rock quintet, "Interstate 5," opening for Lynyrd Skynyrd! (applause, applause, the crowd goes wild!) Alright Jeffster! Bring it on man!*

At least I'm dressed semi-respectably, in my show-announcer navy-slacks, white dress-shirt and tie, and blue-blazer, having just survived another grueling day on the black-top in the Entertainment Center. Following Jeff along the perimeter of one of the most coveted music venues this side of Madison Square Garden, I marvel at the lavish, multi-million-dollar remodel MCA recently completed on the place; mere chump-change for Universal's current parent company, garnered from its global, conglomerate tentacles, which tightly encompass the entire entertainment world.

It seems Jeff feels obligated to give me the VIP-tour before explaining the job description he wants me to fill. He doesn't even stop to introduce me to the two raging-bulls at the fortified, back-stage gate. We push pass them with Jeff's officious nod. It's weird seeing these 'Bubbas' cow-towing to 'My-Man-Jeff;' snapping to attention, as we penetrate the initial protective layers of this buzzing, bee-hive of mega-musicdom, so full of people, each doing something impressive and rushing somewhere important, or so it seems. I am definitely licking my chops, wondering what Jeff has in mind for me.

Further into the backstage complex, we are confronted, then waved on, by two CIA-looking, black-ops dudes, with form-fitting earpieces, sunglasses (indoors?) and clandestine microphones up their sleeves. They look like M.I.B.s, waiting to fend off an extraterrestrial invasion. Either that or they are the extraterrestrial invasion. They check me out head-to-toe, as I follow 'The Boss' into the den of iniquity, the inner-sanctum, the ultimate "Bohemian Rhapsody," the illusive 'Area 51' of Rock and Roll; the hallowed halls of the backstage "Green Room!"

"O.K." Jeff says, still rushing ahead. I hurry to keep up and almost bump into him from behind. He stops before a large, polished, mahogany door, as stately as an entry to any Wall-Street law firm. Suddenly, I find myself standing in a plush, carpeted hallway with massive dressing-room doors on either side.

"Our first stop is the coveted "Frank Sinatra Suite," he whispers in a reverent tone.

"No shit?" I whisper back.

Jeff pushes on the heavy door to our right and peers inside. "It's O.K. Nobody's here yet. Come on...."

I think about wiping my feet, but Jeff quickly pulls me inside, glancing down the hallway before closing the door. Once inside, I am immediately awestruck by its over-arching, tasteful opulence.

"As you can see," Jeff begins, falling into his old tour-guide mode. "Wall-to-wall carpet, floor-to-ceiling mirrors, full-size grand-piano, which had to be taken apart and reassembled here in the dressing-room. It's tuned by the best ears in the business before every concert. Power-jet Jacuzzi, two 'bidets,"

Two bidets? I ask myself. What the hell. If you've got one, you might as well have two! But, I'm not asking.

I follow my new boss into the private living-area of the multi-room 'Sinatra Suite,' as if on a White House tour.

"Full bedroom, king-size, double-plush bed, complete with make-up station, theatrical mirrors and plenty of light... or none at all." Jeff adds, with a whisper and a wink. "This entire wing of the back-stage area is custom-built to be completely sound-proof and guaranteed bug-free."

Something I hadn't thought of actually. But, it makes sense. Anyone with the mega-status of "Frank Sinatra" would need to know their private conversations would stay that way. *What happens in the Greenroom, stays in the Greenroom!*

"The two dressing-rooms down the hall, on the left and right, have similar configurations and amenities," Jeff continues. "Upstairs, the entire second floor is lined with chorus dressing rooms, facilities for the opening-acts, orchestra members and dance companies. Now, if you'll follow me across the hall, I'll take you into 'The Greenroom!"

Hot Damn! The Green room! I've been wanting to check out this 'Den of the gods' my entire life. The famous 'A-List, the 'Cream of the Crop,' 'All-Access-Only' "Green-Room," where the 'elite' of the elite hang out, 'schmoozin or loozin,' before, during and after every show. The closest I've come to this awesome 'center-of-the-known-lyrical-universe,' is an exclusive *Rolling Stone* photo spread. Of course, anything would beat that 'broom-closet' of a waiting-room they give you at "The Mustang;" that old country-western bar on Lankershim Boulevard in North Hollywood, with its stale urine-smell and beer-stained rugs (or is it stale beer-smell and urine-stained rugs). Either way the down-home, trailer-park ambiance grows on you after a while. Me and 'the boys' have been letting it, (grow on us) for more years than we'd like to admit. Playing the open-mic nights, plying our trade as would-be 'Southern-rockers,' with the other 'up-and-comers' who make the rounds of such places. (If you go there on a Saturday night, you'd be well advised to pay your respects to "Joey" the 300-pound bouncer at the door. He once took a broad-head arrow to the shoulder and still beat the shit out of the shooter, after catching him on a dead run. Lucky for the guy, the cops cuffed and booked his drunken ass before Joey could feed it to him on a platter). Needless to say, 'The Stang' caters to a rough crowd.

"Wait until you see this!" Jeff says, leaning into the heavy security-door of the Greenroom, continuing our upscale tour. I quickly follow him into the inner sanctum.

"Again, wall-to-wall everything! Top-of-the-line! Nothing but the best. Full wet-bar; stocked with all the domestic and imported booze anyone could ever want. Plush restroom...."

Twin bidets I'll bet....

Designer couches, catered buffet every night, with anything and everything the Act wants to eat and drink. As you can see, the entire far wall is tempered glass, with sliding-doors leading out to the patio and a killer view of the San Fernando Valley below."

Jeff catches himself and pauses for a moment, to appreciate anew the true splendor of it all.

"Man, when this place is packed with celebrities..." I notice Jeff's faraway look, as he gazes at nothing in particular.

"With the 'Hollywood Sign' lit up and gleaming across the valley, it's quite an impressive place to be" I recognize Jeff's nostalgic tone. It reminds me of the 'good-old-days,' when he and I were both much younger, dangerously naïve and starry-eyed.

I try to imagine what it would be like, hanging out in such close proximity with genuine movie and music legends, all lit up with their favorite flavor of 'interior' illumination, if you know what I mean.

While I take it all in, Jeff rambles on. "You can entertain about fifty people in this room, more with the sliding doors open on a warm, summer night."

Man this is fantastic! I'm noticing the high-tech home-theatre set-up. The video monitors strategically placed around the room. This is where the real shit happens; where the big deals are made, where the road-managers, the agents, and studio execs hang out. Forget about the show man. Whatever's happening on stage is a moot point. The real heavy-weights are holding court here, talking up their next big thing, the newest, mongo, head-banging deal they're working on with 'you-know-who.'

"Of course, he's on-board; that new, up-and-coming-what's-his-name, and whoever else has the cojones to make it happen."

Man, this is it! I muse to myself. *The Taj Mahal of the music world; the Lost Ark and Holy Grail of every ancient, solfeggio, tone ever manifested, all rolled into one! And I'm actually here. My bar-rat buddies at 'The Stang' would give their left nut to be a fly on these walls for an evening! I'm looking around for something with a logo on it… that's not tied down.*

Jeff saunters over to the bar and offers me a barstool. Whipping around the counter, he pops open two perfectly chilled Heinekens from the polished-steel fridge and hands me one, clinking the neck of his dark, green bottle to mine.

"So, what do you think?" he says, with a shit-eating, Cheshire grin. "Not a bad place to hang out huh?"

"Hang out?" I repeat, flabbergasted. "Hell, I could live here and never come out!"

"I'm glad to hear you say that," Jeff chortles, then downs half his beer in one long swig.

"Yeah, man! Sign me up." I say. "Whatever you need." I chuckle, keeping the conversation going while Jeff enjoys his brew. "So, do I get to wear one of those 'charp-looking blazers man? And carry a bitchin' clipboard or somethin'?" I say, in my best Cheech Marin, 'East-LA,' lingo, figuring what the hell, he can only say no. Besides, at this point in my miserable existence, I'd be happy counting paper cups in the concession stand.

Suddenly, I recognize Jeff's familiar, sardonic grin; that same sinister smirk he had on his face when he sent me out to my 'first tram,' as a newbie tour-guide, jam-packed with Japanese tourists, knowing I'd never come back the same again.

"Of course," he says. "You can wear anything you want, as long as you blend in with the crowd for each week's concert."

"Cool! When do I start?" I ask, with the enthusiasm of a freshman pledge.

"Right now." he says in a serious tone. "You're not f---in' going to believe this. Before you dragged your sorry self into my office, I got a phone call from one of my best employees. He worked for me for ten years. That sonofabitch was indispensable," Jeff says, taking another swig of his Heineken.

"He tells me he got a reoccurring role on some prime-time drama and their flying his ass to New York, like yesterday. They gave him two-hours' notice, and he gave me less than that! Then you walk in the door, dressed in your sport-coat and tie, on the first day of the new Amphitheatre season. You're a goddamn answer to prayer!"

Well, if you put it that way. Flattery will get you everywhere. I was going to hold out for more money, but what the hell!

"And the best thing is, I know you!" Jeff continues. "I know you won't screw up. Because if you do, you know I'll beat the living shit out of you, or hire some hulking 'Guido' to do it for me!"

Suddenly, the Jeffster's glowing confidence in my perceived abilities begins to worry me. That, and the pleasure he's having, telling me the dire consequences of my screwing up. *What in God's name is he talking about?* How tough can it be to come up with the correct cup-count after a Jimmy Buffet concert? *Actually, if the rumors are true, Buffet's 'Parrot-Head' fans hold the all-time, galactic record for alcohol consumption at the Amphitheatre. And that's just the 'accounted for' stuff. Not what they sneak in unnoticed.*

"So, Jeff-buddy," I say, attempting to steer him around to the main point of our conversation. "Just what in the hell are we talking about here? You want me to chip gum from under the seats in the balcony or what?"

"Not quite. But, I like your attitude," he says, leaning in for the kill.

"This is it man! Look around you. This is your new office; your playpen as it were! For the next twenty-four hours, or longer if you can handle it, <u>this</u> is your dream-come-true!"

At first, I think Jeff's actually flipped. The poor bastard's been slamming down those Heinekens long before I got here, either that, or there's too many lines on the mirror back at his office. I slide him a sideways gaze, not wanting to take my eyes off him for too long, assessing my strategy for a graceful exit. But, before I can think of the next thing to say, he interrupts my paranoid thought-pattern with the shock of my life!

"You are the new 'Backstage Host! You are it man! One of the most coveted gigs in all show biz! And you start right now! I'll call 'Tiny' at the tour office and let her know you're working for me now. She'll do the necessary paperwork.

Damn. Did he say 'Backstage Host?' What the hell! Or was it 'backstage post?' He's giving me a back-stage post as a security guard!

"Did you say Back Stage Host?" I choke on my last gulp of Heineken.

"Concierge, bartender, 'Confidante to the Stars,' and official, full-time 'go-fer!"

"Did you f---ing' say 'Back Stage Host!' Don't mess with me Jeff, I'm way too close to the edge right now."

"You heard me Bucko! I've plucked you from goddamned anonymity and given you the break of a lifetime! Don't blow it!" he says, with the seriousness of a Mafia Don. "My last guy left me high and dry, and now you're my new guy. Can you dig it?"

"Holy Schitz! You're not kidding? Talk about fate. I need a f---in' aspirin; anything white. Oh... My... God....!" I say, starting to hyperventilate.

'Tiny,' my boss, the beautiful, tough-minded genius who schedules the tour-guides and show-announcers will shit a brick when she hears this! She should be so lucky, after all the corporate ass-kissing she's done for this world-wide gobbler of entertainment companies. But, hey, those are the breaks, right? It's all who you know. Or being in the right place at the right time, or wrong time, depending how you look at it. And this time, I'm staring fame and glory right in the face!

"Now listen," Jeff says, grabbing my collar and getting down to business. "Frank Sinatra" is coming through that door in less than two hours!"

"Frank Sinatra!" I yell, as freaked out as I possibly could be. "You mean f---in' "Frank Sinatra!?" Are you shittin' me?" I squeal like a school-girl, trying to catch my breath.

"The one and only! Jeff confirms. "Now settle down and concentrate," he says, shaking me back to reality. "I've got thirty minutes to run you through everything you need to know. Because I've got a whole shit-load of hot buttons waiting for me back at the office. Can you handle this? At least for tonight, until I can find someone on a permanent basis?"

"Hell yes!" I say, cutting him off. "I'm your Man! Shit, I haven't been giving those celebrity V.I.P. Tours for the likes of Yvonne DeCarlo and Brent Musburger for nothing! But, Jesus! Francis Albert Sinatra!? That's like saying, "God Almighty" Himself is walking through that door and you want me to act natural!" Holy shit, talk about easing into a new gig!"

Jeff sounds a bit relieved, as he loads on the butter. "I've never known you to pass up a great opportunity. Especially one that literally bites you in the ass. Besides, you've got chutzpa. I've seen your creative ingenuity in the face of ball-busting' pressure. Remember when you interviewed that contract-actress for the 'Call Sheet,' praising her major-league hooters and Yale MBA all in the same compound sentence? Only to find out she was the niece of one of the Studio-heads in the Black Tower? Remember how you fast-talked your way out of that one."

"Yeah. Fortunately, he took it the right way, even if she didn't." I say, reminiscing about the old days.

"Or when you tried to auction-off Jane Mansfield's autographed bra for a tour publicity stunt?"

"Hey, I still have that bra. It's classic, and way too valuable to waste on the public-at-large. And I do mean large!"

"Let's face it man. You've been plucked from obscurity for potential fame and glory."

"Either that, or if I screw up I'll never work in this town again, right?"

"Or wake up with a dead animal in your bed."

Thus, my job application, interview, and complete background check, is over in the time it takes to chug a Heineken. I've got the next hour-and-thirty-minutes to frantically prepare, before "The Man" walks through that door. 'The King' before 'The King!' The 'Godfather' of 'Godfathers,' at least as far as the music business or any other branch of the entertainment industry is concerned. The "Chairman of the Board" is in town!

Sweet mother of Raymond Burr! I've got to call my brother before he leaves the lower lot!

Here I am; a certified nobody from little 'Brackett's Landing,' alone in the 'inner sanctum of the music world's version of the 'Holy of Holies,' knee-deep in detailed lists and instructions, strict admonitions, 'specialty riders' and way too many things to do and remember, with nowhere near enough time to do it all, even if I knew what the hell I was doing! Fortunately, Jeff threw me a life-line of sorts, saying that all I have to do is press the panic-button on the secret 'Bat-Phone' under the counter at the bar (the hottest, unlisted, phone number in L.A), and he'll be down in a flash to help me out, any time, day or night. Because, as he sarcastically reminds me, he doesn't have a 'life' either. Which, if nothing else, makes this massive tension-headache building over my pineal gland a bit more palatable to deal with.

Jeff tells me I need to pay special attention to 'The Rider,' which is "the most important part of the 'Artist's' contract." It outlines the unique demands, or more casually put, 'the preferences' for each 'headliner' that plays the Amphitheatre.

I soon discover that Sinatra traditionally opens the concert season at The Amphitheatre, and that the venue is active year-round, with only Christmas day off. So basically, the place is hopping 364-days-a-year, twenty-four-hours-a-day, day in day out, with the 'Best of the Best' when it comes to musical entertainment, both 'oldie' and 'newbie.'

And since the Amphitheatre is located smack dab in the middle of what is arguably the closest you can come to 'music heaven on earth,' any headliner has the best of all worlds here in L.A. They can invite 'Everybody-Who's-Anybody' to the show and, more importantly, to the 'party-after-the-show,' including all the 'A-Listers' from every conceivable sector of the entertainment universe, many of whom live and work right here in what Timothy Leary has dubbed the 'Golden Triangle.' All of them mixing it up here in the Greenroom, schmoozing and cajoling and pitching that fresh new idea, or perhaps another tedious, but monetarily inevitable, retro reunion-tour, now that their solo-careers have wound down to where they were before the band split up in the first place.

I've been told to expect the best 'Italian suits' from both coasts tonight; everyone from music to politics, because this is "Sinatra!" and he naturally brings out 'the Best of the Best!' "'The Rat Pack' has legs!" I read in the publicity materials accompanying Sinatra's rider. And when it comes to those who owe somebody something, or need to be seen with somebody, to pretend they are owed something from somebody else, believe you me, this is the place to be. Of course, in the back of my mind, I'm remembering Jeff's one-time, nuff-said, admonition not to mention anything to do with 'The Mob' or 'Mafia' or make any casual, or even indirect, aspersions in that direction.

"Don't even go there, if you know what's good for you." he said. It seems 'Mr. S.' has been forced to deal mightily with such unfounded rumors and innuendo throughout his stellar career, which has survived and thrived well over fifty years at this point.

"And he don't need no f---in' punk like youz to give him a hard time about it. You got that kid!?" I can hear it now.

Actually, I plan not saying a word to anyone the whole night, unless spoken to of course. The better strategy being just to survive the evening, so I can live to tell my grandkids about it.

So, for the past hour-and-fifteen minutes I've been either on the phone, dispatching my personally-assigned teamster-drivers around the San Fernando Valley, gathering the assorted and sundry items on Mr. Sinatra's contract rider, or stocking and putting things away, and generally familiarizing myself with the layout of the greenroom, the main dressing room suites down the hall, and what I call my 'back-stage office' (and the official 'gofer' headquarters) behind the bar, which I surmise will be the general hub of activity for the foreseeable near 'eternity,' until three or four in the morning!

Suddenly, I realize that the little hand will sweep past twelve o'clock at least twice in this dramatic scenario. Once around the time I fell into Jeff's office, then again tonight during the party after the show. This, despite the fact I've been up since 6:00am, having been savagely beaten and harassed by tens of thousands of tourists during my normal shift as Show Announcer. I guess I'll just think of it as pulling a 24-hour shift, without any real protein to speak of, or mind-altering substances, legal or otherwise, and a pounding pineal gland to boot. But, hey! I'm young. And a college graduate no less! More importantly, I'm a survivor of the 'Grand Brotherhood of the 'Tau!'" (That's "Alpha Tau Omega" fraternity, for the non-Greeks). Anyone who can survive the good-natured hazing of your average college 'hell-week,' with its midnight nude-pyramids in front of the Pi Phi Sorority, and sleep-deprived serenades at the Theta House (singing like drunken hoot-owls, to retrieve our stolen and conspicuously soiled underwear), not to mention those incessant butt-whacks from any upper-classman with a burr in his scrotum, should we forget to address him with that required responsive mantra: "Yes Sir, your Highest Assholiness, Sir!" or "No Sir, you Prickly Bastard, Sir!" Yes by God, any humble 'Plebe' worth his short-hairs should be able to handle a 'piss-ant' music concert. But of course, as the reality begins to set in, this isn't 'any' music concert!' This is "Francis Albert Sinatra!"

(By the way, I hear they refer to it now as 'Help-Week' back on Greek Row. It seems the overt hazing of freshman pledges has been banned and replaced with certain politically-correct, pansy-assed, community-service projects. Those poor bastards, they don't know what they're missing.).

So, naively thinking I've got a decent handle on things; having checked the list twice; verified that everything is laid out, unwrapped, warmed up, or being chilled down, I take a reflective moment to survey the pre-game 'calm-before-the-storm,' from my vantage point in the heart of my now 'known universe,' behind the bar in the greenroom at Universal Studios Amphitheatre, in the hardened heart of Hollywood, glancing nervously at the Bat-phone under the counter.

Let's see… the Heineken's on ice (and I've thrown in a couple long-neck Coors-Lights for my own consumption after the gig is over). The specialty wines are open and breathing. The gourmet food buffet is simultaneously chafing over Sterno and cryogenically cooling. Mr. S's special requests are ready: bite-sized 'Tootsie-Rolls' strategically laid out in ornamental dishes around the greenroom and within easy reach in his dressing room; packs of unfiltered Camel cigarettes, with a book of matches conveniently tucked into the cellophane, placed around his dressing room. I've prominently displayed the funeral home's worth of aromatic, red-rose bouquets, which have steadily been arriving, throughout both his dressing room and the greenroom, each with the 'senders' good-greetings properly displayed, so 'The Boss' can tell at a glance which studio-head or entertainment-mogul has complied with standard 'show-biz' protocol.

The only thing that's got me worried is this strange request for **Homemade-Chicken-Soup**,' which is noted in bold under 'Specialty

Items' at the top of the Sinatra rider. The detailed recipe, which in checking with Jeff is to be made from scratch each night and followed to the 'T' by yours truly!!! (a certified Martha-Stewart-challenged, non-cooking bachelor), with specific fresh ingredients that my trusty teamster-drivers had to track down on a Sicilian scavenger-hunt, from Mr. S's favorite local Italian restaurants and Jewish deli's, each of which turn out to be not so centrally located around the San Fernando Valley. Fortunately for me (My momma didn't raise no dumb kid,' as the saying goes), I immediately got my mother on the phone to interpret the detailed, 'Julia Child-like,' instructions, laid out in the rider, for what I will call "Frank Sinatra's Home-made Chicken Soup."

Firstly, the only fresh chicken-breasts that will suffice come from "Art's Deli" on Ventura Boulevard. The accompanying spices and seasonings had to be precisely measured, with the secondary elements chopped, sliced and diced to a certain, consistent texture. But, most importantly, having been underlined and capitalized, apparently for emphasis, the entire concoction must be 'HOT-AND-READY!' waiting on the bar, immediately prior to show-time, accompanied by a few plain saltine-crackers and two-fingers of "Jack Daniels," no ice. Thus, is the hallowed, pre-show, routine that "Ole Blue Eyes" has been following since time immemorial. And who am I, to be the weak-link in his long and legendary chain-of-glory?

My only problem in this grand, gastronomic equation is the "HOT AND READY!" part! Let's forget that this is my first day on the job, and that the last thing I actually cooked was Top Ramen in college. The main issue at this point is, how to keep the damn chicken-soup 'HOT!' until the strategically appointed time. Never mind my nerves being totally frayed; having worked all day with nothing to eat, but what I could glean without being noticed from the cellophaned, gourmet, food-platters. Then, there's the stark reality that, previously, the highest-ranking celebrity I've had the good fortune to be in close proximity with for any extended period of time is good old "J.P. Patches;" Seattle's legendary KIRO television children's-show icon (the longest-running, kid's show in America at 23 consecutive years). (Not to slight Brent Musburger or Yvonne De Carlo by any means).

Man, I wish "J.P." was here tonight; he and his hairy-legged, mop-wigged, side-kick/girlfriend "Gertrude," and the rest of the 'Patches Pals' from the old 'City Dump.' I'd feel right at home. *Holy Cripe! I must be losing my mind! Get a hold of yourself!*

Having rummaged through every nook and cranny of the greenroom, the dressing-room suites down the hall, and the chorus rooms upstairs, the only thing I could find for heating purposes, was a crusty hot-plate and a new 'Sunbeam' Crock-Pot. So, with sixty short minutes 'til show-time,' I am in a frantic, pre-panic-attack, quandary. The hotplate's ancient, cloth-covered cord started spitting sparks soon after I plugged it in. So, I intelligently opted for the crock pot (being proud that I remembered to wash it out first). Little did I realize, 'crock-pots,' by design, utilize slow-cooking technology, which is definitely not what I need for this frantic, last-minute countdown. And, of course, 'the Jeffster' is conveniently unreachable, tending to some other, more pressing, pre-concert emergency.

"Damn, where is sweet Margaret Hornblower when you need her. Our very own 'Saint Margie;' that southern-fried, slow-moving, but super-efficient, elderly cook we all cherished back at the frat-house. She could whip up two full-course-hot-meals a day, for seventy hungry college boys, five days a week, or more, if the winter snows kept her from going home on the weekends. Margie has probably passed on by now. But, I wish I could tap into her unadulterated horse-sense right about now. If she didn't have enough mayonnaise, she'd whip up a batch from scratch, which tasted better than store-bought any day. And if an important guest showed up for dinner unannounced, she'd produce something 'special' just in the nick of time. No one went hungry when Margie was in the kitchen.

But now, I am staring with palpitating anticipation at the crock-pot, as the condensation slowly gathers under the thick, glass lid, much slower than my own rising blood-pressure, neurotically thinking about my first, face-to-face meeting with the infamous "Jilly Rizzo," Frank Sinatra's big and burly 'Man-Friday'-slash-'Enforcer'-slash-'Body Guard,' remembering what he so sternly related to me only a few unforgettable moments ago.

I was busying myself like a bee in the greenroom, trying to become familiar with things, flying by the seat of my pants with no real guidance from anyone (something I look back on and find utterly ludicrous, and either a testimony to my boss's blind faith in my unproven abilities, or his complete lack of supervisory skills, and in reality, probably both), when suddenly, and totally unannounced, I look up to find myself witnessing an urgent scene straight out of Mario Puzo's "The Godfather."

Like a rush of stale wind from the 'The Bronx,' two large, and obviously 'packing,' refugees from a late-night 'B-movie' appear out of nowhere, nervous as cats and twice as shifty. The brutes were well-toned, well-dressed, with dark greased-back hair, sunglasses, and one hand thrust into the breast pocket of their tailored suits, either holding or attempting to hide, something thick and heavy.

Not saying a word, they went about their business; thoroughly checking the premises from top to bottom, all the while, eyeing my tense and frozen, puny self. They opened and slammed every door and cupboard, check behind the bar, out on the patio, even the restroom, which was empty at the time thank God, confirmed by the fact I heard the toilet being flushed and the seat lifted up and down way too fast to be functionally useful to any bi-pedal hominid. Then again, I shouldn't jump to hasty conclusions.

Apparently satisfied with their routine shakedown, and seemingly as if on cue, it was then that the massive, hulking figure of 'Jilly Rizzo' swept in like a Midnight Zepher. Striding slightly off-kilter, like John Wayne on steroids, with more impending presence than the first two thugs put together, his classic features were those of a Roman Centurion, carved out of marble by Michelangelo himself.

"Who the hell's the kid? were his first words, and probably the last thing I'll remember him saying as long as I live.

"Uh... I'm the new backstage host." I stammer, filling the awkward silence with my weak excuse. "I'm..." I attempt to get my name out.

"You boys checked 'im out?" interrupted the big man.

"We're just gonna do that Boss."

"We'll F----n' A! What're you son's-a-bitches waitin' for? We don't have all f----n' day! We got a show to do. Come 'ere kid!"

"Uh sure…" I whimper, to the giant in the gradient Gucci glasses.

Moving forward with my hand outstretched for a greeting, as soon as I get within arm's length (his, not mine), I instantly find myself whipped around and splayed like a scarecrow; hands on the wall, feet kicked-out sideways like a third-strike felon. In another head-spinning instant, I feel myself being expertly probed and groped by the massive, gold-ringed hands of "Jilly Rizzo," the honor of which, as I look back, I will forever cherish as some special initiation or rite of passage.

"Jilly," as he confirms I should call him (and as everyone in 'the business' will tell you) is Frank Sinatra's loyal and trusted sidekick, bodyguard, and long-time personal confidante, and has been (he'll remind you) since the old days. If Mr. S. wants it done, "Jilly" is the man in charge of seeing that it is.

Thus, having been so intimately introduced to one of New York City's most famous night-life characters; the long-time proprietor of "Jilly's," that famous Manhattan watering-hole just off Broadway's theater district on 52nd Street, and one of Sinatra's favorite nightspots, I am thoroughly briefed on the 'rules of the road,' as far as what's expected of me during Mr. S's run here at the Amphitheatre.

"Nobody's 'compted' to a Sinatra concert! Ever!" Jilly impresses upon me, in no uncertain terms. "Even the Boss' Mother, God rest her soul, paid her own way. And everybody else does the same. You got that?" My head hasn't stopped bobbing in agreement, since Jilly's well-rehearsed lecture began. "And if I find anyone in here without a ticket, they're out on their ass. No matter what f----n' credentials they have, or how impressive their bra-size! You got that kid?"

"Yes Sir!" I say.

"And don't mind 'the Boys' here," he says, nodding to the two guerillas still bouncing on the balls of their feet. "They're just doin' their f----n' job, if you'll pardon my French." *And of course I did.* "The Boss never walks into a room that hasn't been checked out, top to bottom." he says, hitching his shoulder with a twitch. "If you know what I mean." *And I did.*

"And another thing…" he continues, after a long enough pause that causes me to flinch. "You got 'The Rider' kid?"

"Yes Sir. I went over everything and double checked. The flowers, the "Tootsie Rolls," the cigarettes, "Perrier," "Jack Daniels." Oh, and the homemade chicken soup, right from the recipe, just like it says."

"Good! Just make sure it's good and hot, Goddamnit! That little prick in Vegas last night couldn't understand 'hot' from a hole in his head."

"Yes Sir… I'm working on that right now," I say, with the shaky confidence of a federal snitch. Under the circumstances, and despite my general 'being-in-the-presence-of-celebrity-nervousness,' I don't think Jilly could actually tell I was 'shittin' bricks' about this whole, damn, frickin'-a, chicken-soup business… *if you'll pardon my French.*

Just then, and again without proper warning to my weakened heart, Francis Albert Sinatra, suddenly appears through the greenroom door, well within barfing distance, had I not already been scared so thoroughly shitless, as previously noted. Sinatra is dressed in a casual open-collar golf-shirt, carrying his tuxedo in a garment bag over his shoulder. My first impression, which I will surely take to the grave as another badge of honor is: *My God, his eyes really are 'that Blue!'* That, and the impressive presence that he so effortlessly carries with him, without saying a word.

"Who's this?" Sinatra says, in a commanding tone, but without much fuss.

"He's the new kid, the green-room 'go-fer.'" Jilly explains. "He's clean. We're just going over the details with him."

"Nice to meet ya, kid." Sinatra says to me. *To me!* Before I could say a word (like fat chance I could have), Mr. S. disappears back out the door and down the hall into the dressing-room named in his honor. Jilly and the Boys dutifully drop me like a rock and follow 'The Boss,' to begin the business of going over the evening's rundown. It took me some time to fully assimilate what had just happened. It's not every day that one is shaken down by thugs, frisked by Jilly Rizzo and warmly greeted by Frank Sinatra, in a matter of moments. 'Slam, bam, thank you ma'am!'

With only minutes remaining, I find myself back in the present, pale-faced, and staring at the barely steaming lid of the crock-pot, starting to really worry.

What about the frickin' chicken soup?

It's got to be hot! Something about helping to clear Sinatra's throat before he goes on stage, with plain soda-crackers, and a shot of Jack Daniels to cleanse his palate. *Damn...* and what about Jilly's crack about the 'prick last night in Vegas' *with the hole in his head?* I am trying hard to convince myself his off-hand comment was only a colorful figure of speech. *Oh jeez...!* What the hell have I gotten myself into? I really shouldn't be here. I'm not ready for this. I couldn't even utter a coherent word in 'His' presence. What the hell's wrong with me? Nothing that a tall shot of Jack Daniels wouldn't cure. But, not now. I've got to figure this out, and fast!

I uncover the crock-pot and let the soup's aromatic mist curl under my nose. I dip a hesitant pinky into the broth. *Shit...!* It's only luke-warm. And it's been steeping for over an hour! *Oh...! My...! Lord...!* With the buzz-saw of doom looming ahead, and everyone rushing around with no time to answer, or even to ask, any questions, I frantically continue with the remainder of my duties, the sweat pouring conspicuously from my brow, praying to God and Jesus, on my mother's grave (though she's not even dead yet), for a certified miracle to happen here tonight in Hollywood.

The first guests of the evening begin to arrive and park themselves at the bar as if they owned it. I am attending to the last-minute, pre-concert details and attempting to cater to each of their needs. Very quickly, between the deafening throbs of someone's heart pounding in my ears (undoubtedly my own), I'm educated regarded the brutal realities of 'show business,' including: 'This <u>Guy</u>,' who turned into '<u>The</u> Guy,' who later becomes '<u>That</u> Guy,' who left her with massive post-nuptial debt and a sore heart; or... "Did you see that prick at the back-gate, staring down my cleavage, undressing me goddamnit, with his f----n' eyes, like a common slut! Who does he think he is? I'll have his f----n' job, if he gives me any shit again. I'm on the "A-List" goddamnit! I've <u>always</u> been on the A-List. I've paid my dues in this town! That's right... f----n' a, that and more. I'd do it too. I know people! Hell, I <u>am</u> People! How do I look? Have you seen him? Has he seen me? Jeezus, I'm freekin' nervous. You got a light? Hey, Barkeep! Got a light?" I lean in close to light her cigarette, trying not to stare at the famous cleavage she is so unabashedly presenting to the world tonight.

At the end of the bar, two 'Suits' from a mega record label are nursing their scotch-rocks. "The boss sent me in his place; to apologize for not being here in person. Some big-shit deal in the Caymans. Let's face it, when was 'The Ole' Man's' last hit record? Before my bar mitzvah. Hey, I hear Michael Jackson might show tonight. Let me know if you see him. I've got a message from some heavy-hitters. Yeah, highly-placed. Damn straight!"

All this and so much more, is flowing in one ear and out the other, as I fake the role of the anonymous 'Backstage-host-slash-bartender,' and default 'Shrink-at-large,' tending to the liquid and emotional needs of the 'old' and 'new;' the half-crazed 'has-beens' and the 'up-and-comers,' the 'lost-souls-with-killer-bodies,' all vying for the same finite amount of attention from 'anybody-who's-somebody,' or those who pretend to be.

I've got just what they want: beer, wine, champagne, gin, scotch, rum, and all manner of exotic combinations thereof. All 'gratis' of course, 'on-the-house,' courtesy of MCA/Universal or the latest multinational corporation in the process of consummating its next hostile, take-over bid. Most people assume that the music industry's drug of choice is cocaine; 'coke,' 'smack,' 'blow,' or whatever its latest hip moniker happens to be. But, from my standpoint at ground-zero, in the pits as it were, where the lipstick meets the collar, the real grease that turns the cogs in this magnificent glory-hole of sin, sex and stardom, is good, old-fashioned, unadulterated alcohol: booze, brewski, hooch, the hard-stuff. Everything from beer to cognac and the expensive or even prosaic Champagnes. This is what kindles the true spirit of Hollywood.

It flows like water, day and night. And tonight, among other things, I neurotically find myself the humble water-bearer.

And why not? This is 'Rock and Roll Heaven' man! It doesn't get any better than this, at least not down this rabbit hole. This is it! "The Greenroom" backstage at Universal Studios Amphitheatre! So, drink-up and be merry while the band plays on. Primp yourself, adjust your cleavage and suck in that gut. Because when the show is over out there, the 'Real Show' begins back here. Indeed, this is where the 'Big Fish' are fried and the 'Multi-Mega-Deals' are made, somewhere between midnight and three in the morning; the 'witching hours' of musical 'famedom,' at least here on the left coast. (I hear things don't get started until after three a.m. in the east). Pull up a strategic barstool or stake out a few advantageous square inches of the most expensive real estate this side of Nashville. You can actually feel the ominous presence of those musical giants who've come and gone before you, hovering just over your shoulder. Waiting with stale, alcoholic breath for you to vacate your seat. Planning their next poorly calculated comeback or lame, last-chance reunion tour. Humming some vague, haunting tune. That next monster hit! The one you'll claim copyright for if given half the chance. Because you've got perfect-pitch and a "Memorex" mind. If only you can beg, borrow or steal enough venture-capital for that new demo you've been pitching around town. "Hell yes, the vocals are lined up! Michael McDonald's one-time, fill-in, back-up, 'chick.' They used to be tight years ago. If she'd only return my damn calls!" *She probably thinks you're stalking her by now.* And you really don't mind all the stress and constant hassles, because you know damn well there's only so many certified 'mega-hits' allocated to any one, or perhaps two, generations, in the great, cosmic scheme of things. And if you can write just one future 'Golden Oldie.' Or hell, even co-write it. Then Bam, just like that, with the residuals, royalties, and perpetual digital rights, you're 'King of the Hill' again. 'Living the Dream' on 'Easy Street.' From Vegas to Branson and maybe back to Vegas again for 'The 30th Anniversary Tour! If it's really got 'legs,' and if you've still got the guts. Assuming you can continue getting your 'prescription' from that horse-doctor, to get rid of your 'gut.' Then, eventually, when you 'bite the big one,' it'll be your turn. Nay, consider it your sweet, multiple-Grammy-nominated obligation, to haunt these same hallowed halls, imparting whispers of poignant, new melodies and vague promises to the next generation of 'hipsters,' 'gangsters' and 'who-knows-what's-next-sters,' all believing they're spreading some fresh, new gospel to the masses. If someone would only listen to you, you bloated, old has-been!

Thus, it is, riding this frenzied wave of musical trepidation, that my ultimate experience in show-business continues to unfold.

Everyone has been cleared from the greenroom by Jilly and the Boys, and sent to their high-priced, reserved seats, the least of which isgoing for more than I make in two-weeks, so Mr. S. can get down to the serious business of preparing for 'The Show.'

Shit, I wish I could leave too... just disappear into the crowd with all those back-stabbing bastards.

I really should, and never look back. Just "UPS" my show-announcer outfit back in a box, crawl back to Disneyland and beg for my "Shaker the Country Bear" costume back. I'd do it too, if I thought I'd survive the leap from the patio down to the back-lot.

Instead, I resign myself to the reality that this is it; the moment of truth! All the hours of preparation are done. I've been sorely tested by the current elite of Hollywood weirdness, and so far so good. Except for the goddamn chicken-soup! Geez.... It's a little hotter than the last time I checked. It tastes good, if I do say so myself. The saltines are pre-arranged on the soup-plate at the bar, the salt and pepper shakers next to them, the porcelain soup bowl, the silver spoon and cloth napkin all arranged. And the shot of Jack Daniels; two fingers, in a clean glass. I even duct-taped the damn crock-pot lid to seal in as much heat as possible. Nervously, I stare at the accumulating condensation, dripping in slow rivulets down the underside of the glass cover.

Suddenly, the 'road-manager' pops his head into the greenroom; that efficient young-man who seems to be in charge of the actual show, and yells, "Two minutes!"

Double-damn, 'two minutes!' *What the hell does that mean?* Two-minutes until show-time? Or two minutes 'til 'soup-time?'

Maybe there's not enough time for chicken-soup tonight, this being L.A. and all; opening night in the entertainment capital of the world. Perhaps things are running a little behind. I wouldn't be offended if Mr. S. cuts his pre-show routine short tonight and goes straight to the stage.

Shit, I'd better start ladling the soup into the bowl, just in case.

If it gets too cold, I'll pour some more at the last minute. I've got plenty.

Then Bam! The heavy oak door bursts open with flare and authority. My first perception is filled with the large, rose-colored glasses of Jilly Rizzo making a bee-line toward me at the bar... always the first to take a bullet for 'The Boss.' Swiftly, in his wake, comes Mr. Sinatra, tuxed-to-the-tee, impeccably tanned and coifed, his electric-blue eyes fixed on the task at hand. The two bulging bruisers bring up the rear in military formation. Needless to say, their bold entrance scares the shit out of me, again. Fortunately, it looks as if I've professionally anticipated their entrance with a perfectly timed culinary presentation. I withdraw the empty ladle from the bowl just as the entourage arrives at the bar.

Not a word is said as Mr. Sinatra slides onto the barstool in front of me. Jilly stands at attention next to him, while the body-guards check every line of sight and look for anything out of place. Suddenly, I realize that any potential line-of-sight to Frank Sinatra would necessarily include myself in its trajectory, with or without any 'magic bullet' like the one that got JFK and Governor Connelly. But, it's too late to think about that now. I am frozen in my tracks, smiling like a lemur, in sickening anticipation of what is about to happen before my very eyes. 'The Boss' raises his soup spoon; the best I could find amongst the mismatched cutlery in the bar drawers, only minimally used, except for special occasions like this, or when urgently demanded by some twisted opening-act upstairs for some undefined purpose, never to be seen again. Without hesitation, Mr. S. plunges his spoon into the hopefully hot liquid, not even waiting to cautiously touch it to his lips. He slurps a substantial spoonful with no discernible reaction one way or the other. There is no change of expression on his famous face. I know, because I'm as close to 'The Man' as Jilly Rizzo's intimidating arm-length.

As He takes a soda cracker, I notice the beautiful, gold, ring on his ring-finger; tastefully simple, not gaudy. He takes the cracker in one bite, like a Communion Host. Then, a few more spoonful's of soup, chocked-full, I proudly notice, with meat and spices and full-bodied broth from the bottom of the bowl. Wiping his mouth with the linen napkin, he downs the Jack Daniels in one gulp... all under the close scrutiny and watchful eye of Jilly Rizzo.

Damn, the thought suddenly occurs to me. I wonder why Jilly doesn't taste-test the sacrificial offering before 'Old Blue Eyes' partakes in what could be his 'Last Supper,' should I turn out to be some mind-controlled "Manchurian Candidate," raised from birth for one fiendish purpose. I quickly dismiss the fleeting paranoid reflection as a random misfire of my over-taxed imagination.

In a moment, Sinatra is gone, in a rush of big men on a mission, disappearing through the greenroom door and down the corridor to the stage entrance, with nary a comment. In the blink of an eye, I'm alone again. Shaking in silence.... Watching 'The Man' take the stage to tumultuous applause, on the large television monitor in the corner of the greenroom.

By now, I've been awake and 'on-point' well beyond my normal working day. And I realize my job has just begun! In reality, this is the proverbial 'calm before the storm.' In a few hours, I'll be up to my earlobes in wall-to-wall diamonds, expensive cleavage, and pent-up testosterone (or is that 'pent-up cleavage' and 'expensive testosterone') either way, I'll be 'flicking my Bic®' and pouring double-time, hosting one of the most prestigious parties on the planet, with four-score and more of the most famous souls this side of Jupiter, right here in my greenroom, packed into the luxury suites down the hall, and overflowing onto the patio, on this warm summer night in L.A., until the wee hours of the morning.

Son of a bitch! It looks like I did it! Man, what a head-trip! Wait 'til everyone hears about this; my Mom back in 'Opieville,' my funky movie-costumer-brother, and my fellow, starving rockers, playing tonight's sleazy gig without me, somewhere amongst those millions of bejeweled lights twinkling in the Valley below. Slugging it out on that chicken-wire-stage, filling their lungs with the rarified blend of cigarette smoke and cheap perfume, in the mud and the blood and the beers, hoping to draw enough of a crowd to pay for their own drinks at the end of the night.

Jeez...! I need a drink!

Startled from my glazed stupor, sitting on the designer couch in the middle of the greenroom with a crisp Heineken in my hand, I turn to see none other than the 'Don' himself, Jilly Rizzo, bursting through the door looking a bit spent, but all business and ready for his own first drink of the evening.

"Scotch rocks; three fingers, and snap it up!"

I rush back to my humble station behind the bar, apologizing for abandoning my post in his time of need. Jilly pounds down the Chivas in one long, lingering gulp and stares me straight in the eye.

"Look, kid... The Soup.... Let me make this perfectly clear. It's gotta be Hot, Goddamnit! I mean f----n,' steaming Hot! To-burn-the-hair-off-your-balls-Hot! Do I make myself perfectly clear?"

"Yes Sir. I'm so sorry. This is my first time, and the crock-pot..."

"Tut, tut, tut. There is no excuse I haven't heard before. Do you know who you're talking to kid? I was splitting heads and taking names before you were born, you f----n' punk!"

Suddenly, in the blink of an eye, my puny, insignificant life flashes before me... and everything goes black.

I finally feel my toes easing back down to the floor, as my eyes flutter open to find Jilly Rizzo slowly releasing his giant left-handed grip on my shirt and tie, and minimal chest hairs, his sudden burst of terror and savage swiftness having run its course. My first thought is one of incredulity that I am still alive, though not actually breathing at the moment.

"F----n' a'," Jilly says, in a melancholy tone, so close to my face, I can taste the Chivas on his breath. His massive, ring-covered hand gently smoothes the polyester wrinkles he had so shockingly gathered in my shirt and tie; quite an incongruent scene I'm sure, if gazed upon at a distance.

"Sorry kid..." Jilly mumbles, as sincere as an altar boy. "Shit! Forget about it." he says, looking at nothing in particular; displaying a lifetime of duty and pride and infinite pain on his face. "You do your job, and I'll do mine."

At this point in the game, I'm way too freaked to tremble, or smile, or respond in any meaningful way. So, for the longest time and, strangely, for some of the most intimate moments of my life, it's just me ('the kid') and Jilly Rizzo ('the Capo') alone together; he, nursing another Chivas and me, wiping down the bar. Two terrified souls, for two apparently different reasons, thrown together at this weird moment in time. I, feeling his pain, and preferring to feel it vicariously on my side of the bar, and he, no longer afraid to share his. Here in the "greenroom," in the hardened-heart of this fame-and-glory vortex called 'Hollywood."

It goes without saying, that Jilly Rizzo scared the shit out of me again. And I'm not embarrassed to say, almost literally this time. Despite my strong intent to sneak out around 3:30am and never be heard from again, 'the Jeffster' catches me loading up a quick ham-and-Swiss-on-stale-rye before I can make a clean getaway. The greenroom looks like the burnt out crater of a 'huntersthompsonian' Las Vegas hotel suite after a grueling gonzo-journalism assignment that necessarily included massive quantities of illicit substances and plenty of fresh grapefruit.

"So, what do you think?" Jeff eagerly fires at me, with a knowing camaraderie that only a handful of souls can share.

"Was that a trip or what? You ready to start over fresh in six hours? Hell, if I were you, I'd spend the night right here on the couch! That's what I used to do. You can freshen up in the morning in one of the dressing rooms. There's everything you need. I'll have Wardrobe bring over a fresh suit in the morning."

"Son of a bitch Jeff!" I finally burst forth, in a much-needed psychotic break-down. "Are you shitting me? Are you kiddin' me man? A guy could get killed in here! You don't know what went on here tonight. I almost got 'whacked' in the line of duty! And the funny thing is, no one would have ever known! Where the Hell were you man? I was f----n' drowning in here!"

"Calm down. You did just fine! I was checking on you all night long, on the security cameras and through the backstage guards. Besides, I didn't want to bother you on your first night. You did great, Man! If you can survive this, you can survive anything!"

"Yeah, 'if!' That's the operative word. Where were you when I was dangling with my eyes bulging out from Jilly Rizzo's impromptu gallows? Jeff, these people live in a whole different world. And believe me, it's not a normal place to be. Not even for a little while. Shit man! I'm way too frazzled to even <u>have</u> a panic attack, which I'm way over due for by the way, to get me over the crest of this "Far Side," "Twilight Zone" nightmare I just had. You say the guy who had this gig before me got an acting job and blasted out of here with no notice? Shit, I can see why! I can personally verify he's the most motivated actor in New York right now, just to keep his sorry ass out of this 'Hell-Hole' for good!"

I stagger to the nearest greenroom couch and fall exhausted, with the fully-packed 'ham-and-Swiss' clasped to my chest. The room starts spinning, as the blood rushes to my head. Funny, I only had one beer all night and a small bowl of Mr. S's chicken soup. I vaguely recall rambling incoherently, with unconnected impressions; like the exotic shade of Victoria Principal's lipstick; Willie McCovey's massive physique; Burt Reynolds' really nice toupee; and finally, "The Jeffster" tip-toeing out of the room, dimming the lights, and the sound of the greenroom door locking behind him, as I slide with complete surrender into blissful oblivion.

The next thing I know, I'm startled awake by the frickin' roar of an industrial-strength vacuum-cleaner blazing back and forth next to my head! The blinding morning sun is beaming through the patio glass. My focus is drawn to a short Mexican guy, dressed in studio Maintenance-Department garb, going about his business, cleaning up the place. Actually, I'm amazed at the transformation he's already accomplished. Everything is pretty much back in order, as if nothing out of the ordinary happened here last night; like some surreal, "Ralph-Steadman'esque," dream.

I sit up slowly and acknowledge his presence with a vague nod of my fuzzy head. Reaching over the bar, he presses a single button on the phone and continues vacuuming. Eventually, I make it to my feet and stagger to the door, only to be bum-rushed again by Jeff bursting into the greenroom, his clothes looking as rumpled as mine. No doubt, from sleeping in his office all night. It immediately becomes obvious that Jeff instructed the maintenance guy to buzz him as soon as I stirred. *Damn, show-business is a tough way to live!*

"O.K., I let you sleep in. It's nine o'clock. You've had plenty of rest. I've ordered a great breakfast for you from Food Service. A fresh outfit is on its way from Wardrobe. I tracked your brother down on the lower lot. He's got you taken care of, new underwear and everything."

New underwear! That's impressive.

"Hold on Jeff," I say, slamming my crusty ham and rye onto the credenza next to the door, still clearing the cobwebs from my brain. "I haven't said yes yet, you know."

"I'll double what you make as Show Announcer, plus tips!" He fires back.

Plus tips? I do remember those insane tips last night.

"Free food and drink!" Jeff continues. "And at the end of the run, if you do a good job, you'll get a bonus from the Act! On top of all this fame and glory!"

"I'll think about it."

"Your brother's on his way from Wardrobe. Why don't you get showered and shaved and talk to your brother; see what he says. C'mon man, you owe me at least one week's run in the goddamn trenches with the rest of us heartless zombies. Remember that contract actor you interviewed for the Call Sheet who wanted your nuts on a platter for printing that stuff about his first career being in XXX films? Huh? And who bailed you out with that script-continuity Babe in the Producer's Building? C'mon Man! It's only one week of your life. Then, if you don't want the gig, it'll give me time to find someone else. And you can go back to Show Announcing for all those adoring tourists who think you're a big movie star. Huh? What do you say Bucko? "Buy the ticket, take the ride...."

It's just like Jeffster to use the words of my literary hero against me. *Damn you Hunter S. Thompson, wherever you are.*

"Shit.... I could be headlining 'The Landmark' you know, all this week! What if some A&R guy from one of the Labels shows up looking for fresh talent?"

"Yeah right," Jeff interrupts. "I was there the last time you headlined that sleazy joint, and the year before that, and the 'Go Go Cafe' and the 'Maverick.' I've always supported you guys. But, face it man. It's not how good you are. It's who you know! And what better place to get to smooze with highly-placed people in the music-business, than right here in this churning, god-forsaken, cauldron called 'The Greenroom!' It doesn't get any better than this man. And that's the sad truth. Take it or leave it. But, give me one week!"

"Well, when you put it that way. Shit...."

"Welcome to the 'Big Dance." Jeff says, with a smile that I know I'll eventually regret.

The next six days and nights pass like a time-warp blur of pins and needles, caviar and lobster and a few 'up-close-and-personal' brushes with actual fame and glory. Punctuated, of course, with an additional near-death experience or two. Eventually, I learn not to flinch so much when Jilly enters the room. And I try everything under the sun to get the damn chicken-soup hot enough for Mr. S. I can personally attest to the fact that Frank Sinatra must have steel vocal chords! I come in earlier and earlier each day to duck-tape the crock-pot shut and wrap the whole thing in aluminum-foil to keep the heat in. It takes all my feeble brain-power to keep dancing one step ahead of impending disaster, juggling all the balls without losing my own.

Between almost being bludgeoned to death by a major-league, alcoholic, has-been-actor hell-bent on having one more drink before attempting to drive home (I finally flattered the s.o.b. into a free limo-ride, compliments of the Studio), running interference for the back-stage guards as to who should or should not be allowed backstage, and being glommed onto by Jilly Rizzo each night, giving me a bluntly descriptive lecture on the soup not being hot enough ("Goddamnit kid!"), it seems I am putting out fires and hiding the matches at every turn.

But, sprinkled amongst the angst and the ecstasy, there are those amazing, hope-sustaining, moments, when I actually marvel at the unspeakable bliss of what real 'show-business' is all about. Like when I finally gathered enough nerve to check on Mr. Sinatra in his dressing-room before the show; catching him in a quiet moment, reading a hand-written card from a simple glass vase with one red rose in it, touchingly watching "The Chairman of the Board" wipe a tear from his eye before he was aware of my presence.

"Sorry Sir..." I say, clearing my throat and acting as if I just opened the door. "I was wondering whether you needed, anything."

"Kid... come in."

"I haven't seen Jilly, or the Boys, so I was just checking..."

"Do me a favor, will you?" *As if he had to ask.*

He took his Mount Blanc fountain-pen from his tuxedo and scribbled something on the card he had just been reading, put it back in the envelope, and wrote "Muffin" on the front, in his signature 'printing-slash-cursive' style.

"Put this in Nancy's dressing room will you? Oh, and give her that big bouquet with it," he says, casually wiping his cheek and pointing to the hugest, most impressive bouquet of deep-red roses I have ever seen, sitting stately on the grand piano like a flowering bush.

"Yes Sir." I say, taking the envelope from him and carefully wrestling the outrageous bouquet off the piano.

Seeing my difficulty attempting to navigate my way out of his dressing room through the foliage, Mr. S. opens the door for me.

"Don't strain a gut now."

"Thank you." I say, grimacing in the midst of the fragrant, prickly blooms. Just then, I remember why I came to his dressing room in the first place, and I say as I pass through the doorway, "Uh, ten minutes Sir."

"Thanks kid." he says, as I grope my way down the hall to Nancy's dressing-room.

"Wait a minute!" he says, remembering something else. I, of course, do as I'm told, propping myself against the wall for support. Mr. S. quickly reappears from his dressing room clasping a full-blooming, pixie-ear-pedaled, white gardenia. I stand back to attention as he places the delicate flower, with its heady perfume, in the midst of the generous bouquet, as a kind of 'piece de resistance' to the entire masterpiece.

"Thanks kid, she'll like that." Mr. Sinatra smiles and pushes open the door to his daughter's dressing-room for me.

Nancy is still on stage, pulling the opening act for her father as she has been doing all week. Her dressing room is empty and quiet and sweet-smelling. I ease the massive bouquet onto the thick, glass coffee-table in the front room, so she'll see it as soon as she opens the door. I place the card prominently in the stick-holder and think briefly of opening it. Then, just as quickly, I dismiss the idea. Instead, I make a mental note of this moment as being one of those fleeting 'chances of a lifetime,' which periodically, unexpectedly, come along. But, which also, must be allowed to flutter away unmolested. Some things are still sacred I think, even in this jaded 'Business of Show.' I hope to think so anyway, and wish to keep it that way… at least on my watch.

There was also the night, when I and the legendary composer/songwriter, Sammy Kahn, were alone, together, in the greenroom. Me wiping down the bar, like Jackie Gleason's "Joe the bartender" to Sammy's "Frank Fontaine," as 'Crazy Guggenheim,' singing to Mr. Dunaheeeeey. Sammy was playing around with his ('state-of-the art' at the time) "Casio" mini-keyboard, arranging one of Sinatra's musical numbers in front of me at the bar. Man, that scene will last forever in my mind. Pure timelessness, like Gleason and Fontaine themselves. Back when television was pure 'Art,' every Saturday night at eight o'clock… and <u>live</u> to boot.

Or the night I felt like an honorary member of the famous 'Rat Pack!' It was after the show, and the greenroom crowd was sparse, but still, individually stellar. 'The Boss,' Jilly Rizzo and the Boys, Dean Martin, Peter Lawford, Angie Dickenson, Joey Bishop, and a few privileged others. Dean Martin and Peter Lawford were hanging out with me at the bar. Joey Bishop was nervously pacing the greenroom carpet. And classy Angie Dickenson was sitting on the edge of the Gucci couch. Everyone was watching "The Tonight Show" with Johnny Carson on the greenroom television, waiting for Sammy Davis, Jr. to go on.

Mr. S. had made it a point to end the show earlier than usual, to not miss the airing of Sammy's scheduled appearance on the West Coast at 11:30pm. Everyone was on edge and burning through their exotic deodorants, because Sammy had vowed not to cancel his 'Carson gig,' even though he could barely <u>walk</u> the night before. I, had to personally help Sammy to one of the greenroom couches as he hobbled gingerly between me and his wife, Altovise. We propped him up with pillows and he sat there in agony all night; his lower back having seized-up the day before. No one could believe he was even walking the next day, let alone attempting to perform his famous, animated version of "Candy Man" on national television!

I remember holding his slim, muscular arm and easing him down to the couch, thinking how small a man he really is, and how frail he was in his current condition. It must be devastating for a vivacious personality like Sammy Davis, always so confident and full of 'good vibes,' to be physically dependent on others. But there he was, gutting it out, not wanting to miss any of the action, especially since "The Boss" was in town.

Everyone had complete empathy for the guy; each of them having achieved 'celebrity status' long enough to know how devastating a low-back seize-up can be, and how it can wreak havoc on a busy schedule, let alone a 'nearly invincible' reputation like Sammy's. But, they also know Sammy's legendary resolve, and his tenacious, 'the-show-must-go-on,' attitude, which has served him so well all these many years.

Angie Dickenson, in particular, is wearing a truly concerned look on her ageless face, not even caring to hide it.   Jilly is standing nervously at his Boss' beck and call, mumbling into his scotch-rocks, "That crazy son of a bitch." And Peter Lawford, usually suave and composed, is sporting a prominent set of Nantucket-tanned worry-lines over his upraised eyebrows. Dean Martin is trying not to watch, distracting himself with his drink at the bar, but eventually finding his eyes glued to the tube with the rest of us. Mr. S. is standing stiff-legged at the center of the room, still in his show-tuxedo and immaculately shined shoes, steeped in compassion and concern for Sammy; his long-time friend, through thick and thin.

Eventually, a reverent hush falls over the greenroom, like high-mass at St. Francis' back in Hoboken. It's quite a scene, given the circumstances, the people present, and the unique location. Everyone is pulling for Sammy to just get through what everyone knows could be a national 'crucifixion' in the press. Each of them know full-well how fleeting fame can be, and how long it takes to obtain, or re-obtain it, once it's been lost or fumbled away.

It's not easy watching a bona fide "Star" on a free-fall 'fizzle-out' from the celestial heights. Some flash-out quickly in a grand, meteoric blaze. Others fade away with the oncoming twilight. Eventually, most are never seen or heard from again. But a few, so very few, like Francis Albert Sinatra or Sammy Davis Jr., and most everyone else currently in the Greenroom, have boldly carved out their own everlasting constellations. Each of them have given us the lasting impression, and the fleeting hope that they will shine on forever, as a blazing testimonial to what we all recognize as true, unadulterated, God-given, 'Talent,' with a capital 'T!' They are the very few, whose 'star-dust' will never to diminish in our collective mind's eye.

That's how I think of "Stars" like Frank Sinatra and Sammy Davis, Jr., Dean Martin, Peter Lawford and Joey Bishop, Judy Garland, Lauren Bacall, Marilyn Monroe, Shirley MacClaine, and Angie Dickinson; all 'Rat Packers' extraordinaire! They've become so much more than '<u>just like us</u>.' They've become 'much more <u>than</u> us!' They've become the very thing we'd like '<u>us</u>' to be… and always knew we '<u>could be</u>,' '<u>if only</u>.' The truth is, we need <u>them</u> far more than they need <u>us</u>. We need them all, just to survive the day-to-day grind of living and loving and dying and carrying on in this world; this crazy 'world of show and 'tell' and 'things hoped for.'

This, and so much more, I muse to myself in the midst of it all, in the greenroom, backstage at Universal Studios Amphitheatre, in the swirling eye of the twisted vortex that is "Hollywood."

The first commercial break abruptly ends on the 'Carson Show' and everyone in the greenroom is preparing for the worst. Johnny Carson begins his glowing introduction of Sammy Davis, Jr. The tension is stifling and potentially career-ending, as each certified 'Legend' squirms in their seat.

"He shouldn't do this to him," Sinatra says, sternly regarding Carson, his steel blue eyes fixed on Johnny's image. Joey Bishop tries to diffuse the moment with a short quip, "You couldn't keep Sammy away from something like this for all the money in the world." Then Dean Martin adds sarcastically, "And he'd sue you for all the money in the world, if you tried."

"Shit, here we go..." whispers Jilly.

"And now, ladies and gentlemen, the one and only, the incomparable: Sammy Davis, Jr!" (thunderous applause, applause, applause)

Suddenly, the Tonight Show's multi-colored velvet curtain slaps open with Sammy bursting through it, either about to fall flat on his face or just being his old, loosey-goosey self. Initially, it's hard to tell. The entire greenroom gasps a collective breath of shock, as "Doc Severinsen and the NBC Orchestra" jump into Sammy's well-known arrangement of "Candy Man." Inexplicably, Sammy strikes his traditional, show-stopping pose... and begins to sing:

"Who can take a sunrise... Sprinkle it with dew..."

"Holy shit!" Jilly proclaims for everyone.

"Indeed," adds Peter Lawford, in the understatement of the evening.

"Cover it with choc'late and a miracle or two;
The Candy Man... Oh, the Candy Man can...."

Every jaw in the greenroom is gaping wide-open, while Sammy continues to sing and dance and gyrate like his old self. Even better!

"Is this on tape?" Sinatra says. "It's gotta be on tape!"

"Hell, if it is, he should archive it forever." Dean Martin throws out from his barstool. "He's looks real good!"

"That's the same tie he wore last night in the greenroom, I can tell you that." Angie Dickinson notes, with disbelief.

Joey Bishop rolls his eyes to the ceiling, "That crazy bastard! How does he do it? Last night he was knocking at death's door. And now look at him!"

"He is amazing! What a trouper! Now that's a 'Star!'" are just some of the awestruck accolades heard from the privileged and dumbfounded faces around the greenroom.

"'The Man's' solid gold in my book," Sinatra proclaims, with an enthusiastic slap to his thigh. "That's what I call chutzpa!"

"That's what I call some damn good medication," Martin whispers to me under is breath, with a wink. Then turning to the crowd, he raises his glass, as Sammy begins his big wind-up, "I'll have what he's having!"

The entire greenroom bursts into enthusiastic, heart-felt applause, as Sammy flawlessly punches the finish with a classy, but conservative, pirouette and dramatic "Mr. Bojangles" bow of his head. Then, with much relief and renewed admiration for Carson, everyone smiles knowingly at each other while Johnny goes straight to a commercial break. Upon returning, Johnny makes the further gracious comment that Sammy couldn't stay to be interviewed tonight because he had to rush to another benefit performance across town. Johnny then repeats all the generous accolades that were heard around the greenroom, giving appropriate voice to the collective admiration of the millions of viewers who just witnessed another of Sammy's stellar performances. Now, that is an evening I'll never forget.

And finally, there was one particular evening or most probably early morning after the show, with Jilly Rizzo seated at the bar repeatedly dialing then slamming down the receiver of the 'Bat-phone,' wildly thumbing through his 'little black book' with a frantic look of consternation on his rosy, Italian cheeks. Looking back on this fleeting, but significant, episode in my life, I suppose I should have been flattered at the time. But, it happened so fast and resolved itself so quickly, I continued on with business as usual, not fully realizing how close I may have come to true 'fame-and-glory...' either that, or really foolish 'fear-and-loathing.'

"Yo, kid," says Jilly, leaning delicately toward me over the bar. "Listen, I seem to find myself inextricably double-booked, if you know what I mean." He punctuates his perplexed look with repeated slaps of his black book into the palm of his massive, gold-ringed hand.

"F----n' a...!" he exclaims. "And it always happens when you don't want it to! Otherwise, under normal circumstances, I could handle 'em both... bid-a-bing, bid-a-boom!"

I nod casually, as if I could somehow relate to his quandary. Jilly continues spicing his spontaneous midnight-confession with a flurry of Sicilian sign-language and sound-effects that cause me to flinch again and again, until I realize his machinations are intended for 'punctuation' and not 'pummelization' purposes.

"So, shit...! What do ya say kid? How's about a night on the town? All expenses paid. With a classy broad from the Bronx. Huh? Blonde, lonely, tits to here! Horny as hell. We'll double-date, you and me."

I can't remember whether I was still reeling from the shock of Jilly's proposal, mulling over the potential ramifications of his use of the term 'double-date,' or whether I was trying to formulate some lame excuse. Either way, within another life-saving split-second the phone rings again and Jilly crams the receiver to his thick ear.

"Yeah? Babe! No, no, no, you don't apologize for nothing.' It's O.K! Sure.... Listen, when I get back, you and me, we'll do the town, huh? Yeah, I know. Blondes do have more fun! Love yoooooooz. Bye."

"Shit, kid! Don't hate me for this. But, it's all worked out. Maybe next time, huh? Whoa, F----n' A! The Boss'll be done any minute."

With that Jilly was off like a pit-boss to a high-roller, slicking back his thinning hair and adjusting his fine, Italian suit. My initial reaction was one of relief. But, the more I ruminated on the situation (and believe me, I did ruminate) the more aghast I became at how close I had come to one of those (most-definitely) life-changing forks in the road. This time the sign-post had reared up and flashed by so quickly, I had missed it all together. Whether it was meant to be a tempting 'life-saving' short-cut or a costly 'life-shorting' detour, I'll never know.

And so, it comes down to this one last, surreal 'moment-of-truth' on a sultry Saturday night in Hollywood, backstage in the greenroom at Universal Studios Amphitheatre, on the closing night of a long, full week of Frank Sinatra concerts. For some fateful reason, I find myself still alive, and still working on getting the homemade chicken-soup hot enough for Mr. S's incendiary taste.

This is it! My final chance to impress "Ol' Blue Eyes" and get it right, knowing full-well that any 'tip,' which may or may not be coming my way at the end of Mr. Sinatra's run, as well as my future employability in the greater Los Angeles basin, and/or more importantly, my potential ability to father children in the future, may well be on the line.

I make an extra effort to really nail the proprietary recipe tonight. And to tell you the truth, I think I'm getting pretty good at it. I mix the broth precisely, exactly per instructions, chop and dice the ingredients to perfection, pick the best, most tender, parts of the special-order, flame-broiled chicken and chunk them up just right, when suddenly... like a bolt out of the blue... it finally occurs to me!

Shit... I've been playing around with small caliber firearms in this little ceramic slow-cooker, which of course, is totally suited for its intended purpose of slow-cooking all day long. What I really need is a nuclear-powered, atom-splitting, particle-collider that doesn't mess around; something that comes straight to the point, like Jilly Rizzo himself. Slam-bam thank-you-ma'am!'

That's when my eyes fell upon the holy-grail of my week-long quest for show-biz redemption. I can't believe it! It's been here all along and I didn't recognize it as the answer to my fervent prayers. There, in the corner against the full-length mirror at the back-wall of the bar, is the biggest, baddest, double-burner, 'mother-of-them-all,' industrial-strength, "Bunn" coffee-maker, staring me straight in the face!

"Oh... My... God...!" I think to myself, and I might have even verbalized it. That's it! Suddenly, a giddy, euphoric feeling overwhelms

me. *But, shit...* I think again.... *It could kill him! Or ruin his voice for life!* Do I dare?

Just then, Jilly Rizzo's nightly admonition rings loudly in my ear. "It's got to be HOT, <u>GODDAMNIT</u>!" *Hell yes...! I think I should.* But, there's no time to loose! I've been messing around with the crock-pot since well-before noon, and it's almost show time... for the last time! So, with the deftness my mother would be proud of, I ladle the soup broth into a stainless-steel coffee carafe that I found under the bar. I then plot my plan; calculating, from the thin recesses of my memory just how long it takes for a steaming pot of coffee to come to a full boil through the major-league mechanical, monster behind me. Realizing of course, that everything will have to be perfectly timed, to accomplish the task without the ever-hovering 'bar-flies' comprehending what I am up to.

"Two minutes!" I hear someone announce from the hallway; way too early, compared to my watch!

"Shit...! I kick into over-drive.... At this point there's no turning back. Stealthily, and with one clandestine move, I pour the soup-broth into the top of the massive coffee-maker, flip on the red switch, and start praying like a Franciscan monk.

With only precious minutes remaining, I place Mr. Sinatra's ceramic soup bowl directly onto the coffee-maker's built-in hot-plate, right under the spigot, to catch the fiery liquid, which instantly starts pouring from the machine's coffee-grounds holder.

"Holy Shit...!" I forgot to change the filter! A brackish-brown mixture of chicken-broth and rich Asian/Pacific blend starts dripping like molten-lead, sizzling into the soup bowl on the hotplate. I quickly flick-off the red switch, frantically slide out the scalding coffee filter full of grounds and precious, not-to-be-wasted, soup-broth and flip the whole damn mess, like a flaming roman-candle, into the trash-bin next to the bar. The resulting "thunk" causes some concerned heads to turn my way, only to find me humming and dutifully washing my hands at the sink.

With only mili-seconds remaining, I jam the naked filter-holder back into the coffee-maker. No time to wash it out. Flip the switch again, and wait for the soup-broth to start dripping... this time, much slower than my racing heart! Thank God, it's coming out clearer this time, pouring like a flame-thrower, directly into the soup bowl.

Immediately, I start ladling the chicken-stock, with its special herbs and spices and chicken chunks, into the bowl, hoping against hope that the ceramic bowl doesn't shatter, either from the laser-hot soup pouring down from above or the scorching, industrial-strength, hot-plate beneath.

Holy shit…! It's too damn Hot! I've got to cool it down before 'He' gets here. Quick the ice…!

Bam! Too late…. Jilly Rizzo's hulking figure blasts into the greenroom. "The Boss" is close behind him, with 'the Boys,' like eager puppies, bringing up the rear.

'Frickin' a…!' Here goes nothing.

I gingerly grasp the rim of the soup bowl, trying to keep a few subcutaneous layers of my finger-prints intact, and clank it down on the waiting soup plate, which is already rimmed with saltines. I then pirouette like a ballerina and deftly place the entire ensemble, like a skittish jar of nitroglycerin, onto the bar, slapping the big silver spoon down on the starched napkin, just as 'The Boss' slides onto the barstool and Jilly takes his station beside him.

Holy shit…! Mother of God…! This is it! There's no way out, except over the bar, past Jilly, onto the patio and a death-defying leap to the Valley below. To this day, I'll never know what kept me from doing it. Sheer stupidity I think. It wasn't brains.

I stand frozen, watching in utter horror with my eyes bulging like saucers, as the 'Chairman of the Board' takes his first saltine cracker and crunches it in his mouth. Finding a strange joviality at the edge of insanity, I note the sound is quite similar to the muffled, crunching noise my neck will most probably make, when Jilly gets his massive, Sicilian, hands on me. Mr. Sinatra then plunges his silver spoon into the boiling-caldron-of-death before him, raising a heaping load of spiced-broth and chicken-chunks to his mouth, shovels it in and swallows! My eyes grimace shut like a blind-fold before the firing squad. *Holy Jesus…!*

The end did not come as swiftly as I hoped. I open one cautious eye to find 'The Man' still alive and unfazed, working on his second, then a third, 'X-Class-Solar-Flare' spoonful of soup! He takes one last soda cracker and casually dabs the corner of his mouth with the linen napkin. His Rancho-Mirage-tanned fingers reach for the Jack Daniels and he downs the two fingers in an instant, as usual, as if he were strolling through the park. Then, with Jilly leading the way; turning the whole yacht around, Francis Albert Sinatra and his entire entourage flow swiftly out the door.

For a long time I stand there… alone in the greenroom, leaning against the back-counter of the bar… surveying everything that has now become so strangely familiar to me, during this past week of high-pitched, balls-to-the-wall, show-biz pressure… just waiting for my heart to come down out of my throat.

No one will ever believe this! I wouldn't have believed it myself, had I not seen it, and experienced it with my own eyes.

I keep reminding myself: that soup was hot enough to strip paint off the wall! I definitely lost layers of my finger-prints just getting the bowl to the plate.

What I just witnessed is totally insane!

And he didn't say a word. Not a wince or a pause. And multiple, heaping, spoonfuls, without even blowing on it first!

Oh… My… Word…!

No wonder he's been singing at full-voice for over fifty years! That's what hot, home-made, chicken-soup and a full-hour of vocal-exercises will get you; total 'ENT' invincibility! Hell, no puny cold-virus could ever hope to survive that. His personal cook must wear 'Haz-Mat' protective-gear, to achieve such 'surface-of-the-sun' temperatures on a regular basis.

The rest of the evening is pretty routine, if you can call turning away last-minute, celebrity ticket-smoozers on the phone and frantically hunting for, then finding, a misplaced piece of sheet-music for Vinnie Falcone, Mr. S' music-director, routine.

Nancy comes into the greenroom after her opening gig and hangs out with me at the bar, along with the gorgeous Angie Dickinson and the lanky, athletic, Mrs. Sinatra; the former Mrs. Barbara Marx. But, the person I really want to see... I think... is Jilly Rizzo; that big 'Bronx-Bruiser' with the rose-colored-glasses, just one last time. He doesn't appear for his normal medicinal dose of 'scotch-rocks-after-The-Boss-hits-the-stage,' which I take to be either a good or a bad thing, depending which way my over-taxed, paranoid brain is leaning at the moment.

Thus, the final concert of Frank Sinatra's run at Universal Studios Amphitheatre is over before I know it. The greenroom instantly fills again with all manner of celestial celebrities, politicians and music-industry demi-gods, all wanting to be <u>seen</u> supporting "The Man" on another of his successful... whatever he wants to call his sold-out concert series this time; one of his many resilient comebacks or just another 'clam-bake' for his friends.

I have never seen such a gathering of luminaries in my life. The unique mixture of musical-persuasions in attendance is almost comical. At the bar to my left is the 'funk-master' himself, 'Rick James,' deep in some high-brow conversation with a gray-haired, conservatively-suited MCA Executive who you would never think in a million years would know, let alone understand, what 'Funk' is all about. The tall and dapper Gregory Peck with the tanned and handsome Michael Landon chat like old friends in the center of the room. The ever-gregarious Dean Martin and the miraculously recuperated Sammy Davis, Jr. are cutting it up, trading humorous barbs and grab-assing each other out on the patio. And the one and only Michael Jackson, sans his entourage of body-guards, shyly holds down the end of my bar to the right, a diet Coke in one hand and a curvaceous, green-eyed brunette at the other.

Everything that <u>is</u> "The Greenroom," is in full swing. I am dispensing beer, wine, champagne and all manner of mixed-drinks to the pressing crowd. It's shoulder-to-shoulder-celebrity all the way out to the patio, packed to the gills with famous, flirtatious pheromones on this warm breezeless night in L.A.

In my sanctuary behind the bar, I work amongst the kick-around-clutter of empty boxes, bottle-caps and buckets of back-up, emergency ice. It is during one of those mindless-moments of automatic-action that I look up to find Jilly Rizzo's impressive figure spreading himself thick on the barstool in front of me.

"F----n' A' kid!" he says, as I flinch in surprise. "We did it, Huh?"

Jilly slams his meaty fist on the bar for punctuation. Give me one last 'scotch-rocks' for the road." I quickly comply and slide a generous, tinkling, low-ball in front of him, retrieving my hand swiftly, just in case he's playing coy; waiting for a careless move on my part. Then, for the first time in the short life-time that I've known him, he seems a bit relaxed, almost human... almost.

"Hey kid! I could set you up tonight?" says Jilly, in his endearing 'Brooklynese.' "You know, make up for jerking your chain with that Blonde the other night. What do you say?"

Jilly fumbles in his breast pocket for his little black book.

"I got plenty of Broads who owe me big-time, just waiting for the call. Shit, we should celebrate, now that it's over. What do you say?"

I quickly beg off with the only excuse I can think of; that I need to be up early to get ready for the next run of shows.

"Bonnie Raitt," I say, which is a complete lie (not the Bonnie Raitt part, but me being anywhere near this place in the morning).

I figure 'Jeffster' must have found a replacement for me by now, in the form of some 'head-banging-long-hair' who can live this 'twenty-four-hour-rock-and-roll' lifestyle, without a second thought about a life of his own.

"And besides," I wink to the big 'Bronx Hammer,' with a little chutzpa of my own. "You see that curvaceous, green-eyed, 'Babe' with Michael Jackson?" I whisper, with a confident, shit-faced grin. "She's going home with me tonight!

"F----n' A...! Jilly declares. "Good for you kid!" Jilly adds, giving me a thick thumbs up.

"Listen," he whispers, leaning in closer and nodding toward Michael Jackson. "If he gives you a hard time about the Broad... just let me know. F----n' a."

I smile hesitantly and attempt to look grateful, as the massive man seals his support with a serious Sicilian wink and screeches off the leather stool to leave. Then, in a flash, he returns and slaps a large manila envelope on the bar and slides it in my direction.

"Shit, I almost forgot!" he says. "This is for you, with The Boss's finest regards, for a job well done!"

I stand frozen in mid-pour, dumbfounded at Jilly's sudden, unsolicited, flattery.

"Just a small token of our appreciation for taking such good care of us."

"Oh, and kid..." Jilly adds, suddenly serious again. "Next time you're in Vegas? Give me a call. I owe you one!"

With that he disappears into the undulating crowd like a sounding whale, his large void filing instantly with demanding new-comers.

My anticipation to open Jilly's envelope gnaws at me the rest of the evening; for another couple hours at least. I finally shoo away the last of the bar-flies (those few unsuccessful show-girls and a couple nerdy music-company interns) a little after 3:30am.

Damn... that curvy brunette with the emerald eyes is nowhere to be seen.

Finally, in utter exhaustion, I flop onto the big couch in the center of the greenroom, kick off my show-announcer shoes and pop open my first beer of the evening; an icy-cold Coors Light that's been chilling all night. I take a long, refreshing swig and direct my attention to the manila envelope that Jilly gave me earlier in the evening.

Damn that beer tastes good!

What the hell could this be? Hopefully, it's an autographed photo.... Yes, it is!

"Hot damn!" I exclaim out loud.

Will you look at that; a personally autographed, 8 x 10, color-glossy of "Ol' Blue Eyes" himself, regally sitting on a stool on stage, in Vegas no doubt, holding a glittering, gold "Shure-SM58" microphone, belting out some classic number like his signature "My Way," with characteristic style.

And more…!

The inscription on the photo reads: "To Michael – Thank you! My very best to you – Frank Sinatra."

I sigh a huge wave of relief.
Oh Thank God!
What a relief. What a treasure! Wait until the boys see this, and my brother and mom back home.
And something else!
At the bottom of the envelope is a plain piece of stationary, folded and paper-clipped. I retrieve it and remove the clip. Suddenly, and inconceivably, I find myself staring at more, crisp 'One-Hundred-Dollar' bills than I have ever seen in my life!
"Holy Shit!" I scream, quickly looking to see if there is anyone I can share my disbelief with.
Oh Man....
This is more money than Jeff was offering to pay me for the whole damn month!
Unbelievable!
On top of the tips I garnered behind the bar during the past week; this long week of pure, unadulterated, paranoid confusion, I could buy a nice used-car! But, Hey! All of a sudden, it seems almost worth it. Now that I'm still alive to tell about it, and my potential future progeny have been reprieved.

Then, something else catches my eye. Beneath the crisp, fanned-out, 'Ben Franklins,' I notice that the folded stationary has something written on it. I stuff the wad of bills in my shirt pocket and focus on the now familiar hand-writing.

There, scrawled in Sinatra's own recognizable combination of cursive-printing, is something I will always treasure from this entire amazing experience... an affirmation of sorts... a testament to hope and ingenuity if I do say so myself; like when the shit (or the hot-soup) hits the fan, and all you've got is duck-tape and an "Oral B" toothbrush.

The note says: "Best soup I've had in a long while – great flavor – nice and <u>HOT</u>!" signed, "F.S."

"F----n' A..." I think to myself, and smile.

Chapter 18

MOVIE DEBUT

Janice Margaret Flannery is bright, young and ambitious; one of those rare individuals who lights up any room she enters. But, not in an over-bearing or presumptuous way. By some fortuitous luck of the draw or, perhaps, divine designation, Jan is blessed with the gift of 'relationship.' She can relate to everyone she meets, and who they really are, not just their outward appearance. Jan is a 'people-person!' And one who is wrapped in a very pretty package... a quite handsome package indeed.

Jan learned about the filming of Somewhere in Time from a local television newscast. Not knowing much about the movie business or acting, but being fascinated with Hollywood and the 'business-of-show,' Jan threw together a travel bag, kissed her bewildered husband goodbye, and flew out the door to answer the casting-call to be an 'extra' in a new movie starring Christopher Reeve, Jane Seymour and Christopher Plummer. The only detail anyone knew about the film, was that a handsome, young man supposedly falls in love with the photograph of a beautiful young woman who lived in 1912, and somehow he travels back in time to find her. Of course, everyone knew the dashing and handsome Christopher Reeve from his recent fame as the 'Man of Steel,' in the critically acclaimed "Superman" film.

Jan jumped at this 'chance-of-a-lifetime' with the characteristic gusto and naiveté that had served her so well during the previous twenty-five years of her, up until then, rather normal life. Driving like a maniac, without a map, and much too fast for her own comfort, she was horrified enroute to find that the last ferry to Mackinac Island would leave the mainland way too early to match the speed-limit and distance she had to travel to get there. Miraculously, and with the kind assistance of a State Trooper who took pity on her enthusiastic story during a short traffic-stop, Jan made it on 'a-wing-and-a-prayer,' throwing her hastily-packed bag and her harried self onto the last ferry of the day.

And now here she is, assembled with the rest of us on this quaint, sun-drenched summer-isle, each from various departure points, all pleasantly surprised to find ourselves intimately involved in what has turned out to be a very unique movie production. Small and intimate (personnel-wise). But, classic and memorable (Hollywood-wise), with the Grand Hotel as the luxurious back-drop for this beautiful story of romance and adventure, of desperate devoted-love and mind-bending time-travel from 1979 to 1912.

And here I am, either dreaming all this upstairs in my hotel room or, and/or, experiencing some haunting déjà vu reality, seeing the beautiful and engaging Jan Flannery again, conflicted as a young man again, still clinging to the mild discontent of a middle-aged husband and father-of-four, attempting to navigate my own desperate, time-traveling mid-life crisis.

Jan Flannery is arguably the best-looking woman on the island, besides of course, the lovely and engaging Jane Seymour. Each so incomparably gorgeous as to deserve Captain Renault's famous line to Ilsa Lund in the classic movie, "Casablanca:" "I was informed you were the most beautiful woman ever to visit Casablanca. That, was a gross understatement."

Jan's beauty is so approachable and alluring, both within and without. Her natural attractiveness turns heads even without the aid of movie make-up or an expensive wardrobe. And with the addition of a few feminine enhancements, it's downright difficult to take your eyes off her. At least I couldn't, back in 1979, and obviously still can't now back in 1979, again.

Jan's amber-blonde hair is equally enticing, free-flowing at her shoulders or pinned up old-fashioned style. Her glowing cheeks and electric smile provide the perfect foundation for her sparkling, blue eyes, which dominate her pleasant appearance. The grace with which she carries herself, her movements and intentions, suggest a sensual appeal, placing her at the pinnacle of any 'top-ten' list imaginable. And with the sage perspective of these past fifty-odd years, Jan's agreeable persona is even more entrancing than my faded memories would allow. It's such a pleasure just to watch her. But, wait! There's no time to lose! *I'm not letting this opportunity pass me by… again.*

Megan, the Assistant 'Casting-Director,' is hurriedly pairing up the extras and instructing them to walk, casually, the full length of the Grand Hotel's famously long front-porch, to simulate an old-fashioned, turn-of-the-century 'Promenade' (which, apparently, is what people did back then, before cable-television), giving us a chance to practice 'walking' and 'talking' and 'moving naturally' before the day's shooting begins. This initial 'fresh meat' gathering also provides an all-important 'first impression' for the other 'Production Assistants,' who must quickly evaluate the pool of 'undiscovered talent' for the more critical close-up scenes to be shot in the coming weeks.

"The Look" being 'Everything' in this business, these obligatory 'fishing expeditions' have served as a time-honored tradition since the beginning of filmdom. The tedious process having discovered many a fresh face and even launched a few stellar careers; Shirley Temple, John Wayne and Clint Eastwood being but a noteworthy few.

Thus, the pressure 'being-on,' each of us instinctively understand this will be our first, and most likely last, 'best-shot' to create a lasting impression, and that our fates will most likely be 'cast-in-stone' during this very first competitive audition.

Megan is noticeably distraught, rushing here and there with her clip-board jammed with disorganized papers and a dog-eared copy of the 'Somewhere in Time' shooting-script. Her name is written in thick "Sharpie" on the back: "Megan – Assistant-Casting." She has the unenviable task of babysitting us twenty-or-so atmosphere-actors who have eagerly arrived at the crack of dawn, to be cut, coiffed and costumed like prize Pomeranians for the first day of filming.

Jan is living a dream-come-true. She must have been the first in line at the woman's costume trailer, as she is definitely sporting the best outfit for today's filming. It is an elegant pastel-blue, turn-of-the-century dress fitted splendidly at the bust with accentuating ruffles and bows, complete with a matching 'parasol,' reminiscent of Scarlet O'Hara in "Gone with the Wind."

Frankly Scarlet, you look pretty damn stunning! I think to myself, standing only a few intimate feet away, admiring how well Jan fills her fetching ensemble.

At this point, I am still a 'single-entity' by design, not yet having been paired with anyone, just milling around biding my time. Jan is waiting next to a pudgy, middle-aged fellow with a 'handle-bar' mustache dressed in the style of a "Monopoly" game-board banker. I surmise him to be an insurance agent in real life. Either that or a lawyer. Jan is waiting for her cue to promenade the length of the hotel's picturesque front porch.

I remember this scene as if it were yesterday. Even though in my old reality it took place over twenty-five years ago. I also remember not being picked to be Jan's promenade partner that day either. Something I intend to rectify this time around, if at all possible.

I glance around, evaluating my last-minute chances and notice that one of the banker's boot-laces is untied and tantalizingly trailing behind him. I quickly crouch down to take advantage of the heaven-sent synchronicity, pretending to tie my own shoelace. Instead, I tie his errant boot-string solidly to the leg of a large wicker chaise-lounge next to him.

Megan pauses momentarily from her exasperating walkie-talkie conversation and cues Jan to begin promenading. Suddenly, and hardly noticeable in the jostling crowd, the portly banker leans his bulk into a sharply-abbreviated first step and promptly falls flat on his face. Not missing a beat, I slide into Jan's suddenly vacant elbow, and match her stride for stride. I urge her on with an assuring; "Allow me…" all the while, calmly displaying a 'The show-must-go-on' attitude, like a seasoned veteran.

Jan's momentary concern for her downed partner seemingly belayed by my firm-grip and tenacious charm, we continue down the long veranda. Despite the initial confusion, each of us manage to stay in character and pretend to carry on a casual conversation, as we move together.

"Who are you? And what the hell are you doing?" Jan whispers tersely, still smiling and attempting to act natural.

"I'm promenading with you." I say, as if it were my next line in the script.

"I've come a long way to be here..." I say, finishing the sentence inaudibly, "...*with you again.*"

"Well, so have I, Buster!" says Jan, with certain indignation. "And I don't want to blow this chance for anything. So, look sharp and make it work. Or this will be your last curtain call if I have anything to say about it!" With that, she quickly looks away and serenely pretends to admire the stunning view of Lake Huron below.

So, for the time being I content myself to merely enjoy the moment, feeling my youthful muscles again, striding out with a beautiful girl on my arm and a spring in my step.

We do fit well together, I muse to myself; Jan and I, both in our mid-twenties, matching each other's movements, swaggering forth on this glorious summer's day in one of the most romantic locations anyone could imagine.

Glancing to my left, as if 'directed' to do so, I too admire the breathtaking view of the deep-blue lake strikingly laid out beyond the hotel's sprawling front lawn. But, my attention is quickly drawn back to the beautiful Jan Flannery, intimately clinging to my forearm, moving gracefully beside me. Her bright, flowing dress candidly displays 'the best' of what nature has abundantly provided her, allowing us few fortunate souls, in close proximity, the unique pleasure of apprehending her exquisite beauty. Fortuitously, in my case the view is indeed up-close-and-personal.

Having traversed the entire length of the hotel's six-hundred and sixty-foot front porch and having settled into a mutually agreeable pace, Jan and I pause a moment, alone, at the far end of the porch. On our return promenade, we've been instructed to use the front portion of the porch nearest the railing; the side closest to the seemingly bored Assistant-Directors, who are waiting at the hotel's main entrance to check us out, individually, and as a couple, as we pass by. Jan gives me a guarded smile and takes in a deep breath laced with blooming lilacs, then exhales with a sigh of nervous energy.

"Well, that wasn't so bad," she says, trying to convince herself of the adequacy of our first nerve-racking pass. Her brilliant blue eyes flash down the length of our return route. I quickly shift positions, slipping my right-hand under her left elbow so she would be closest to the judges on the return promenade. Then, in my best Rhett Butler characterization, I reply: "Not bad, indeed, my Dear."

Jan stops short and momentarily steps out of character, her eyes locked to mine with genuine curiosity. I can almost hear her thoughts...

Who is this strange person I suddenly find myself partnered with, on this, potentially, 'one-of-the-most-important-days' of my entire life?

Leaning closer, where the sweet scent of lilacs mingle with the nape of her neck, I whisper without the accent, "Frankly, you look wonderful!" She takes my compliment surprisingly well and responds with a full-faced blush, despite the nervousness of the moment. Gathering herself with a flutter of her laced glove, and forcing us back on task, Jan calculates the pace of the promenading couple in front of us, to allow for our own maximum exposure when we arrive at the sleepy-eyed Assistant Directors. Cinching my arm firmly to her side and displaying an adorable look of determination, she announces for my benefit, "Now, let's make a good impression for the 'Close-Up' test, shall we?"

Then suddenly, and perhaps for the first time in my adult life, I resolve to follow an overwhelming urge that flashes through my body like lightning. I pull Jan firmly to me in a frontal embrace and kiss her exquisite lips for the eternity of an ever-so-fleeting moment, before, instinctively, she breaks away with brilliant sparks of emotion. Surprisingly, she allows a further moment of bliss, as I hold her in my determined arms. Before she can speak, I take advantage of the stunned nano-second it takes to calculate her appropriate indignant response, and quickly shift positions again back to her right side, taking her right elbow with my left hand and usher her forward toward the waiting Directors. Fortunately, for the moment she is flabbergasted and mute, still contemplating her outrage and sorting through the mixed emotions so expressively displayed on her radiant face.

Effectively upstaging Jan for the moment, I walk between her and the front portion of the porch, where the Assistant Directors are waiting just ahead of us to the right. It's a calculated move on my part. My strategy being, to give them a good, long look at Jan's beautiful, expressive face looking in my direction; so they will see what I have always seen and so lovingly held in my mind all these years.

Jan is simply glowing for her first 'live-action screen test,' as we approach our crucial close-up pass. At the last second, I nonchalantly drop back a step, allowing an unobstructed view of Jan's natural beauty and grace for the blasé 'movie-types.' As we flow effortlessly in front of them, Jan is lit perfectly by the sun reflecting off the lake, and stately framed by the entrance of the Grand Hotel behind her. I notice one of them nudging his neighbor and mouthing an exaggerated, "Bingo!" not able to hide his enthusiasm for Jan's stunning countenance.

Continuing past the now huddling 'Assistants,' I hear a muffled buzz emanate from their midst, followed by the urgent crackling of walkie-talkie conversation.

When Jan and I reach the end of our strolling audition and exchange guarded smiles of relief, Megan, the Assistant Casting Director, rushes up to us in a flurry of shuffling papers, yelling into her walkie-talkie, frantically trying to convey something seemingly important. All the while, she is making frantic hand-motions to her 'Assistant-Boy-Friday,' who has been shadowing her all morning like a baby duck.

"Yes, yes, I've got them!" Megan confirms into her walkie-talkie.

She then gives us a quick head-to-toe look-over and continues her shouting conversation.

"Right, pastel-blue dress and cream colored suit. O.K. Alright!"

Jan and I look at each other dumbfounded, realizing that someone seems to be talking about us over the walkie-talkie.

"What are your names?" Megan barks at us, absentmindedly forgetting she's not yelling into her walkie-talkie.

Her 'Second-Assistant' fumbles for a new page on his own messy clipboard and follows up. "Uh, yes, your names...?

Before either of us could respond, Megan shifts back to her walkie-talkie.

"Yes Sir, I'm getting all that now. Right...O.K!"

Megan tries to match the energy level of whoever's giving her orders on the other end of the line. Then, as the crackling conversation ends, Megan resumes her jaded, movie-crew personality and addresses us with no-nonsense instructions.

"Give Steven here your names; first and last, and where we can reach you, day or night, for the next few weeks."

Megan then storms off, re-claiming her demanding Assistant Director persona, yelling into the 'S.W.A.T. Team' megaphone strapped to her wrist.

"People? People! Work with me here..."

Jan and I match each other's wide-eyed surprise, as I think to myself, *the next few weeks!*

"Oh, Man," is all I can utter.

"Did you hear that?" Jan whispers through her teeth, trying to contain her enthusiasm, as Steven struggles with a pen that seems to be out of ink.

"The next few weeks?" she says, almost hyperventilating, "Oh my God... Oh my God!"

Not wanting to blow this unbelievable opportunity, I jump in quickly for both of us, directing my focus to Steven giving him a pen from my own suit pocket.

"Her name is Jan Flannery. That's "J," "A"..."

Jan interrupts me, having gathered herself sufficiently to proceed with the pertinent details.

"The last name is, F.L.A.N.N.E.R.Y. I'm staying here at the Hotel, room 117." Jan double-checks to confirm that the 'obviously-inept-Steven' is spelling her name correctly and writing her room number legibly. Steven then turns to me, as Jan quickly adds, "And

I'm available any time, day or night! Just let me know... or leave a message at the front desk... really.... Thank you."

"Uh, me too," I say. "Anytime!"

I then confirm my name and room number as well.

"O.K." he says, in a timid attempt at show-biz authority. "Someone will be in touch with you."

"People! Listen up!" Megan screams into her megaphone, collectively addressing our small brood of 'Atmosphere Personnel.' "We need everyone down on the front lawn for some wide-angle establishing shots! Listen up! We need everyone for placement in twenty minutes. Take a quick break and be down in front of the hotel at seven-forty-five! Thank you."

Assuming her 'below-the-line-mandatory-union-brake' mode, Megan then lets the megaphone dangle from her wrist and cracks open the large bottle of "Extra-Strength Tylenol" hanging on a string from her clipboard and slugs back a few horse-pill-size tablets. Grabbing an Evian water from her fanny-pack, she strides off gulping with a constant stream of technical conversation crackling from the walkie-talkie bouncing at her hip.

Everyone disperses in various directions to find a few moments of calm before the full day of filming ahead. I turn to Jan with a humble, self-congratulatory smile on my face, only to have it swiftly removed by a well-placed slap of her gloved hand to my cheek. Then with a swish of her dress, she turns in a huff and strides off toward the Hotel entrance. Shaking the cobwebs from my brain, I hold the affronted side of my face and marvel at the wallop Jan packs in her dainty hand.

"Wow...!" I say, just as Jan turns around to make sure she has the last word.

"I... am a married woman!" she states, indignantly, but with a slight lack of conviction.

With that, she storms off into the hotel lobby.

Licking my wounds, trying to 'de-frag' my reeling middle-aged brain, I mentally click back and forth between the perceived realities of 1979 and 2005. Eventually, I wander over to the gorgeous view at the front porch railing and take in the green expanse of the hotel's manicured lawns and the deep blue of the lake beyond. Gazing and musing on the moment.

If I had a choice, would I stay here in this extraordinary situation?

After a while, still not resolving the matter, I hear myself say, quietly, soberly, "And I'm a married man as well, somewhere in time."

From the vest pocket of my cream-colored movie costume, I retrieve my iPod and look at it dispassionately. In an irrational attempt to end this entire time-travel charade, I fixate on the urge to throw the damn thing as far as my seething anger will allow. Rational or irrational, I find myself swimming in self-doubt and fear, not knowing what to do, or what not to do. For the first time in my life, I find myself speechless and numb.

As I stand at one of those major "Y's" in the road, without a clue which way to go, or whether to proceed at all, one of Yogi Berra's exasperating conundrums bubbles up through my subconscious, providing a confusing guidance that I could take or leave... for the moment.

"If you come to a fork in the road, take it."

Instead of chucking my iPod, I slip one of the earbuds into my ear, close my eyes and turn my face to the sun.

Even if I don't know which road to take... by not going back, I've already decided that either path ahead is better than merely backtracking on a life poorly lived.

Soon, the soothing, 'Hemi-Sync,' white-noise fills my weary head. I drink in the summer breeze and linger in the moment. Eventually, a subtle smile forms on my face, prompted by another classic Yogi Berra-ism:

"If you don't know where you're going, you will wind up somewhere else." *Amen....*

Down on the front lawn, in the heat of the day, the cast and crew assemble for the film's expansive establishing shots, which are being artistically choreographed to showcase the Grand Hotel and its extensive, verdant grounds. This is the memorable scene where the two Chris's; Christopher Reeve and Christopher Plummer, engage in a duel of wits, over the engaging Jane Seymour, as Elise McKenna.

Both Jan and I are fortunate to be in this rather complicated scene. Initially, Christopher Plummer begins the shot in a close-up, regally standing in front of the hotel, having his photograph taken. His character, W.F. Robinson (Ms. McKenna's shrewd, and overly-protective, agent/business manager) then leisurely strolls amongst the lawn's brightly canopied tables, as a few of us 'hotel guests' partake in a leisurely open-air breakfast.

It's at this point, in the middle of Mr. Plummer's casual stroll, that I am allowed to expend a precious few of my allotted, Andy 'Warholian,' 'fifteen minutes of fame,' sitting at a white-wicker table, with three of my atmosphere personnel colleagues, eating and pretending to be engaged in casual breakfast conversation. At one point Mr. Robinson passes next to our table, walking-stick in hand, to confront Richard Collier who is enjoying his morning paper and a light breakfast at the table next to ours. Ironically, at the same time, Jan has been directed to stroll in the background, just behind Richard's table.

Jan has quick-changed into a beautiful turn-of-the-century riding outfit, complete with a lengthy dressage-dress, riding crop and lady's top-hat with a matching chiffon bow. I'm surprised and pleased to see that Jan has been upgraded to such an exquisite and definitely noticeable costume. My brother's colleagues in the women's costume department have outdone themselves on all the ladies' movie costumes, including the extras. Jan's new outfit is both authentic and stunning at the same time. I notice she is paired with a different partner for this scene, and obviously has been instructed to pass by Richard Collier's table while he is engaged in conversation with the cantankerous Mr. Robinson.

There is no way that either one of us can be edited out of this scene. We'll definitely have something on the 'Silver Screen' to show our grandchildren one day. And this is only the first day of filming! Additionally, given the camera angle and the placement of the shot, I'm pleased to discover that Jan and I will appear in the scene at the same time; myself in the foreground and she in the background. I am grateful as well that our simultaneous appearance at this moment in time (her in 1979 and me fresh from 2005) is being memorialized forever, no matter what happens from this point on.

As the day wears on, and our scene is shot over and over again from different angles, with various pacing and direction, I actually find myself becoming tired of sitting. The lawn chairs are comfortable enough. But, it's the intensity of having to 'look natural' for so long time that becomes unnatural in itself.

I can tell by Jan's flushed cheeks, and her partner's ever-slowing pace, that their repeated 'strolling' is taking a toll on them. Especially Jan, in her full-length, woolen, outfit. Eventually, by late afternoon, the shadows become too long to match the shots taken earlier in the day and, thankfully, exterior filming is wrapped for the day.

It is certainly a fickle thing, this movie-making business. I had hoped to be Jan's partner for today's beautiful breakfast scene. Instead, I content myself to being happy for her, as she experiences her first, much-deserved, moment in the sun… in an actual Hollywood picture!

Chapter 19

LADY OF THE LAKE

Instead of attending tonight's catered dinner in the hotel dining room, I decide to take some personal time off. And since I have not been tapped to participate in the evening's tuxedoed ballroom scene, I decide, *What the hell... I'm going fishing! Besides*, I remind myself, *whose 'mid-life-crisis' is this anyway...* or Hemi-Sync nightmare or whatever this is.

I originally came to Mackinac Island, to the Somewhere In Time weekend, to get away from it all, and to think things through. Something I've not had much time to do since my lazy college days. It's a little disconcerting to think about my advancing years, back in my youthful body again, without the old aches and pains I've become so accustomed to, that I don each day with a certain middle-age pride.

I still can't believe I've bumped over the half-century mark, a gray-haired baby-boomer, tentatively looking over his shoulder, wondering where his life went. My "Lost and Found Generation" is still shell-shocked from having stared with innocent eyes into the brink of nuclear Armageddon and lived to tell about it, having been raised with the stark absurdity that one 'magic bullet' could end our shining season of Camelot, and disillusioned by realization that psychedelic drugs and free sex are not all they are cracked up to be (or was it free drugs and psychedelic sex). The fact that I can't remember is proof enough I was there. Frightened to still be alive, with our heroes and gurus and their white-hot flashes of insight now co-opted, franchised and reduced to 'Pavlovian' sound-bites that eventually rang as meaningless jingles and slogans, until they became trite and unmotivating.

But, perhaps that is what a good mid-life crisis does for one; causes you to think and reminisce and sort things out. Fifty-three years-old can feel like ninety-three when it comes to counting how many good 'fishing years' you've got left on this planet.

I still can't believe it's been twenty-six years since I last visited this beautiful, enchanting place. And, inexplicably, back in my youthful twenties again, re-living that carefree summer as a 'movie extra' on this sun swept isle on America's 'north coast' in 1979.

The minimal fishing gear that my brother optimistically stashed in his studio costume-trailer is fine enough for me. And since he'll be busy filming late tonight, I'll have the full-moon over Lake Huron all to myself. Just me, a custom-built fly-rod and an "Elk-Hair Caddis" or two, or perhaps a "Woolly Bugger."

Besides, I originally came to Mackinac Island to do some serious thinking. And given my present condition; having just encountered one of those major "Ys" in the road of life, the 'serious thinking' aspect of my pilgrimage has taken on a much deeper meaning.

I soon find myself thigh-high at twilight in the shallow flats in front of the Grand Hotel, rhythmically casting to the classical-music wafting from the Hotel's dining-room windows, waving a seven-foot, six-weight "Ray Gould-Special" to a three-count waltz, matching the eternal rhythm of the waves lapping upon the shore. Long loops of lime-green fly-line whip and whisper past the brim of the old hat I found in the bowels of Greggy's costume trailer; a 'Herbert Johnson Hatters' brown-felt fedora. The same style Harrison Ford wore in those classic, "Indiana Jones," adventure films. It fits like a glove, both size-wise and heart-wise, with a warm, 'broken-in' feel, as if it has been waiting for this very moment to be worn on this magical summers-eve.

Suddenly, it occurs to me that the same analogy might be apropos in my case. Have I not been waiting for such a time as this? A chance to relive my life? To 'do-over' a portion of what has made me... me? To make it better or different somehow, or right. What an awesome opportunity. What a fearsome responsibility! And with the added perspective of time, I seem to be experiencing more temperance and patience this time around. Two admirable qualities I could've cared less about in my younger days. For some unkown reason, I find those qualities more admirable now. Not just for the moment, but for the long term. I want to make an actual difference this time around, for my own eternity, and for those I love; for all those I love.

This concept has become glaringly clear to me now... now that I've been given this second chance at such a major 'do-over.'

Son of a bitch...! "I've got one!"

The weight-forward line snaps taut as silvery beads of lake-water slide down its quavering angle, pointing to the ghostly commotion circling and splashing not more than ten-yards away, in the reflection of the harvest moon-rise on the lake. A good-size walleye makes its desperate run. I heft the rod high in the air, as it forms a perfect parabolic curve above my head. I fight to retrieve the clicking reel. Five, six pounds maybe....

Now this is what I'm talking about! What a perfect ending to a magnificent day! Dancing with a walleye on the shores of Mackinac Island, to "Mahler" in full symphonic-bloom, beneath the glow of a smiling moon. If this turns out to be one big dream, it'll be one for the record books as far as I'm concerned.

Suddenly it hits me with dumbfounded amazement...

What the Hell am I doing? Why am I in such a hurrying? Shit, I've been waiting for a perfect moment like this all my life...!

The last time I fished at all was with the kids in the blasting sun at Fish Lake, just beyond the quaint Bavarian-town of Leavenworth in the Washington 'Cascades.' I was so busy keeping the kid's hooks wormed-up and rowing for shade that I barely had time to fish myself.

So, in the mid-fight, I resolve that tonight, I will exact my just reward. Slowing myself down, I take a long, deep breath and allow the feisty fish to take the line again, on another daring run against the drag of the reel. I stand and watch and relish the power and grace of another of God's incredible creatures, so awesome and fearfully made, placed here like me, perhaps, for this very moment. I vow to honor this fish tonight. To play the cards just as they are dealt, as if this were my last, best hand.

As the 'backing' of the large-arbor reel begins to roll out, I slowly turn the fish, and begin the next phase of our exhausting 'give-and-take-ballet.' Reeling in and letting go. Keeping enough tension on the line for the long retrieve. But, not too much, as to blow my chances at landing this beautiful monster.

For a few precious moments, I glance around me, taking in my glorious surroundings; the primal smell of the lake, the magical moon, the stars, and the sparkling lights of Mackinac Bridge, just savoring the moment. I smile.

Man, this is as good as it gets. And I'm going to enjoy every sacred second of it... as time allows.

Eventually, after trying, then countering, every trick in the book, at both ends of the line, the exhausted walleye slips silently into my hickory hardwood net, creating a mind's eye photo that will forever be bookmarked in my memory-bank.

I tuck the rod under my arm and carefully work the 'Woolly Bugger' from the side of her mouth. What a beauty! So sleek and golden-yellow. Shimmering in the moonlight. I ceremoniously raise her glistening body to the star-studded sky and watch the moonbeams play through the majestic spread of her dorsal-fin, like candle-light through a Chinese fan.

Suddenly... so sudden it takes my breath away... a shooting-star paints a golden arc across the hazy-band of the 'Milky Way,' seemingly, just beyond my outstretched arms. I stand mesmerized, watching the majestic Lady-Walleye swim, whimsically, like a goddess through the heavens.

Joyously, I bellow into the night, "Yes...! Thank you!" giving voice to the uncontrollable emotions welling in my soul.

The stardust residue of the shooting-star fades as quickly as it appeared. Seemingly so close, yet so very far away.

Indeed, that is what it's like to experience one's life over again; living at arm's length in a reality that is light years away.

And for some reason there *is* a reason for it, somewhere out there, just waiting for me to discover... this time around.

Ceremoniously, I kiss the fish's nose and lower her gently into the darkness of the lake, moving her sleek, golden body back and forth until she revives. Then, with a slap of her tail and a flash, she is gone... back to the deep, with an incredible story to tell to all those who will listen. *Bless you Lady Walleye. Will-o'-the-wisp. Lady of the Lake....*

I wait for the longest time. Not wanting to move, or think. Letting everything wash over me; the night… the stars… the lake… the Golden Lady… All of it… like stardust from Heaven. Perhaps, this is what 'Life' is all about; catching and releasing, experiencing and forbearing, taking time for the small moments, so, that the big, important 'decisions-of-a-lifetime' don't catch you with your waders down.

Chapter 20

BUFFO BREAKFAST BUFFET

The next morning the cast and crew are up before dawn, to take advantage of a full day's daylight for filming. I slept like a log, even though it wasn't long, waking again in 1979, as confirmed by my brother's belongings still characteristically strewn around the room. As usual, he's up before me, already out and about. Still in my new (or old) youthful body, I find that I'm getting used to this 'doing things over again' scenario. Fortunately, I've retained a comforting level of middle-age memory lapse, so the day's routine events still retain a certain freshness and spontaneity. I'm just hoping I get an appropriate moment to apologize to Jan Flannery for my overzealousness yesterday.

To my utter surprise, at the early-morning breakfast-buffet, Jan strolls in with my brother, Chris Reeve and Jane Seymour, like they are old friends; laughing and joking.

Of course, I'm not surprised to see Greg and Chris paling around. Greggy is Chris' personal-costumer. He attends to every detail of Chris' on-screen appearance. As a matter of fact, my brother is in charge of the one and only outfit that Chris wears throughout the entire movie; a light-brown/canary-yellow, three-piece, pin-striped suit, with a brown bowler hat and two-tone, high-top, shoes. Greggy also has many duplicates of each of these articles, to ensure that a replacement is ready, should Chris soil or damage an item of clothing during filming.

I marvel how quickly Jan has skyrocketed to the top of the Hollywood social ladder. Of course, my brother saw me promenading with her during yesterday's opening ceremonies. And given the opportunity, he most likely singled her out for special notice during last night's filming of the ballroom scene. Neither one of the Hall boys are shy when it comes to beautiful women. Of course, with the quaint atmosphere here on the Island, its Victorian architecture and the historic ban on motorized vehicles, everything lends itself to a slower, more personal, pace and a genuine feeling of camaraderie.

I nod to my brother and slip in casually behind them at the buffet line, tagging along as if I belong. Attempting not to let my nervousness show at being in such close proximity to 'Superman' and the legendary 'James Bond babe,' from "Live and Let Die, I try to give the impression that having breakfast with certified Super-Stars is no big deal. Fortunately, I find Chris and Jane to be very regular people, who enjoy eating and hanging out with the tight-knit cast and crew.

Greg introduces me, offhandedly, and each of them graciously put me at ease with their friendly demeanor. Even the stately Christopher Plummer; Captain Von Trapp from the classic 20th Century Fox film, "The Sound of Music," is surprisingly approachable and congenial. In a matter of moments, it's as if I've known them for years.

Jan, of course, is completely enthralled with Chris, the former silver-screen 'Man of Steel.' But, who wouldn't be? Being a single guy, I can tell that Chris appreciates Jan's wholesome good-looks as much as I do.

Jan allows our eyes to meet and charitably breaks the tension between us. I nod, to offer my unspoken apologies in response to her initial volley of reconciliation. For the moment at least, I seem to be forgiven. So, I concentrate on enjoying hobnobbing with the upper-crust of Hollywood filmdom.

I scoop a perfect pair of Eggs Benedict from the warming tray and peruse the full complement of delectable delights the hotel has lavishly provided us so early in the morning. With keen anticipation, I slide into the glorious aroma of crisp, thick-sliced bacon, biscuits-and-gravy, hotcakes, sausages, hash-browns, toast, and pure Michigan maple syrup. Fresh-brewed coffee is calling to me at the end of the white-linen table, drawing my puffy eyes toward its welcoming bouquet. I pour a thick stream of maple syrup over everything, grab a cup of 'Joe,' and glance around for a place to sit.

Like the good younger brother he's always been, Greggy insists I join him with Chris, Jane and Jan at a private table with a breath-taking view of the sun rising over the lake. Chris and the girls take one side of the table and Greg and I hold down the other; I across from Jan next to the picture-window and Chris between the two ladies.

Greg and Jane begin the conversation, commiserating about their memorable experiences together, working on the original "Battle Star Galactica" television series. Greg was the show's costumer and Jane was cast as "Serina," an inter-planetary news reporter. Jane amusingly expresses relief that her character was killed off shortly after the pilot episode, allowing her to unobtrusively leave the show to pursue her film career, and fortuitously, before the series was unceremoniously axed after the first season.

Greggy reminisces on his favorite 'Battle Star' character; the little mechanical dog, or 'daggit,' called "Muffit," and the trained chimpanzee he had to stuff into its costume every day.

Not to be left out, Chris throws in some stories of his own about his summer-stock days with the legendary Katharine Hepburn, while Jan and I content ourselves just being part of the group.

To my surprise, I learn that the filming last night didn't go as late as anticipated. So, on the spur of the moment, Chris took Jane, Jan and my brother on a moonlit flight in his private plane (which he stealthily hid at the island's small airport). They flew to the mainland and went bowling, ate pizza, the whole works.

Jan even commented they saw the most glorious shooting star on their outbound flight, which she took as a special sign, having made a wish that she chooses not to immediately share with us.

Listening with jealous admiration about their late-night/early-morning escapades, I can't believe they are actually up and awake, given that they must have returned to the island only a few hours ago. Both Chris and Jane are remarkably resilient for this early hour. Only time will tell how they will hold up as the long shooting day progresses.

I doubt Jan slept at all last night, after her real-life Cinderella experience. I admire her radiant after-glow as she sits across from me, floating on cloud nine.

Although I wouldn't have wanted to miss my own adventure last night, I'm definitely disappointed to have blown another of those 'chances-of-a-lifetime.' Thus, I relegate myself to vicariously enjoying Jan's fairy-tale, with a twinge of jealousy.

But hey! I think to myself, trying to put a positive spin on the situation... *last night my dance card was filled by destiny, with the 'Lady of the Lake.'*

I'm surprised to find that despite his lanky frame, Chris packs a major-league appetite, having no problem keeping up with the 'Hall Boys' when it comes to packing it away. Between Chris and Greggy and I, we look like the Detroit Lions at 'training table.' Jan and Jane look out of place, sandwiched between the three of us, wolfing down the carbs like there's no tomorrow. Only periodically, do either one of us pause to cleanse our pallets with never-ending tumblers of ice-cold milk.

As our initial gastronomic attack settles to a more satiated pace, I begin to muse upon the many coincidental synchronicities that must have taken place to bring each of us together this morning. With the unspoken perspective of my fifty-plus years, crammed into this twenty-six year old body, I am amazed how intertwined certain lives seem to be. It's interesting to note that all of us have the proud distinction of being similarly situated on the crest of the massive baby-boom wave (having been born between 1946-1964), along with those other 78-million souls who flooded this 'third rock from the sun' after World War II. (the largest influx of intention to this little planet in recent, recorded history).

Jane is only slightly the oldest among us, then myself, then Chris (who is only twelve days younger than I am), he having made his entrance, stage-left, in New York City in 1952, and I, stage-right, in Walla Walla, Washington.

Then comes Greggy, born just before Chris' younger brother, Benjamin; not quite a year later.

Then Jan, the baby of our boomer-bunch.

It's intriguing how some aspects of our lives have paralleled each other. Perhaps, not the same intensity or fame-factor, but at least mimicking some basic patterns. With a few fortuitous twists of fate, we brush closely by one another with strikingly similar life-patterns, as if we are long-lost cousins... even soul-mates.

Jan's and my life-stories seem to have placed us on similar paths long ago. Her unquenchable enthusiasm for life, her willingness to drop everything to pursue her dream, no matter how crazy or unconventional, are personal traits all too familiar to me. Her enduring connection to Mackinac Island also parallels my own, seemingly unintended, life-journey.

In another interesting coincidence, Chris' publicity materials indicate that his blue-blood genealogy traces back through his mother to the landing of the Mayflower at Plymouth Rock; having descended from William Bradford, the famous leader and chronicler of that early pilgrim community. My own paternal line is documented back to the Mayflower, having descended from the oldest Mayflower passenger, John Chilton, and his twelve year old daughter, the youngest passenger on the ship, Mary Chilton Winslow, who has the distinction of being the first European woman to set foot onto the new world. Some of Mary's notable progeny include the singer Pete Seeger, Marjorie "Betty Crocker" Child, actors Vincent Price and James Dean, and as rumor has it, Abraham Lincoln.

Chris's and my parents were both teachers; our fathers each having received their doctorates from Columbia University in New York City. Chris began his acting career at the tender age of nine at the private "Princeton Country Day School" in New Jersey, at the same time I landed my first leading role at the "Agnes Russell School;" a private grammar school at Columbia University (Horace Mann Hall), where the children of the staff and administrators of Teacher's College, Columbia University, Union and Jewish Theological Seminaries and Juilliard attended.

When Chris was accepted to Cornell, I was accepted at Harvard (but had to opt for Washington State University because of lack of funds for an ivy-league education). Additionally, Chris's further studies at Juilliard (with his roommate, actor/comedian Robin Williams) seems no small coincidence, as the campus of the famed

New York city performing arts school was literally around the corner from Greggy's and my childhood, 'Morningside Heights,' neighborhood on 121st Street (between Amsterdam and Broadway). Our little block spawned other famous personalities, such as actor Eric Estrada, the noted Catholic theologian Thomas Merton. And it was subsequently nicknamed "White Harlem" by another fellow '121st Street alum,' comedian George Carlin.

When Chris was touring the summer stock circuit, I was traveling the world as Master of Ceremonies of "Up With People." At the time he auditioned for the role of "Superman," I was honing my theatrical skills with tramfuls of tourists on the backlot at Universal Studios.

By the time Chris was racking up critical acclaim on the silver screen and Broadway, I had opted for law school, moved back home, and settled into helping that curvaceous, green-eyed babe, who became my wife, raise our four kids in small-town U.S.A.

So, what's wrong with this picture? I don't know that there's anything wrong with it. But, it does poignantly illustrate how separate lives can closely parallel one another for a time, converging in the same general proximity, only to diverge again and continue on their own separate ways. It's only natural to wonder *what if...?* What would life have been like if things had turned out differently? Not that I'm complaining or anything.

Alright, I probably am.

But, then I realize, *What have I got to complain about?* I've had a good life so far, even with my current situation being a bit tenuous. I'll probably wake up soon anyway.

I think about Chris's life; so filled with successes and well-earned accolades, only to be changed forever in the blink of an eye with his riding accident at an equestrian competition. I think of my brother's terrible bipolar tribulations, which are still to come. I contemplate whether I should warn Chris of his looming fate; his future life as a paraplegic. A very famous paraplegic to be sure. But, bound to a wheelchair and dying way too young.

Then, I ponder... would I change lives and circumstances with Chris? Jump over this table and exchange places, now that our lives are brushing close together again? Would I give up all that has become me... for everything that is becoming him? Even if it were possible, I really don't know the answer to that question. I am sure I'm not capable of contemplating the full ramifications of such a reality.

Chris smiles that 'knowing' Christopher Reeve smile and I sigh my 'unknowing' sigh…. Who am I to presume we are not all intricate players in some greater, more meaningful plan; some grand, cosmic production, the actual script of which none of us has any clue about, and probably never will.

Chris finally throws in the towel, leans back and stretches his long arms over his head. Greggy and I follow suit, allowing for a few silent moments to digest the morning's copious delights. The girls having long-since conceded to our conspicuous gluttony.

Chris finally mentions that Greg tried to find me last night; to go flying with them. But, he found my 'Gone Fishing' note in our room. With genuine curiosity, Chris inquires about my evenings fishing expedition.

"So, where'd you go?"

"Uh… right down in front of the hotel, in the shallow cove across from the front lawn. Seems it's been a local hot-spot for generations."

"What kind of gear did you use?"

"I borrowed Greg's split-cane fly-rod. Seven and a half foot, six-weight… hand-crafted by a friend back home."

"Really? Hand-split cane? I'll bet that set you back a pretty penny." Chris says to Greggy.

"I grew up with the rod-maker's son." Greggy responds. "Otherwise, I couldn't afford his classic, parabolic creations."

"Kind of light tackle for this area isn't it?" Chris continues, with his probing questions.

"Yeah, but I load up on the tippet and take my time. Actually, I don't care if I catch anything. I just like being out there on the lake."

"Liar…." Chris says, with a wink and a smile.

"What kind of flies...?"

"Weighted 'Woolly Buggers,' buck tail streamers, and some homemade stuff."

"Really? You tie your own flies?"

"Yeah, well…"

"I tried that once… for about ten seconds. Takes way too much concentration. Drove me crazy. What are your homemade patterns called?"

I glance around the table self-consciously….

"Promise you won't laugh?"

"No really, I'm intrigued."

"I call them my "Hallywood" series. You know, H.A.L.L…. Kind of a signature thing, in case they ever catch on."

Chris pauses, contemplating my willingness to be transparent and throws out:

"You mean like, 'Hallywood Bugger…?'"

Chris struggles to keep a straight face, while Jane, Jan, and Greggy crack up at his quick wit.

"Or 'Hallywood Nymph!" he adds, causing Jan to urgently preempt the spraying of a mouthful of milk with her cloth napkin.

"I've actually known a few of those," Jane chimes in, with her delightfully-dry, English humor.

"Exactly…" I say, joining the merriment at my own expense.

For the next half-hour, we talk about fly-fishing and other important 'life-things,' relaxing with steaming refills of aromatic coffee generously laced with heavy cream and pure maple syrup.

Eventually, with Chris' continued prompting, I end up relating my magical evening in the moonlit cove, most probably under their very wingtips as they flew to the mainland in Chris' private plane. I confirm that Jan and I must have seen the same breathtaking shooting-star. And that I witnessed its fading stardust through the fanned dorsal fin of a golden Lady Walleye, suspended in my outstretched arms, beneath the awesome expanse of the Milky-Way. I describe my midnight dance with the 'Lady of the Lake' and the sweet moments of bliss that washed over me like moon-dust on the sand.

Suddenly, I find myself a bit conflicted, feeling that I don't belong here; having recently flashed back from 2005 to 1979, or living in the midst of a very lucid dream, sleeping off a bad hangover.

Witnessing life with such dual perspective makes whatever I say, or think, even the most trivial things, seem more meaningful. At least in my own mind. As if I have stereoscopic vision.

This time-travel-thing is definitely disconcerting; trying to assimilate my limited knowledge of the future into my day-to-day existence in the past. Then there's the temptation to use your knowledge to play with the various scenarios that Yogi Berra conjured up when he said, "If you don't know where you are going, you will wind up somewhere else."

Or a variation on the same theme: *If you know where you'll end up, should you attempt to alter the way you're going?*

These fleeting notions seem to be pulling me to a higher perspective. What if, since our lives on this planet are so short-lived, in comparison to the stark reality of eternity, and since both science and religion tell us we are much more than our physical senses can perceive (with 90% junk DNA?), it makes sense that our puny life-experience is not the full story; neither the beginning or the end of our actual reality. What if everything we are, and all we do, amounts to a mere sentence or two in just one chapter of some <u>great</u> book, or one of <u>many</u> great books of life that are still being written, revised and edited, simultaneously, as we struggle on unknowingly, living and dying and eating breakfast as miniscule, but carefully crafted, footnotes lovingly contemplated and created with pride, diligently cataloged for future expanded sequels and prequels on some highly-revered bookshelf by the 'Great Author' of all time, space and dimension. Perhaps, the ultimate outcome of our existence is not so important as how we arrive at our destination, and the attitudes we embrace along the way.

Not knowing exactly when I slipped into the fugue state I now find myself returning from; sipping coffee with my breakfast companions, apparently in mid-sentence, I suddenly realize that Jan and Chris and Jane, even my brother, are staring at me, seemingly captivated by the thoughts my words have either consciously or otherwise provoked in their minds, and still linger on their faces. I have no idea which of my daydream-musings may have bubbled-up into verbal expression, beyond my simple intent to relate a memorable fish story.

"Whoa..." Chris says. "Sounds like we're the ones who missed out last night."

I self-consciously poke at the vestiges of my Eggs Benedict, not fully realizing what I may have said, thinking I've gone way overboard in monopolizing the morning's conversation. Jane finally rescues the awkward moment with a smile and a quip across the table at Greggy.

"Well, the next time we knock off early, I'm going fishing with your brother!"

"Me too," says Jan, enthusiastically, to my surprise.

No matter what else happens here on Mackinac Island, my experience thus far has got to be a major highlight of whichever life I still have to live. Indeed, hanging out with the stars, both literally and figuratively; in the moonlit cove and working with them on this special movie, has been memorable to say the least. It's easy to get swept away in the romance and adventure of it all, realizing that moments like these will never come again. Except, evidently in my case, where I <u>am</u> living them again... for what reason I have yet to discover.

Chapter 21

UP THE WAY....

The day turns out to be another gorgeous one for filming. The sun is bright and not too hot. A cooling breeze off the lake periodically breaks through the lazy feeling that permeates the island this time of year. Chris and Jane spend the morning shooting a montage of beach scenes, with us atmosphere personnel filling in the back and foreground.

These are the romantic scenes where Richard and Elise become better acquainted on their first actual 'date.' I take advantage of the relaxed pace and sidle up to Jan whenever I can. They have her costumed in an elegant white dress with a sheer sunbonnet. I was able to bypass the early morning scramble at the costume trailer because Greggy allowed me to take my cream-colored suit back to our room after yesterday's filming. That way, I can dress directly into my costume each morning and catch an extra thirty minutes of sleep, which I definitely appreciate.

"It'll only work," he admonishes, "if you keep the damn thing clean and presentable for filming." I keep this in mind, as Jan and I sit and walk and clump together in the background, during Chris and Jane's romantic beach scenes.

Jan and I dutifully follow each whim and direction of the various assistants in charge of such things as placement of atmospheric personnel. I seem to have been bumped up the thespian food-chain from a mere 'extra' to what I hear described as a 'featured background actor.' The credit for this minuscule, but meaningful, promotion I can only attribute to the forgiving heart of Jan Flannery, who has mercifully acquiesced to me being her on-screen partner for the day's filming.

As the morning drones on and the lake dapples hypnotically in the sun, I notice that last night's lack of sleep is beginning take a toll on Jan. Chris and Jane still have their intimate lighthouse scene to film during the height of the afternoon sun. They will definitely earn their paychecks today. Of course, it was their choice to stay out late, carousing with my brother until the wee hours of the morning.

I feel a natural lull myself, having gone to bed after midnight, which is way beyond my normal, middle-age bedtime. I guess you'd call it "time-lag," instead of "jet-lag."

I glance behind the camera and notice my brother nodding off in a wicker chaise-lounge, cat-napping with an old-fashioned straw hat over his face.

I admire the stamina it takes to perform at this level, with such consistency and intensity, day after day, let alone remember your lines without the benefit of eight hours of sleep.

But hey, that's why movie stars get paid the big bucks! Right?

Then I realize, *they also get to suffer the slings and arrows of the 'critics' and the 'live-or-die' decisions of the studio-heads, and many times, the unforgiving movie-going public.*

What a pressure-cooker it is to survive such a life, day in and day out. But, I have a feeling neither Chris nor Jane nor Christopher Plummer would have it any other way.

We as fans should be grateful for their fortitude in the face of such daunting uncertainty and insecurity... and applaud every accolade, nomination and award they are fortunate enough to garner.

By early afternoon, after we've heartily consumed a well-earned box-lunch on the beach, all unessential on-screen personnel are given the afternoon off, while the crew sets up for Chris and Jane's intimate scenes at the old-fashioned light house. Hopefully, they can catch a cat-nap before resuming work in an hour or two.

I see that Jan is fading fast and could use some rest and quiet, out of the mid-day sun. I suggest we take advantage of the time off and check out the island's historic theatre. The old playhouse will play an important part in the Somewhere in Time script later on, when Elise gives her 'performance of a lifetime,' secretly professing her love for Richard before a packed, opening-night audience.

In another interesting twist of synchronicity, the 'Orpheum Theatre' has historic significance for me as well. It was at this same auditorium here on Mackinac Island, that "Up With People," had its humble beginnings. It was in the early 1960's, when as a positive statement by the then youth of the world, an original idea was birthed to bring together young people from around the world, to create a performing group with a positive, uplifting theme, promoting international goodwill and communication. At the time, the idea was rather countercultural, with all the anti-establishment protests and the 'down with this, down with that' attitude of the era.

As a college student in the early-seventies, I thought to myself, *not a bad idea for a guy who hasn't yet declared a major course of study.*

Besides, when in doubt... travel the world!

Thus, by happenstance... either that or a touch of Yogi Berra's sage advice... I eventually found myself the master of ceremonies and a featured performer in Up With People, along with a hundred and thirty other enormously talented and unforgettable youth from around the world.

In my case, it meant going from the small, sea-side town of Brackett's Landing to headlining at Heinz Hall and the Super Bowl, and many more unbelievable stops in between. Our musical 'United Nations' performed over 300 shows a year in every imaginable venue; from musty high-school gymnasiums to blazing, bullfight arenas, inner-city ghettos and sold-out coliseums. We even pulled off what had been touted as one of the best Super Bowl half-times ever, launching the modern-era of fully-produced, half-time sports spectaculars. What a whirlwind tour.

We lived with host-families wherever we traveled; rich or poor, from every socioeconomic stratum imaginable, performing in multiple languages and different cultures in whatever foreign country we found ourselves.

Along with my "Somewhere In Time" movie-making experience, my time on the road in "Up With People" is something I'll never forget. It's so strange that both these memorable life-changing experiences are inextricably tied to one place... Mackinac Island.

A bit of pride grabs me, as I show Jan the plaque posted in the theatre lobby commemorating Up With People's historic beginnings here on the island. As we walk into the dimly lit theatre, a rush of nostalgia greets me like an old friend.

I remember the harried days of 'staging,' putting the show together from scratch, in the hot, July sun back in 1974. Funny, but Up With People seems a lifetime away from my subsequent experience here on Mackinac Island, which occurred five years later in 1979. Though the two experiences were only a few short years apart, 1979 seems a lifetime away from 2005, and the thin reality I left behind only yesterday.

Jan and I sink into adjacent seats in the front-row of the theatre, leaning back, stretching our legs, and resting our brains in the cool dimness of the theatre. Jan removes her bonnet, placing it on the seat next to her. Suddenly, I remember I have my Up With People cast-album on my iPod, along with a few other mid-life-crisis-must-haves, like the Beatles 'White Album,' Chicago, America, Crosby, Stills and Nash, Linda Ronstadt, and selected works of Joe Cocker. Without trying to explain in 1979 terms what an iPod is, I offer Jan one of my earbuds, to share some of my favorite "Uppie" songs, digitally re-mastered of course, from their original vinyl. Something else I won't take time to explain.

"Would you like to hear some Up With People 'Oldie-but-Goodies…?'" I offer.

"Sure," she says, more relieved than anything to be sitting in a cool, restful spot.

"I always wanted to travel with Up With People," Jan reminisces, surveying the empty stage before us.

"I went to the concerts whenever they came around. I even have some albums from the old 'Sing Out' days with "The Colwell Brothers" and "Herb Allen."

I smile at Jan's enthusiastic recall and relax into the seat next to her.

"You would have been wonderful in Up With People," I confirm without hesitation.

"I can see you now," I muse, nodding to the stage before us.

"See..?"

"What?" she asks, amused by my playful attitude.

"No really." I say. "Look closely. I can see you in some parallel-universe, singing and dancing up a storm."

Despite her exhausted condition, Jan is pleasantly intrigued with the idea of living out her dreams and desires simultaneously in another dimension, only slightly out of phase with this one. I've been mulling over such strange possibilities myself, as a potential explanation of what is happening to me.

I punch up the "Cast B-1974" cast-album, as Jan eagerly places an earbud into her ear and I put the other in mine. We lean back in the soft theatre seats and close our eyes for a few moments of respite, before picking up some 'second-unit' work, later in the afternoon. My last recollection comes in a soothing flood of memories from a more carefree, yet purposeful time, covering me like a warm blanket....

There are many roads, to go...
and they go, by many names.
They don't all go, the same way.
But they get there, all the same...
And I have a feelin,'
That we'll meet some day,
where the roads come together,
up the way...

(Words by Paul Colwell, music by Paul Colwell & Herb Allen, ASCAP, Copyright 1971 Up With People, All rights reserved)

Chapter 22

WHAT ARE YOU DOING IN MY DREAM?

BAM! We hit the stage in a coordinated blast of syncopated sound and kaleidoscopic color; some cast-members dancing down the aisles, others singing in the balcony. Don't look now, but there's one right next to you, wherever you happen to be in the audience. Young people of every size, race and religion, all moving as one syncopated force.

It would be difficult to sleep through the opening of an Up With People concert. The multi-colored costumes, the brilliant lights, the performers representing every human personality imaginable, all flowing together, laughing and smiling and for all intents and purposes, having the time of their lives.

It's opening night at Heinz Hall, Pittsburgh, Pennsylvania! Our cast has traveled all night on the bus, again, like so many other nights, in three deluxe Greyhounds. I slept comfortably, swinging between the luggage racks in my hammock, a few inches above my sleeping colleagues, swaying to the rhythm of the road.

Tonight is a big performance. Our local sponsor has booked us into Heinz Hall, which is reminiscent of Carnegie Hall and located in the heart of Pittsburgh's Cultural District.

So far, everything is going along planned. I just finished my opening monologue as "M.C.," welcoming the black-tie audience to the show with my nightly stand-up routine; relating a few good-natured jokes that are calculated to put the crowd in a receptive mood.

I then introduce the first featured performer, the handsome heart-throb Gerald Stevens; a golden-throated, guitar-playing soloist from Midwest America, who swiftly beckons the hearts of every female in the house with his handsome good-looks and intimately expressive performance. He gently prompts the audience to contemplate the socially relevant words to his song. Indeed, even the male ego is vicariously aroused, by his pleasing presence and good-natured machismo. And this is just the beginning of our nightly, two-hour, musical extravaganza called "Up With People!"

I love all this... I really do! I love the music, the message, my fellow cast-members and the fascinating people we meet every day on the road. In the bright lights, I flow with the upbeat music, stepping in time, twirling with my cast-mates, dancing and singing my heart out for those thousands who have come to be entertained, challenged and motivated, and to perhaps, make the world a better place.

Quite lofty ideals for a young man still in his twenties, fresh out of college, with limited worldly experience. But, then you couldn't ask for a better environment to grow and mature in. Nor could you ask for better role-models than our Cast-Directors and Staff, or any greater people to learn with than my fellow "Uppies;" representing more than 30 diverse cultural groups from around the globe. It's mind boggling really. And I'm relishing every minute of it!

One of the great things about being the show's 'Master of Ceremonies' is I can be a 'floater.' During the musical numbers I'm not directly involved in, I move around the stage pretty much where I want; sharing a microphone with friends in the Band, spinning off-stage (then back on) from the wings, taking a turn near the orchestra pit, moving across the apron, dancing with whoever I wish. If you haven't been to an Up With People concert, I can only describe it as 'magnificently controlled chaos' in a kaleidoscope of sights and sounds, choreographed to an infectious beat, and wrapped in a unique, soul-stirring message.

There's Jan Flannery, that cute girl from Michigan. The Band strikes up the lively 'World-Medley' portion of our show. I move in Jan's direction. She and I are scheduled to be partners tonight for some dances-numbers in the World-Medley montage. I love dancing the 'Boogie-Woogie' with Jan, in her 1950's sock-hop outfit. Then, a lightning-fast quick-change, dancing the 'Charleston' together, her in a 'Roaring-Twenties' flapper dress. We usually tease each other while we dance, knowing our steps by heart, having performed the same routines night after night. A little levity keeps things fresh and exciting.

"So, what are you and your host-family doing after the show?" I whisper to Jan, between breaths, whipping her across my back in a locked-elbow barrel-roll.

Not missing a beat, grabbing my hands and pushing back and forth, jitterbug style, Jan says, "Are you asking me for a date, or just bored with the show?"

"Only if you're available," I say, holding her cheek to cheek, now synchronized to Chuck Berry's rockin' "Johnny B Goode." I then quip, "I'm never bored with the show...."

Before Jan can accept or reject my proposal, we brace ourselves for the number's climatic ending, where we and two other costumed couples take the momentary spot-light, lifting and swinging our partners from hip to hip, between our legs, then high into the air, in a precarious shoulder-stand with each girl's shapely legs pointing up to the catwalks, hopefully without flipping over the top (which happens periodically, necessitating a few strategically-placed cast-members as spotters at the critical moment).

We finish on time with the music, Jan plopping down on my knee, and all of us punching the air with upraised arms to thunderous applause. We congratulate each other with a smile, hold hands for a bow with our chests heaving in and out, then bound offstage to change back to our show outfits.

At the women's quick-change area, Jan pulls me aside and catches her breath.

"It's a date," she confirms. "We'll coordinate the details with our host families...."

"You're on," I shoot back, letting her hand slide from mine and turning toward the guy's quick-change area.

Before jumping behind the quick-change curtain, Jan stops with a quizzical look and whispers, "By the way, what are _you_ doing in _my_ dream...?"

Incongruously, Herb Allen, the show's legendary musical director, looks at me from his position just offstage and sarcastically points to his fellow Up With People Co-founders, the Colwell brothers, standing next to him and says,

"Probably the same thing these guys are doing in my dream!"

Steve, Paul and Ralph Colwell, who have been waiting patiently in the wings to go on with Herb, look innocently at each other and begin their signature 'arguing routine' amongst themselves:

"Herb's dream? I thought this was your dream."

"I thought it was yours."

"Actually, I thought it was my dream!"

Then spontaneously, all four musical legends break into a comic version of Woody Guthrie's "This Land is Your Land," substituting their own ad-libbed lyrics...

"This dream is your dream, this dream is my dream
From the dreams that you dream, to the dreams that I dream
From the dreams that they dream, to the dreams that we dream
This dream was made for you and me."

Milking the reprise in slow, four-part harmony; Steve on guitar, Paul on mandolin, Ralph on his standup bass, and Herb at his magical xylophone, they croon together...

"For... you... and... me...!"

Without missing a beat, Herb sarcastically points his xylophone mallet in the direction of his life-long friends and musical collaborators and dryly intones, "See what I mean?"

Chapter 23

WAKE UP AND SMELL THE COFFEE

Suddenly, I'm awake... like in a natural chapter-break in one of those old novels I love to read again and again. I startle myself and inadvertently wake Jan in her theatre seat next to me. We must have fallen asleep, as her head was resting on my shoulder. I catch her sweet-smelling fragrance as she stirs next to me. Each of us still has an iPod earbud in our ear, the soft Hemi-Sync white-noise droning on in the background. I typically add soothing white-noise to the end of each musical selection I record because I usually nod off half-way through whatever I'm listening to. It seems to help me sleep better.

Jan stretches, provocatively, providing a precious moment to admire 'her charms,' as they would have been prudently described at the turn of the century. The earbud falls from her ear and bounces off her shoulder as she stretches. I quickly wrap the earphone wires around my iPod and place it into my vest pocket.

"Wow," Jan says, her blue eyes blinking in amazement, "I just had the strangest dream!"

"So did I," I start to say...

"And you were in it," she continues.

Jan's bubbling enthusiasm trumps my own fuzzy thoughts. So, I wait for her to tell her story.

"No, I mean you were really *in* my dream. And I was really *in* Up With People! I was singing and dancing. I was one of the featured dancers. And I was dancing, with you!"

Jan gazes longingly at the stage before us, as if her fleeting Up With People experience was still taking place... somewhere in time. A sweet combination of joy and disappointment crosses her face.

"It was so real." she says, gazing into nothingness. "Just as I imagined it would be...."

I stand and sympathetically take Jan's hand, relating to her pain. Indeed, I've had my own moments of heart-wrenching longing, that have haunted me over the years; wishing I was back on the road, under the lights, performing before an audience, large or small, in far-flung places, living with a new host-family every few days (most of them memorable and hard to leave, some of them challenging and hard to forget), sleeping in strange beds, bus-napping on long road-trips, living out of a suitcase and learning about life first-hand as it happens… like drinking water from a fire hose. Those were the days. The excitement and newness of it all. Waking each day to a bold, new adventure to be lived to its fullest.

Comically, in my own recurring dreams, the show is about to start and I can't find my pants anywhere. Although I was never late for the stage in real life, the residual anxiety seems to have stuck with me all these years.

I think about explaining my version of our seemingly-shared dream, but then, decide not to tread on the sweet afterglow of Jan's intimate reflections. Instead, I let her revel in the last vestiges of her precious reverie, as my tired brain struggles to catch up with my own circumstances.

Man, this Hemi-Sync© stuff can do some strange….

I check my pocket watch and find that we have slept for a much-needed two hours. Jan sees me checking the time and shifts back to reality.

"What time is it! Are we late…?"

"It's only two o'clock," I say, clearing the frog from my throat. "I don't think we've missed anything. Chris and Jane are most likely still filming down at the lighthouse."

Jan suddenly realizes I still have her hand in mine. Slowly, she lets her fingers to slide away, allowing a dreamy residue to linger between us.

Not wanting to share Jan with the rest of the world just yet, I interject, "Hey, they said they don't need us back at the hotel until dinner time. Why don't we sneak over to the lighthouse and watch Chris and Jane do their romantic scene together, just from a distance? It'll be fun to see them work alone; just the two of them, without any distractions."

My heart skips a beat, as Jan's face brightens with child-like excitement. Blinking the sleep from her eyes, she says,

"Why not? I can't think of a better way to spend the next few hours."

To my astonishment, she takes my hand again and pulls me up the theatre isle, bouncing with renewed vigor from our midday nap.

"Besides," she says on the run, "I want to see if they can pull it off with only four hours of sleep!"

We laugh and run together like children embarking on some glorious adventure.

After a brisk walk to Biddle's Point at the south end of the island, we are surprised to find there is no one there. No film crew, no equipment, or any sign they've been there yet. Just the picturesque red and white saltbox-style lighthouse gleaming in the afternoon sun.

Sporting a fresh coat of paint, the old lighthouse is actually located on the northern tip of Round Island, which is only a discus throw from the southern shore of Mackinac Island. The Round Island Light protects the shipping lanes in the Straits of Mackinac, as well as the island itself. Situated in the Hiawatha National Forest, the historic place brings to mind verdant visions of Henry Wadsworth Longfellow's "The Song of Hiawatha" and his epic tale of that great First Nation mediator, his epic adventures for peace, and his wife; his "Laughing Water," Minnehaha. "By the shore of Gitchie Gumee, By the shining Big-Sea-Water…" [where…]

> "… the heron, the Shuh-shuh-gah,
> From her haunts among the fen-
> lands,
> Screamed, "Farewell, O Hiawatha!"
> Thus departed Hiawatha,
> Hiawatha the Beloved,
> In the glory of the sunset,
> In the purple mists of evening,
> To the regions of the home-wind,
> Of the Northwest-Wind

> Keewaydin,
> To the Islands of the Blessed,
> To the Kingdom of Ponemah,
> To the Land of the Hereafter!"

("The Song of Hiawatha," Henry Wadsworth Longfellow © 1855)

Jan surveys the empty scene before us and is as perplexed as I am, crinkling her nose ever so slightly.

"Didn't they say they'd be filming the lighthouse scene next...?"

"That's what I heard." I assure her. "Looks like a last minute change of plans."

I attempt to ease her disappointment by adding,

"Like my brother says, movie-making is a 'hurry-up-and-wait' business."

Then with a little levity, I attempt to imitate Greggy's frenetic mannerisms and his abrupt, staccato-style speech:

"And just because it's on the call-sheet, don't mean it's going to be shot that way."

We both laugh, then pause to take in our picturesque surroundings. The smell of the lake fills our lungs, cutting through the brain-fog of our mid-day cat-nap.

"Hey, look!" I shout, running down to the beach.

"We could do our own scene! Here's the wooden boat."

I grab the varnished bow and lift it slightly, testing its seaworthiness. Jan reluctantly draws herself to the shore, as I continue my impromptu inspiration.

"Let's row out to the lighthouse and pretend the film crew is here, and we're the ones acting out the scene...."

Jan rejects my crazy proposal with a sideways smile and a dismissive wave of her hand.

"That'll be the day... you and I in a film together? I'm afraid it wouldn't be very interesting. Probably go straight to video just to break even. Besides, we don't even know what the scene's about? We haven't seen the script!"

Not wanting to let on that, like any good S.I.T. aficionado, I know the Somewhere In Time script by heart. And not wishing to allow such a small detail to dampen my enthusiasm, I grab the wooden-skiff and push it stern-first into the lake, enjoying my youthful strength again. Something I forgot I possessed, back in 1979.

"Don't worry... We'll make it up as we go!" I say, holding the bow of the boat as it floats in the shallow water. I doff my Panama hat and give a regal bow, continuing our whimsical fantasy.

"Your vessel awaits Madame...."

I extend an assisting hand to Jan with my best Christopher Reeve 'irresistible look' (like when he won't take no for an answer from the reluctant Elise McKenna). Jan acquiesces by taking my hand and steps elegantly into the skiff, striking a picture-perfect pose sitting at the stern.

Continuing our swashbuckling adventure, I shout a hearty "Heave-ho," sending the boat drifting backwards, almost tipping the shaky craft, and getting my boots wet in the process. Then, manning the stout wooden-oars, I lay my back into a few initial awkward strokes, turning the ship around and sending us on our way.

"Who knows," I say, glancing over my shoulder toward our intended course of travel. "Maybe we'll make it big on cable, like Somewhere in Time did!" I abruptly catch myself in mid-stroke, just as the words leave my mouth. I keep on rowing. I feel Jan's curious inquiry, even before she forms it on her lips.

"What do you mean? she says quizzically, from under the shade of her lace parasol. "The movie won't be released until next year."

I nonchalantly continue pulling at the oars, looking around, pretending to assess my bearings. But, Jan persists with a look of concern in her eyes.

"How do you know how well the movie is going to do... or not do?"

"Oh, well..." I stammer, stalling for a reasonable explanation to come to me....

"I just assume this small, romantic picture won't be the blockbuster that "Superman" was... that's all."

I attempt to divert her attention, by quickly glancing over my shoulder, feigning an earnest effort to keep the lighthouse in the general direction of our forward progress.

Jan is about to continue her line of questioning, when I add preemptively,

"And it stands to reason that the cable-tv audience would better appreciate this beautiful love-story."

With my vague explanation lingering in her mind, Jan thankfully lets the perplexing moment hang on the doldrums of the warm, summer air, while I continue the task at hand.

Gently, the peaceful beauty of our intimate surroundings washes over us, infusing our silence with a deep, reflective meaning. I notice that Jan is lost in her own significant reminiscences, mesmerized by the rhythm of the oars dipping into the lake. I find myself transfixed on her poetic figure... her luxurious fingers trailing on the surface of the water.

This could definitely be a dream, I think to myself. *Or a perfect, parallel reality.*

Whatever it is, I'm loving every perfect moment I can drink into my soul.

I allow myself a museful moment.

What if this were to become my new, permanent reality? A whole new life....

What if I am destined to live my life over again from this moment on? A middle-aged mind in a young man's body. What would I do differently? I hope I would do things differently, given the way things turned out the first time around. The opportunities missed, the wrong turns taken. But, I'm not completely confident I would make any better choices the second time around, or the third or fourth for that matter.

One thing is for sure. I won't be in such a hurry this time. If allowed to linger here in my past, I vow to concentrate on actually 'being here' this time. Caressing every thought, savoring every moment, taking each experience as it comes.

Then, as if I planned it perfectly, my final oar-stroke beaches us pleasantly on the sand of Round Island, not far from the lighthouse. Neither of us moves for a contented moment, collecting ourselves from the thought-provoking crossing.

I help Jan ashore and we walk the beach together, just like Richard and Elise; holding hands while we walk, thoroughly enjoying each other's company. As the mood presents itself, I lead her into role-playing one of the classic scenes from the movie.

Jan looks stunning in her movie costume, with her parasol and the blue sky behind her... and the deep-blue of the lake. So natural and so wonderful at the same time.

"Is it you?" Jan whispers with exaggerated diction, redeeming Jane Seymour's original, truncated line from the film (when Elise meets Richard for the first time). We both enjoyed watching Chris and Jane film those initial scenes in front of the hotel.

"Yes," I respond, in my best Richard Collier imitation.

"Yes, it is," I intone with impeccable timing, having watched the video in my middle-age existence so many times.

We sit together in front of the old lighthouse, like Chris and Jane will soon do for one of the film's famous publicity shots. These are the timeless, romantic scenes where Richard and Elise engage each other's heart and soul for one overwhelming purpose; to be together for this one moment in time.

Of course, Jan has no idea that our current reality closely parallels the movie script we are so innocently acting out.

I must find a way to tell her the truth... who I really am... where I have come from, and why I'm here.

The answer to the last question being something I hope Jan and I can work out together. Hopefully, she feels the same way I do.

If not, I am truly lost in time, without hope... or a way home.

As the sun leans toward the horizon, we seem to connect at a deeper level for the first time, feeling so comfortable in each other's presence. For the moment, time stands still. Nothing else matters, as Jan's eyes lock with mine with knowing approval and acceptance. We feel and say the same things, as our words swirl around us, confirming our deepest thoughts....

"Have you ever wished for more time to experience all that there is?" I begin.

Jan agrees, and adds, "Life seems much too short when you think about it."

"One minute you're born and grown, and still wondering what life's all about." I say.

"Then, you think you <u>know</u> and you take that path for a while." says Jan.

"The well-trodden one... the one with the brightly posted signs."

"Then, the road begins to bog down."

"So, you trudge another way, eventually losing your bearings altogether."

"And wonder if you'll ever find your way home."

"Or whether you want to go back at all."

"It's there, in that lonely place, you think, 'What have I done with my life?'"

"What do I have to show for it; all the hard work, the pain and pride?"

"Looking ahead, you only see more of the same, with nothing more promising on the horizon."

"So, you sit at the crossroads and take stock of things."

"And maybe for the first time...."

"You realize what you really need from life."

After volleying our thoughts back and forth, I take the lead, sharing my innermost feelings with Jan.

"I was there not long ago; at that crossroad. Not knowing which way to turn. Then, I came to Mackinac Island and found a different me. A whole new life. Wrapped in fantasy, with movie cameras and real life celebrities.

That's when I found you. You've shown me things I only dreamed of, but never knew existed. It seems I've known you forever... somewhere, deep inside. I don't want to go back. I don't want to lose what might have been. I don't know if there are answers to my feelings. But, I'm blessed to have found you to share them with."

With nothing more to say, I envelope Jan's shoulder in a sideways hug, leaning together, staring at the blue of the lake.

Finally, Jan sighs and asks, "What time is it?"

Reluctantly, I open my watch.

"Four twenty-five. I suppose we should be getting back...."

Before I can lift my eyes, I feel Jan's tender arms around my neck and her warm lips pressed to mine, embracing in a kiss from heaven.

I pull her to me and feel our bodies meet in a moment of indescribable ecstasy.

Where am I? Am I really holding her, kissing her welcoming lips, on this lost, summer isle?

In an instant she pulls away and dashes down the beach leaving my mind reeling. I pop back into my body from some unimaginable somewhere and scramble after her in the sand, grabbing her around the waist. We laugh and whirl together.

Then, hand in hand, we make our way to the boat and back to reality. Jan is married. And so am I... in another place and time. But, for this one moment, we have found each other. And now I know, neither of us would change that for the world.

Chapter 24

TIMELESS

Jan and I leisurely walk through the Hotel's main entrance, into the crowded lobby, and are surprised to see so many new faces. Everyone is milling about, attempting to look natural, as no doubt they've been instructed to do, evidently having recently been added to the pool of newbie extras.

Funny... no actual filming is taking place. The cameras and the lights aren't even set up yet.

I chuckle to Jan and say, "They must have recruited a new bunch of 'green' extras."

Considering ourselves now seasoned 'background actors,' we allow ourselves the privilege of watching the new group, while they attempt to recreate an authentic turn-of-the-century scene.

I am impressed though at the large number of people my brother and his cohorts have costumed and made-up during the short time that we were away.

I lean toward Jan, lowering my voice,

"Looks like they've been instructed to promenade the lobby, to get into the whole 1912-thing."

Jan grabs my arm and immediately falls into character.

"Well then, let's show them how it's done."

Smiling coyly, she adds,

"Perhaps, this time, we'll 'both' be picked for the best scene of the day."

Taking her good-natured ribbing in stride, I bow and reply in my best Richard Collier, "Shall we...?"

Jan locks my arm to her side.

"Let's..." she says, in her best 'Elise McKenna.'

Together, we stride into the posh world of 1912 Victorian society, dressed-to-the-nines, feeling like seasoned professionals, mingling with the amateur wanna-bees.

Glancing around the ornate lobby, I notice many of the old furnishings have been replaced with gorgeous period-pieces by the set designers for today's filming. If you didn't know better, you could easily imagine yourself back at the turn of the century.

Humorously, Jan and I check out some of the rather extreme-looking individuals who have been drafted for the evening's shooting. Most of them obvious 'locals,' dying for their first chance on the silver screen.

I compliment a rather plain-looking woman as she passes by on her "Exquisite hat," eliciting a nervous blush and a quick flutter from her ornate fan. Jan punches me with her lace-covered fist and retorts in a thick Victorian accent,

"Let's not over do it my dear!"

"How'd you like to wear one of those all day?" I whisper, directing Jan's attention to a particularly hefty woman negotiating the crowd with an outrageously large "bustle," comically bobbing to and fro behind her.

I dryly add with a straight face, "Looks like a Volkswagen trying to pass a cow in the middle of the road."

Jan erupts with laughter and instantly muffles her mouth with her gloved-hand, burying her dainty fist into my shoulder again in humorous agreement.

Until instructed otherwise, already knowing the drill, we join in the fun, pretending to be rich and married, just having arrived from 'The Hamptons' or 'Cape Cod,' after venturing west for adventure and romance.

I pretend Jan and I have known each other forever, predestined to share our lives and love from the beginning. I lose myself in Jan's elegant beauty, as she walks next to me holding my arm, as if we belong together.

I fancy myself the most envied man in the room.

Indeed, seeing the way these resident goons are staring at Jan, there's no doubt I am.

That's how I always feel when I'm with her... like when Richard Collier first gazes at Elise's portrait in the Grande Hotel's "Hall of History."

How can such a feeling of peace and fulfillment be anything but right?

Here we are, both married to other people in different places in time; Jan in 1979 and I in 2005, living completely separate lives, so far from each other.

But today, in our pretend movie moment, I couldn't be closer to anyone than I am to Jan right now. It's such an eternal feeling, not a fleeting fancy. A real, soulful place of rest. If I could, I'd will myself to stay in this alternate reality forever, sharing my happiness with Jan, in our own literal dream-come-true.

Seizing the moment, I stop in the middle of the crowded lobby, with everything moving around us, and take Jan by her delicate shoulders, drawing her blues eyes to mine. Intuitively, she seems to know my thoughts and only half-heartedly attempts to break our connection. I persist with unabashed affection exuding from my every pore. She pauses, allowing our emotions to mingle. I am flushed with feelings for her; deep, longing feelings of wanting to be together forever. Jan has inexplicably intrigued me from the first day we met, on this enchanted island so long ago.

I draw her to me softly, blocking out everything but her. I lean forward to quench myself in her delicious aura, as if her very being is calling me home; home from some long ago, arduous journey. I sense her welcoming my every intention, anticipating my deepest thoughts, as if they are her own.

Unable to dissuade my aching emotions any longer, I begin the sweet journey to her perfect lips like a forever-lover, returning from the quest of a lifetime. Then, as fate would have it, another reality intrudes on our eternal moment....

I feel a persistent tapping on my shoulder... like a rude suitor cutting-in on the last dance. I turn with a start to perceive a well-kempt, middle-aged gentleman, with a gold name-badge displaying the title: *"Mr. Biehl, front desk,"* sporting an affable smile and repeatedly calling my name….

"Mr. Hall? Oh Mr. Hall…? Please forgive me."

I blink and pretend not to skip a beat.

"Yes…?" I declare, through the blatant incongruence.

"It's so wonderful to see you again, Sir." Mr. Biehl continues apologetically, seemingly out of place, away from his station behind the registration desk.

"Welcome back to The Grand Hotel!" he announces, fawning over Jan and I for no apparent reason.

"Or should I say, 'welcome home again?'" he adds, smiling at Jan, and nodding with the familiarity of a family friend.

"I always say, it's never quite the same until our regular summer guests arrive to make this palace feel like home." Mr. Biehl enthusiastically shakes my hand and turns to kiss Jan's glove.

"Madame it's so nice to see you again."

The dapper gentleman then dutifully leads us to the registration desk.

Following his lead, Jan and I glance at each other, impressed with this well-seasoned actor's impeccable performance, seemingly for our sole benefit. I do wonder though, how he knows my name. I don't recall meeting him on the set. Perhaps we met and I forgot. Not too surprising, since I'm still operating under the handicap of my fallible, middle-aged brain. Either that or Greggy has put him up to it, as an 'inside' joke.

In any case, as "Mr. Biehl" continues his convincing act, pretending to resume his duties behind the registration desk, I think to myself,

Three can play at this game!

I didn't squander my meager tour-guide wages on all those acting classes for nothing.

With a nod to Jan, I playfully signal her to play along with the gag.

"Why uh, thank you Mr. Biehl." I say, jumping into the improvisational banter.

"I do hope you and yours have been well while we were away?"
Ah, yes, the projection, the tone, it's all coming back to me.
If only the gang could see me now....

It was the middle-seventies. A small cadre of working actors would gather weekly at the North Hollywood studio called, "The Performers," to hone their craft between jobs, or in my case between tours on Universal's back lot; just biding our time, waiting for fame and glory to catch up with us. We were a close-knit bunch of mostly unknowns at the time, along with some downright talented people; a few of whom were house-hold-names, or soon about to be.

Robert and Lorene ("Shields and Yarnell") had already starred in their own CBS prime-time variety show, having begun their careers as San Francisco street mimes. The glamorous Veronica Hamel would eventually garner multiple Emmy nominations as the intelligent, hard-driving, public-defender, "Joyce Davenport," on the long-running TV series "Hill Street Blues." The bright and spunky Dee Wallace would soon land the starring role as Elliot's mother in Steven Spielberg's classic film "E.T." And the old sage himself, Dennis Weaver, the Emmy Award-winning "Festus" from television's "Gunsmoke" (one of the highest-rated, longest-running, television series in U.S. history), could always be counted on to lend supportive praise and constructive criticism to his fledgling thespian colleagues.

Maybe I can find someone on the island with a camcorder... Not likely, I suppose, in 1979.

I pitch a knowing smile to Jan and encourage her to join in the impromptu conversation.

"Uh, yes... Mr. Biehl..." Jan adds. "How is Mrs. Biehl? I do hope we can have tea together soon?"

Mr. Biehl picks up on our free-flowing improvisation and further elaborates,

"She's quite well, thank you. She will be delighted to hear you've finally arrived. She will most assuredly want to pick up where you two left off last fall. Of course, she's as busy as ever, with her social groups and good causes. And of course, young "Arthur" over there has grown like a weed since you've last seen him."

Lowering his eyes to the guest register, Mr. Biehl rambles on as he works.

"Yes, indeed, five-years-old and as rambunctious as ever." He continues. "Now, let's see...."

Still smiling, Jan and I look at Mr. Biehl, as if something significant has clicked in our brains. We look at each other a bit flummoxed, marveling at Mr. Biehl's seemingly unrehearsed soliloquy. Jan and I simultaneously turn our heads in the direction of his imaginary "Arthur" and are instantly shocked to see a small boy holding a big, red ball, sitting alone on one of the large, over-stuffed chairs... looking bored and dejected.

Jan stars at me and I at her, with astonished faces of mutual disbelief. Turning again, we confirm the very real, young lad. Then back again to each other.

"Arthur?" we whisper in surprised unison.

Mr. Biehl returns to the desk with a room key, which he had retrieved from a wooden cubby on the back wall.

"Yes, the poor lad.... He has a hard time understanding that his father has an entire hotel to run... having been appointed the Hotel's new Trustee and all."

Mr. Biehl purposefully pauses, waiting for our anticipated surprise and belated congratulations.

Jan and I attempt to recover from our momentary skip in reality.

"Well, Mr. Biehl! Hotel Trustee! Our hearty congratulations!" I stammer, shaking his hand.

At the same time, I flashback to something another young 'Arthur' told me about his great-grandfather being cheated out of his rightful position as Trustee of the Grand Hotel.

"Yes, indeed!" Jan says, adding her perplexed congratulations.

"Thank you both," says Mr. Biehl, almost busting his vest buttons.

"It seems that my old railroad connections finally paid off after all these years."

"I do try to keep Arthur out from under the guest's feet and all," Mr. Biehl continues, showing his concern for the young boy.

"It's been a particularly harsh winter here on the island and the little ruffian has been cooped up for most of it. But, now our regular guests are starting to arrive, and everything will be getting back to normal. Arthur is so looking forward to playing with his young friends again."

"It is good to see you again.... Oh, and I apologize for not having your room ready when you first arrived. I almost gave it to a dashing young chap a few minutes ago. Thankfully, my assistant keeps me in line. I trust your afternoon stroll wasn't too inconvenient after your long journey?"

Jan and I direct our dumbfounded expressions to the gold room key that Mr. Biehl is extending to us with pride. *"Room 420...."*

"Your telegram was delayed at the station for some reason. But, I took the liberty of holding your annual reservation anyway... figuring you'd be here on your usual arrival date. I think you'll find everything is in order."

I smile at Mr. Biehl and take the room key, not knowing what to do next, like a flummoxed improve actor fresh out of ideas.

Then Jan seems to have an idea.

"Thank you Mr. Biehl," she says, taking the room key from me.

"By the way," she continues. "May we look at the guest register, to see if our other friends have arrived yet?"

"Oh, by all means, please do," says Mr. Biehl.

He turns the ornate register around and flips back a few pages for our perusal.

"You'll be surprised to see that Dr. and Mrs. Johns have arrived ahead of you this year. They'll be pleased to know you're here."

Mr. Biehl's stunning remark sends a shiver up my spine.

Doctors David and Amanda Johns? Now this is getting way too weird... even for me to handle.

"Oh my!" Mr. Biehl catches himself.

"I almost forgot the most exciting news of all! Miss Elise McKenna is here at the hotel! She and her theatrical troupe are debuting a new production at the theatre this very weekend. I'm hoping the Mrs. and I can break away for at least one performance. Perhaps we'll see you there."

As Mr. Biehl turns to attend to some administrative duties, Jan and I gaze at each other in utter disbelief, attempting to shake the cobwebs from our brains. For an instant, I rationalize this must be a continuation of Jan's dream, which I am obviously still be participating in. That's it. Jan shared my iPod back at the theatre, and the Hemi-Sync white noise….

But, how can I be so lucid and aware, in someone else's dream?

Completely dumbfounded, I watch as Jan runs a gloved finger down the flowery ink signatures on the Hotel's guest register, noting their corresponding checking-in dates and times. Then, in amazement, she pauses at a bright and elegant signature purporting to be the one and only "Elise McKenna!" Beneath that, I note the no-nonsense script of one "E.W. Robinson." With further bewilderment, Jan's finger continues and then stops at the signature of one "Richard Collier, Chicago, Ill, June 21, 1912, 9:18am, Room 416."

Jan searches my eyes with an expression I instantly recognize as my very own, the first time I inadvertently side-slipped through time and attempted to make sense of it all. I extend to her whatever moral support I can muster, being grateful at least we are still together, wherever this particular 'here' happens to be.

Wait a minute! I struggle to regain my senses. This has got to be some very clever joke! Someone, probably my crazy brother, has borrowed the movie-prop 'Hotel register' and put this obviously seasoned actor, "Mr. Biehl," up to the whole thing. Funny though, I don't remember being the butt of such a creative prank back in 1979. At least not the first 1979! And what about little "Arthur" over there, and his big, red ball?

Jan then turns the heavy parchment page to reveal the most current guests listed on the register. Abruptly, her fingers stop at the third-to-the-last entry. I watch, as the color quickly drains from her rosy cheeks. Jan's clear, blue eyes turn saucer-like. Groping for emotional footing, she directs my focus to where her finger is pointing. There, on the parchment page, I read for myself,

"Mr. and Mrs. Charles W. Hall, June 21, 1912, 9:32am, Room 420."

My jaw drops in disbelief!

Jan quickly muffles my contemplated expletive with her gloved hand. I notice that the strange entry is written in a delicate hand that I don't recognize. My baffled confusion turns to amazement, when Jan whispers with a confirming nod,

"That is my handwriting!"

I gulp at her bewildered confession. Then, I tentatively add my own.

"I'm related to a Charles Wesley Hall... I think he's my great-grandfather!"

As our flabbergasted realizations collide head-on, the entire scene is cut short by the rapid approach of what appear to be two overly excited children, competing for our attention. To compound our confusion, the oncoming cacophony rushes straight toward us, and we are confronted by a surreal, youthful chorus, clearly out of breath.

"Mother! Oh mother?"

"Father, father!"

Stopping abruptly before us, crashing directly into our mutual dream, a strapping, young boy in turn-of-the-century garb, approximately ten years old, and a prim and proper young woman, perhaps thirteen, both address us as if attempting to force some unknown connection. Disheveled and gasping for air, the obvious siblings impatiently speak over one another.

"Mother, can we go to the stables and see the horses first?"

"I want to go swimming first, like we always do!" the young man interjects. "Please father?"

Over her brother's objections the young girl continues,

"Oh Mother, you should see the flowers!"

"There are flowers at the beach!" the lad protests.

"And the butterfly house! We must go there next!" says the girl.

"I'll not wade in past my waist. I promise!" the boy emphatically states.

Jan and I are completely overwhelmed at being so intimately accosted by these wayward refugees from some episode of Laura Ingalls Wilder's "Little House on the Prairie." Either they are giving Academy-Award-caliber performances or somehow, they actually mistake us for their parents.

Just as my middle-aged brain is about to burst from its way too crowded, youthful head, lost somewhere between 2005 and 1979, which has now inexplicably morphed to the early nineteen hundreds, the young boy looks straight into my eyes and says,

"Father, the canon at Fort Mackinac are not nearly the caliber that yours were at West Point!"

His sincere statement and the pride with which he delivered this proclamation, stops me cold at the sheer coincidence. My own great-grandfather supposedly attended the United States Military Academy, sometime around the turn of the twentieth century… at West Point! If I recall correctly, family legend has it he played football for The Army and went on to become an electrical engineer.

My searching eyes meet the lad's innocent gaze and a momentary glimpse of genetic recognition flashes between us. Prompted by something totally unknowable, I hold the boy's stout shoulders squarely before me. And almost inadvertently, I address him, "Charles…?"

The handsome child smiles and cocks his head in a manner that wells unmistakably from the Hall family gene pool, and replies quizzically, "Yes, Father…?"

I am suddenly overwhelmed with a rush of significance that flushes my face and dashes to my palpitating heart. Somehow, someway, I am beholding the perfectly youthful version of my very own grandfather… Charles Lindley Hall… the son of Charles Wesley Hall. Here in the flesh! And looking remarkably like me at the same age. The blatant juxtaposition shatters my already weakened psyche.

Am I actually witnessing the juvenile version of my own "Grandpa Charles…" that three-hundred-pound, gentle-giant, who served over thirty years in the Washington State Patrol?

Completely overwhelmed at the revelation, real or not, I grab the boy and wrap him in my arms. Young Charles eagerly accepts my embrace and pats me tenderly on the back with his small, but 'large-for-his-age,' hand.

"I love you father." the young lad whispers from somewhere beyond eternity.

I sigh in response, my voice lodged firmly in my throat, and choke out, "I love you too son."

Jan and the young girl silently witness our tender moment, which outwardly, looks like a meaningful embrace between a father and his son. But which, in reality… as far as reality goes… is something much more amazing and mind-bending.

I release the boy slowly and the young girl, misty-eyed with her own emotion, rushes to me with outstretched arms.

"Oh Daddy, I love you too!" she says. "Thank you for bringing us back to Mackinac Island."

I fight to control these unknown emotions exploding within me, realizing this young beauty must be my grand-aunt "Margaret," my grandfather's only sister, whom I have only seen in ancient family-photos and never known much about. I can only accomplish a faint response, "Maggie, dear Maggie…."

As young girl leaves my embrace, I'm astonished to see that Jan is flashing on some poignant recognition of her own. Taking the young girl's hands in her own, and looking deep into her bright, blue eyes… so similar to her own… she says, "Margaret Delilah Hall… what a lovely name for such a lovely girl."

"Thank you mother," the girl replies, with the foretelling grace of the remarkable woman she is destined to become. Then, as they embrace, like mothers and daughters do, I watch, touched to the core, as Jan's soul is blessed, as if by a kiss from heaven.

This is all too bizarre. But, the pieces seem to fit together so snuggly. Like a giant, multi-generational jigsaw puzzle of intertwining lives and times. Could it be that Jan's and my own genealogies sprout from an identical branch of the same family tree? Is this young girl simultaneously my grand-aunt and Jan's grand-mother? That Jan and I are intimately related through the blood of our great-grandparents?

How utterly unbelievable! And at the same time, so seemingly familiar in a strange way... like a reoccurring dream you can't quite remember.

Young Maggie clings to Jan's motherly embrace, not wishing to let go.

"I love you so much Mother." she says, with complete surrender.

Jan allows herself the moment, feeling the heart of her own, not so-distant, flesh-and-blood, in her very arms.

Not to be left out, young Charles buries his face between both of them, joining their sweet embrace.

Jan holds them tight and whispers, "I love you both so much."

Watching their tender scene, my own expanding consciousness blooms like a mushroom cloud before me.

Jan and I are related through the marriage of our great-grandparents!

What are the chances that such a thing could happen? That my life-long crush on someone I've only known for a few short weeks (if you add up our times together), who's loving memory I've so diligently kept in my heart all these years... turns out to be so intimately connected to my own life? But then, as I've so often experienced again and again, reality is not as clear as it appears to be. Mere coincidence and synchronicity are apparently not rare aberrations after all... but natural, recurring expressions of some universal law of attraction and repulsion... routinely affecting us all, whether we know it or not.

Thus, everything must have significance... and therefore, consequences? How can one live a life of boring anonymity after such a mind-blowing epiphany? That we are all connected somehow; people... realities... Universes...! *My God, I must be going mad.... I have definitely been thinking way too small!*

Just then, another mysterious puzzle-piece presents itself, seemingly out of nowhere.... A young, strikingly beautiful, Asian woman, also out of breath, rushes to us, pleading in perfectly enunciated English, betraying a distinctly ivy-league education,

"Mr. and Mrs. Hall... I am so sorry!"

Slight, but well-proportioned, with a small boy in tow, who displays both Asian and apparently Caucasian features, the woman is dressed in the stylish uniform of an upper-class domestic helper. Self-consciously adjusting the mother-of-pearl combs, which keep her long, shiny-black hair up in style, she attempts to regain her composure.

"As usual, I have had some difficulty keeping up with the children." Then addressing Maggie and Charles directly, she admonishes...

"Young ladies and gentlemen do not run in public places without proper reason! And not wishing to follow your Nannies' admonishments is hardly a proper reason. Especially since young Lewis here (alluding to the smaller boy at her side) has not yet developed your gazelle-like speed. Something, I fear I will also find challenging in time."

The woman dutifully straightens her disheveled uniform and continues addressing all three children.

"And if neither of you wish to conduct yourselves in a proper manner on the hotel premises, I suggest the bridles in the stable could be employed for a more practical purpose."

Charles, Maggie and the little one then burst into giggles of laughter, as the young nanny re-establishes her evident authority over them with her sharp-witted humor.

Maggie, the oldest, instinctively leans forward and gives the young woman an endearing hug.

"Oh Sophie, we do love you. Don't we Charles? We're just so excited to be back on Mackinac Island."

Young Charles grabs Sophie's free hand with a confirming, "Of course we do... especially your Chinese cooking!"

The young woman is taken aback by the children's unabashed display of affection towards her. Quick to forgive, she gathers them into her arms, fighting back her tender emotions. Completing the touching scene, the diminutive lad with the intriguing features, chimes in,

"I love you too Mommy!"

The young Nanny struggles to regain her composure, instinctively primping and rearranging her youthful charges.

"Look at you... all mussed and fussed. There's something awry with each one of you, I do declare."

Jan and I, grasp for each other's emotional support. Having witnessed yet another strange reality played out before our very eyes, we attempt to defrag our brains and understand this latest thread of consciousness, which has surprisingly presented itself.

Jan, displaying her characteristic aplomb and lightning-fast intuition, is the first to take the leap in her new role as the de facto mother of this unexpected family and the evident employer of the bright, young nanny.

"Well...," says Jan, forcing a tone of confidence. "Uh... Sophie? Children? Let's hurry along now. There's much to see! And... all day to see it!"

Jan instinctively herds everyone through the lobby in the direction of hotel's front entrance, periodically glancing to me for emotional stability. Not knowing what to say, I stall for a few moments alone to sort things out.

"Uh, yes... Sophie? Why don't you take the children and enjoy the view on the promenade porch? And uh, we will join you momentarily. I have a small matter to take care of at the registration desk."

"As you wish Sir," Sophie acquiesces, with a dutiful smile.

"Yes, thank you..." Jan says, ushering the children along.

"Now children," Sophie entrains, as she proceeds through the crowded lobby.

"Lewis, please hold my hand. Let's stay together, and no bolting off again."

Sophie and the children gaggle off out of earshot and I grab Jan's arm, briskly walking her back to the front desk to scrutinize the hotel registration book again. This time I run my own fingers down the last page of names, dates and check-in times, stopping to confirm Jan's beautiful handwriting and our names listed as "Mr. and Mrs. Charles W. Hall," registered to Room 420.

Jan suddenly gasps at the next listing, as my finger runs the length of what is written below our entry, in a different flowery script:

"Miss Sophie Wang and son Lewis, Nanny to Charles & Margaret Hall, June 21, 1912, 9:33am Room 418."

The remainder of our day blurs in a rush of juxtaposed emotions, ranging from uneasy trepidation to cautious jubilation. Jan and I find ourselves becoming acquainted with our own, youthful grandparents, from the confusing, yet revealing, perspective of our respective great-grandparents. We accumulate more details about our co-mingled genealogy in the space of a few short hours than either of us had known our entire lifetimes.

Together, as a family, with "Nanna Sophie" lending her devoted support, we thoroughly enjoy what we discover is a long-standing Hall-family tradition; the annual summer retreat to Mackinac Island. Joyfully, we partake in the traditional fun-filled activities of typical island vacationers. We sing together on a brisk buggy-ride along the shoreline. We visit the magical butterfly house. And sit for a family photo at the local portrait studio. Then, a leisurely bicycle-tour, spending a much-needed, relaxing afternoon on the beach, sharing box lunches and gourmet fudge, watching the children splash in the water to their hearts content.

It is all pure nostalgia for me, watching the children play, seeing them enjoy their every waking moment. It seems only yesterday, that I was living my own carefree 'Tom Sawyer' life; those dawn-to-dusk serial-adventures that ran merrily into days and weeks, living multiple lifetimes on faraway shores (or planets), as time flowed slowly in my youthful, summertime world.

'Grown-up time' moves much more quickly, compared to those lazy, sun-dial days of bare-feet and freckles, doing the things children do, exploring the places children explore, even if only just around the block.

The possibilities were endless then, as neighborhood 'sidekicks' gathered daily from their fortresses and castles down the street, perpetuating the fabled legends and odysseys of old, on foreign battlefields, with legions of green-plastic soldiers, vehicles and field-artillery, and brave landings on lonely, pockmarked beaches, against columns of enemy forces, against overwhelming odds... each heroic campaign as close as our own backyards, or the vacant lot next door.

With the aid of our collective imaginations, our glorious adventures to exotic places seemed to last forever-and-a-day before we were finally called, whistled, or hollered-in at twilight, for milk and cookies, to "brush-flush-and-p.j.'s," and hop in bed.

Today, Jan and the children have brought it all back to me; those timeless dog-days of childhood. It seems we have crammed an entire lifetime into one glorious, sun-drenched day. In the quieter moments, we agree that our present condition is like jumping into a full-blown relationship, with its history and traditions and baggage on the very first date. Even more amazing, we take to our newly acquired roles, as husband and wife, and mother and father, as naturally as a cool, summer breeze.

The contentment is so palatable it touches our hearts. We sense a 'foreverness' about the day; something that has always been there, even though it couldn't have been. At least not in the previous reality we have just slipped from. Subconsciously, we sense a connection that underlies our very souls. How can anyone explain the timeless attraction that binds us to those special souls we have such an unknowing familiarity with? Whatever the answer and wherever the source, Jan and I have tapped into it and find ourselves content to drink our fill, slaking ourselves with each other's essence.

That evening, after attending the opening night of Elise McKenna's new theatrical production, with Sophie and the children fast asleep in the suite next door, Jan and I slip like newlyweds into our dimly lit room... finally alone, together.

Jan is more talkative than I, and continues to bubble with enthusiastic praise for Elise McKenna and Richard Collier, and Elise's romantic, ad-libbed dialogue, professing her undying love for Richard, in the final scene of the First Act.

I can only focus on Jan's mesmerizing beauty, not wanting to hide my affections for her any longer. I struggle with my cuff links, while Jan automatically begins her nighttime routine, unpinning, then brushing her luxurious, golden hair, continuing to critique the evening's performance.

"Wasn't it just perfect, the way Elise shuns the rich, old banker for her one true-love? You and I were the only ones who truly understood her ad-libbed lines in the First Act... along with Richard of course. And actually seeing him there, just a few seats away, watching him drinking in her every word. It was so romantic! I can't believe we were actually <u>there</u>, together... you and I."

Jan finally settles into our intimate moment together, catching her breath as our eyes meet for the first time, alone... as husband and wife.

"I can't believe we are actually <u>here</u> together, you and I," I say. Jan melds her presence with mine, taking the moment as our own, relishing it as it approaches. As she undresses before me with patient expectation, I am determined not to take my eyes off her enchanting beauty. I lay my pocket-watch on the bureau, letting its gold chain fall in a mound. Inadvertently, the fob lands on the watch cover and flips it open. Instinctively, I glance at the time... 11:18pm. I reach to close it, when something catches my eye that I've never noticed before.

There, under the ornate watch-cover, an inside edge has sprung away from under the molded lid, revealing a hinged compartment thin enough to hold a small photograph for safekeeping. This is the first time I've noticed this secret feature since the watch was passed down to me from my great-grand-father.

My momentary curiosity distracts me from Jan's enticing charms and prompts me to examine it more closely. Seeing my diverted attention, Jan observes me quizzically, as I follow the intruding impulse.

Pulling open the hidden compartment, I turn the watch to catch the rays of moonlight streaming in through the window. There, revealed in a moonbeam, is a miniature tintype photograph, partially obscured by decades of dust and grime. I wipe the photo with my handkerchief and am delighted to find the portrait of a young couple in turn-of-the-century dress, which I assume I must be related to from my generational past. I struggle to make out their faces, bringing the watch closer to share with Jan. As we focus for more detail, an unfathomable shock hits us both at the same time, swirling ethereally around us.

There, in miniature detail... undeniably ancient from generations of wuthering of time... is the very same portrait that Jan and I sat for earlier today...! On a whim, we had our own photograph taken after the family portrait and Sophie and the children... just the two of us... for posterity.... Little did we know, we were living that posterity with every breath we took.

Just then, like stardust from heaven, the startling truth resonates within our souls, striking us speechless.... Then, I notice something else; something additionally amazing and unbelievable. There, above the photo, etched onto the inside cover of the watch... where it can only be seen while looking at the photo... reads the phrase, engraved in gold script... echoing hauntingly from the past....

"As Time Allows."

Slipping into each other's arms, we share the most indescribable, embracing kiss... confirming everything we have held in our hearts for so long... that somehow, someway, we are meant to be together.

Just then, in a glorious streak of gold, a beautiful shooting star paints the night with a burning, regal arc over the lake... marking our timeless, forever moment.

Chapter 25

WAVES UPON THE SHORE

Jan is so entrancing, lying next to me, her skin glowing in the moonlight that filters through the lace curtains. For me she is a healing; a purging of some long-held debt I had carelessly accumulated during my haphazard life, or lifetimes; the cancelling of a debt with accumulating interest at a usurious rate. She is my reconciliation to everything I have been estranged from for so long.

Holding each other, with the stars blinking above us, we share deep feelings and old thoughts, about life and love… and us.

"What did you wish for?" I ask. "On that falling star…"

"What did you wish for?" Jan returns, coyly.

"That this moment would last forever…" I say. "Here with you, in this enchanted place."

Jan pauses a moment, then decides to share everything.

"I wished the same thing I wished when I saw the first shooting star, flying in Chris' plane."

"Yes…?" I say, waiting.

"To have the courage to follow my heart."

She contemplates her own thought… acknowledging in silence that her wish, and vicariously mine, has come true.

"And so we have…" I say for both of us.

I then lend voice to something that has been puzzling me all day; something that I'm sure Jan has been curious about as well. I mention how strange it is that Sophie's young son, Lewis, shares so many characteristics and mannerisms with Charles and Maggie. Even though they're not related, they act and play together so naturally, like siblings.

Having once been uttered, the vague confession lays silently between us… lingering, as it blooms into its own reality….

"Oh my God," I gasp, with astonished revelation.

"Did my great-grandfather have an affair with young Sophie?"

Such a thing would have been scandalous in the Victorian culture of 1912.

Jan gazes at me... knowingly, but chooses not to interrupt my rising epiphany. I continue to verbalize the swiftly approaching thoughts with dumbfounded amazement.

"Historically, an unwed mother and her unborn child would have been sent away, to live a completely separate life!" I surmise.

Breathing as one, we lay in each other's arms, contemplating the meaning of it all.

Finally, Jan gives form and substance to the words that must be said, to complete the timeless parable.

"Perhaps, there is something to be learned from whatever happened between your great-grandfather and Sophie."

The wisdom of the ages seems to flow from Jan's heart, as she becomes the messenger of the only truth that can reconcile my conflicted feelings. My heart melts at her loving kindness... for me, and for my family's' unspoken, secret legacy.

As I come to the clumsy rationalization of what may have happened between Charles Wesley Hall and Sophie Wang, Jan adds further pearls of wisdom that I need to hear.

"Perhaps in the grand scheme of things, life's little indiscretions are used for some positive purpose. Maybe, the important question is, 'What can you learn from knowing the truth?'"

Her probing words prick at my heart. I have never contemplated such a question, about this or any other issue of real-life importance. Indeed, who has ever cared that I gleaned any significance at all, from life's periodic bumps and bruises, small or otherwise. The stunning realization of the lack of emotional analysis in my own life wrenches my gut, filling my eyes with timeless tears.

I perceive Jan with as much gratitude as one person could ever have for another. I stammer to verbalize my thoughts, as they flow from some unknown source.

"Sometimes, I think life just happens, and you can't control it. You react to whatever comes your way and make the best of things. It's so hard to do the right thing. We all have flaws that keep us humble. But, the most important thing is to acknowledge your own actions and take responsibility for them."

Suddenly, my own words hit me like a ton of bricks, with eternal importance.

When was the last time I apologized for anything?

Or really forgave someone for some perceived wrong done to me. Let alone, actually forgiven myself? Not that I have many apologizes owing. Or do I...?

What about that time I verbally lashed out at my own daughter with sarcasm that cut her to the quick? Or when I inadvertently ignore my son's emotional needs. And those tired, old 'nagging-wife' jokes I relish repeating in front of dinner guests.

If I am truly honest with myself, I must admit, I generally put myself before others. Especially, when no one's keeping score. If I had to apologize for each of my acts of self-centeredness, I'd need another lifetime to accomplish the task.

I gaze into Jan's shining, blue eyes; eyes that reflect so much love and compassion, and let these mind-altering realizations wash over me in cleansing waves of reconciliation.

Suddenly, I am no longer conflicted. An eternal peace presents itself to me like a calming balm, integrating my past, present and future... in this dimension, and every other.

It's as if everything is connected, somehow, someway... everything and everyone!

I now see Jan with the eternal perspective of a man who has both loved her and cheated her, but needs her more than life itself. Carefully, I form the redeeming words to enunciate the timeless confession that erupts from my soul. I whisper to her, and to everything she represents....

"I am so sorry... I have treated you unconscionably. Will you please forgive me?"

A deep sorrow bursts forth from my very essence, as I lose myself in Jan's loving arms, sobbing in broken, contrite, repentance.

Jan holds me and kisses me... and forgives me, with the mercy of the ages, and her timeless, everlasting love.

By accepting my earnest apology in her heart, as if directly from my great-grandfather to her great-grandmother, through the generations, Jan has set me free to really love her. To love her unconditionally, and healing my mid-life-crises at the same time. It's as if the cynical attitude I've had for my perplexing situation and my uncertain future has been dissolved. Through Jan's loving guidance, and my belated atoning for the past, my transgressions and, vicariously, everything that I represent, has been set free!

It must be a universal law; that every woman (and consequently, all that is good and positive) deserves a sincere, heartfelt apology, and every man (and conversely, all that is dark and negative) simply needs to be forgiven.

And so it is that a simple apology from the heart has settled the score for a major wrong that time forgot, but had begrudgingly never forgiven. The unresolved iniquity that had visited itself upon the third and fourth generations of my family, and manifested itself in my own mid-life crisis, has now been released.

Jan's uncanny perception and forgiving heart has lifted the burden of my lifetime of accumulated offenses. And for the first time, I know who I really am and who I want to be. I want to be me!

I don't need to be anyone else or anyone else's version of me. I now realize I am not very good at being someone else. And I am determined to celebrate every moment of this unique 'here and now,' as if it were my last... and best!

A light, airy feeling washes over me, as if a shadow has been lifted from my soul, illuminating a new hope; that perhaps, I haven't messed my life up as much as I feared. The slow realization warms to me...

Today is, indeed, the first day of the rest of my life!

I gaze at Jan and think of our new life together, here in this place and time; this somewhere that has caught our future selves in vague shadows and lingering thoughts, which eventually drew us back to one another. We have participated in the healing that neither of us knew needed healing. Like a gentle, but persistent whisper through the ages, it settled onto my middle-age consciousness, until it was properly acknowledged, recompensed and released by someone, anyone, but this time by Jan and I.

I might have shrugged it off as a necessary stage in the aging process. But fortunately, through the enduring love of Janice Parker Flannery, my mid-life-correction has mediated a loving ripple-effect through our entire family tree, from generation to generation, heart to heart, through time and space and beyond.

I am now ready to live my life to the fullest, here and now, with Jan. Fulfilling that strange longing I felt on the first day we met, this new life, which began as an unexpected, confusing, detour from my desolate, mirage-ladened life-path, has become a glorious short-cut to a more meaningful life. Now that I've seen the road map, with its infinite intersecting routes and alternate, meandering by-ways, I realize we are all connected and that the choices we make affect us all.

Jan stirs in my arms and shares a dream she just had about our life together; the good times and the bad, the great and small things we shared together. I look into her sparkling eyes with as much love as I have felt for anyone.

"How do we do together, you and me?" I ask.

She smiles and pauses... as if to savor her newly revealed life-review.

"We do well," she replies, with an eternal satisfaction in her eyes.

"We do very well. And so do our children and their children and so on. Yes... we do very well."

We kiss again, and she holds me, and I hold her... for the last time.

All at once, the illuminating moonlight grows dim, and ominous storm-clouds roll over the lake. Jan is alarmed and reads the concern on my face.

"Michael.... What is wrong? What's happening?"

The room begins to swirl around us... the bed starts to spin. Instinctively, I reach for my iPod on the bed stand.

"We've gone too long..." I say, fumbling for the iPod, inadvertently knocking it to the floor. Then, the last vestiges of light fade from the room, and I realize... *"It's too late!"*

"Michael...!" I hear Jan's frantic voice. I watch helplessly, as her timeless image fades from my perception... disappearing like water into a thirsty, desolate ground.

"I love you...!" are the last words I hear, as I grasp at nothingness, and reality slips away.

I feel myself dying, rushing, paralyzed in a vibrating buzz, through a hazy space, like a tumbleweed whirling before a storm. I hold fast in my mind to the last image of my beloved Jan... reaching out for me... piercing my heart with her desperate cries for me to return.

Juxtaposed, I see young Charles and Maggie smiling, as I streak through the fog. Then, Sophie and her young son, Lewis, waving as if in a dream. Strange, the lad is listening to my iPod, with the wisdom of the ages in his eyes.

Uncontrollably, I race toward a brilliance that dominates everything, for what seem both an eternity and a nano-second. Then abruptly... it's over.

Chapter 26

TIME STILL RETURNS

With a fearful, pounding heart, my eyes flutter open.... Disjointed and confused, I find myself standing at the quaint, Mackinac Island ferry dock in the cool, autumn sun... embracing the lovely, now mature again, Jan Flannery! Settling into my middle-aged bones, pulling on those old aches and pains, I step back and behold her fondly, as the sad, but fulfilled, realization comes to us both....

We are back where we began, apparently at the end of the "Somewhere In Time weekend," in the fall of 2005. A few S.I.T. stragglers hurry past us with their luggage to board the last ferry to the mainland before the Grand Hotel closes for the winter season. A blustery, October wind grazes my thinning hair.

Jan and I stand, holding each other's hands, speechless, like children at the end of something wonderful, acknowledging with our eyes the eternal love and admiration we have for each other. A love that transcends time and space.

Jan is radiant, even with the gentle passing of time. I am crestfallen, but somehow, strangely satisfied, and truly touched by what we have shared, and what Jan has done for me. Now I know, no matter what the future brings, our lives will forever be connected by the two most powerful gifts of all... 'Love and Forgiveness.'

Jan gently draws us back to ourselves....

"Well... did you find what you came to Mackinac Island searching for?

"Yes... I most certainly did," I hear myself say.

"And with your help, I've discovered many more things, most of which I was totally unaware. I only hope we didn't do anything our great-grandchildren will have to deal with in generations to come."

Jan smiles, as she accepts her own middle-aged self again.

"By then, they'll have a complete cure for the mid-life crisis." she says, then adds,

"Besides, being grateful for what we have... and had... is the most important thing."

"That, and sharing it with those we love," I say.

Suddenly, someone rushes toward us calling my name....

"Mr. Hall...! Mr. Hall! Uh, Michael!"

I turn and see Arthur, the young hotel bell-boy, running up, lugging what appears to be his worldly possessions in an old, leather suitcase and backpack, obviously, heading for the mainland.

"Art!" is all I have a chance to say, before he begins an excited recitation between attempts at catching his breath.

"I'm so glad I ran into you... I've been looking for you!"

The young man drops his load at our feet.

"Hello Jan," he says. "The Somewhere in Time weekend was a great hit again, as usual... great turnout this year."

"Thank you Art," Jan graciously replies.

Art then continues his address to me....

"After you told me about the 'Rule Against Perpetuities,' I did some research. You were right! My grandfather, Arthur, was actually conceived within the statutory time limit to qualify him to succeed his father as the Managing Trustee of the Hotel! He was a 'life in being' before the Rule Against Perpetuities kicked in. According to the language of the Trust, he should have taken over his father's position as Trustee when he turned twenty-one!

I ran the whole thing past a lawyer friend of mine in Cheboygan. He threatened to sue the Board of Trustees if they didn't settle with me, as my grandfather's only known heir.

"So..." Art pauses, as he draws out the anticipation.

"So...?" I say, waiting for the bottom line.

"I'm off to Harvard Law School!"

Art can barely contain himself, as he gives me and Jan bone-crushing hugs, including us in his impromptu celebration.

"Oh my word!" Jan says, in astonishment.

"Well... congratulations!" I blurt out, totally non-plussed and amazed.

"It turns out one of the trustees has connections at Harvard. They agreed to pay for everything; room, board, tuition, the works! As long as I can hack it...."

"Oh, I have a feeling, with your innate intelligence and enthusiasm for life, you'll do just fine." I say.

"Your grandfather would be very proud of you."

Our celebration is cut short by the blasting of the ferry's departure-horn.

Art quickly gathers his things, then takes one last moment to extend his youthful hand in gratitude.

"It wouldn't have happened, if it weren't for you. Thank you for the Rule Against Perpetuities... on behalf of Arthur."

I shake his grateful hand.

"Don't thank me... thank your great-grand-parents for conceiving Arthur on time," I add, with deflecting humor and a wink to Jan.

"You're going to make a great lawyer," Jan says, giving him another farewell hug.

"Just like someone else I know...." Jan smiles at me, then back at Arthur.

We wish him well, as he rushes to board the ferry.

"Carpe diem!" I yell after him, as he strides away.

Arthur spins around with a questioning look.

"What's carpe diem?"

"Seize the day!" I translate, with my fist raised, in gonzo-style solidarity.

"Carpe diem!" Arthur throws back, with his own celebratory fist of victory.

Jan then turns to me in what we both realize must be our own, fond farewell.

How do you say goodbye to someone who has become such an important part of your life? Not only since that first magical summer in 1979, but for what feels like an entire lifetime... even generations and more.

For a long, precious moment we put off what we must do.

Jan takes my hand, and to my surprise, she places my great-grandfather's gold pocket-watch, with its chain and fob, into the palm of my hand, closing my fingers around it with her own. Then, mimicking the elderly Elise McKenna to the young Richard Collier, at the beginning of the Somewhere In Time movie, she whispers, sweetly...

"Come back to me...."

This time Jan's plea is not from a treasured lover at the end of her life. But rather, as a rhetorical question, between forever friends... who already know what the answer must be.

I open the watches secret compartment to reveal our ancient, time-worn portrait and the precious inscription inside. I turn it to share with Jan one last time.

"As Time Allows..." she says.

"As Time Allows..." I smile.

I re-clasp the watch and place it in the chest pocket of my motorcycle jacket, next to my heart.

The earthy smells of autumn rush to us in the wind. We gaze into each other's forever eyes, and embrace in a long, all-encompassing kiss. Then, I turn to leave....

"See you up the road," I say, kicking my cycle to life.

"I'll be there," Jan says, with eternal optimism.

"Make sure you stop to pick me up." she adds, over the revving throttle.

"Where "The Roads Come Together," I say, quoting the old 'Up With People' song.

"Up The Way...." she adds, finishing the line to herself, as I pull away.

I roll onto the Mackinac Island ferry, conflicted, with a heavy heart and soaring spirit, as if something wonderful has painfully awakened within me.

I park next to the familiar vintage, Indian motorcycle owned by my two Ph.D. friends from Whidbey Island, and lean 'Sophie' next to it. Funny, how differing realities so freely commingle themselves, unknowingly.

I look around and see Dr.'s David and Amanda standing on the upper-deck at boat's railing, silently acknowledging their pledge to return again next year, to renew their own time-honored vows. They give me a knowing nod, perceiving somehow, that I am leaving behind something of eternal importance, but realizing also, I have found something as well… something bigger than myself. I wave to them with a smile of gratitude. They smile back in honor of my private moment.

I brace myself as the ferry muscles away from the dock. Jan and I reconnect with our eyes again and take in each other's entire being, as we slowly depart, receding from each other's senses. Not wanting to say goodbye, but needing to do so, we exchange half-hearted waves, as if to provide for a swifter return.

Watching Jan's essence flow away from me, with the enchanting island and The Grand Hotel growing smaller and smaller, I stand alone at the railing, my collar against the wind, cherishing it all. Thinking and dreaming of another place, somewhere in time….

The End....

"Somewhere In Time (A Mid-Life Memoir)"
Copyright 2016 Michael W. Hall ™. All rights reserved.

Printed in Great Britain
by Amazon